D1423355

# Human Resource Management in Ageing Societies

# Human Resource Management in Ageing Societies

## Perspectives from Japan and Germany

Edited By

**Harald Conrad**
*Sasakawa Lecturer in Japan's Economy and Management at the School of East Asian Studies, University of Sheffield*

**Viktoria Heindorf**
*Research and Teaching Associate at the Japan Center and the Faculty of Business, Munich University*

And

**Franz Waldenberger**
*Professor of Japanese Economy at the Japan Center and the Faculty of Business, Munich University*

First published 2008 by
PALGRAVE MACMILLAN

Palgrave Macmillan in the UK is an imprint of Macmillan Publishers Limited, registered in England, company number 785998, of Houndmills, Basingstoke, Hampshire RG21 6XS.

Palgrave Macmillan in the US is a division of St Martin's Press LLC, 175 Fifth Avenue, New York, NY 10010.

Palgrave Macmillan is the global academic imprint of the above companies and has companies and representatives throughout the world.

Palgrave® and Macmillan® are registered trademarks in the United States, the United Kingdom, Europe and other countries.

ISBN-13: 978–0–230–51545–1 hardback
ISBN-10: 0–230–51545–2 hardback

This book is printed on paper suitable for recycling and made from fully managed and sustained forest sources. Logging, pulping and manufacturing processes are expected to conform to the environmental regulations of the country of origin.

A catalogue record for this book is available from the British Library.

A catalog record for this book is available from the Library of Congress.

10  9  8  7  6  5  4  3  2  1
17  16  15  14  13  12  11  10  09  08

Printed and bound in Great Britain by
CPI Antony Rowe, Chippenham and Eastbourne

# Contents

v

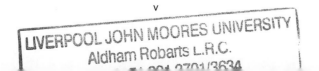

# Figures

# Tables

# Acknowledgements

The plan for this book goes back to the conference 'Demographic Challenges for Human Resource Management and Labour Market Policies – a German-Japanese Comparison' at the University of Tokyo in October 2005, organized by Harald Conrad and Viktoria Heindorf. We would like to thank the University of Tokyo, the German Institute for Japanese Studies, the German Federal Ministry of Education and Research (Förderkennzeichen 01OA0502), the Japan Foundation, the Embassy of the Federal Republic of Germany in Tokyo, the Japanese Ministry of Health, Labour and Welfare and the Friedrich Ebert Foundation Tokyo Office for their financial and organisational support of the conference and book project.

# Note on Names

In common with international bibliographical norms, the names of the authors of this volume are listed with their given names preceding their family names. The transcription of Japanese sources into the Roman alphabet follows largely the modified Hepburn romanization system, but Japanese words that have been adopted into English, for example Tokyo, are written without macrons.

# Notes on Contributors

**Harald Conrad** is Sasakawa Lecturer in Japan's Economy and Management at the School of East Asian Studies, University of Sheffield.

**Uschi Backes-Gellner** is Professor at the Institute for Strategy and Business Economics, University of Zurich.

**Marjaana Gunkel** is Assistant Professor at the Faculty of Economics and Management, Otto-von-Guericke-University Magdeburg.

**Viktoria Heindorf** is Research and Teaching Associate at the Japan Center and the Faculty of Business, Munich University.

**Yoshio Higuchi** is Professor at the Faculty of Business and Commerce, Keio University.

**Holger Luczak** is Professor emeritus at the Institute of Industrial Engineering and Ergonomics, RWTH Aachen University.

**Gerhard Naegele** is Professor of Social Gerontology at the University of Dortmund.

**Jiro Nakamura** is Professor at the Advanced Research Institute for the Sciences and Humanities, Nihon University.

**Keisuke Nakamura** is Professor at the Institute of Social Science, University of Tokyo.

**Isao Ohashi** is Professor at the Chuo Graduate School of Strategic Management, Chuo University.

**Atsushi Seike** is Professor of Labor Economics, Faculty of Business and Commerce, Keio University.

**Nobuyuki Shintani** is Assistant General Secretary at the Japanese Electrical, Electronic and Information Union.

**Marie-Christine Stemann** is Research Assistant at the Institute of Industrial Engineering and Ergonomics, RWTH Aachen University.

**Stephan Veen** is Research Assistant at the Institute for Strategy and Business Economics, University of Zurich.

**Franz Waldenberger** is Professor of Japanese Economy at the Japan Center and the Faculty of Business, Munich University.

**Sebastian Wenzke** is a Project Manager at Chemserv Industrie Service GmbH in Linz, Austria.

**Birgitta Wolff** is Professor of International Management at the Faculty of Economics and Management, Otto-von-Guericke-University Magdeburg.

**Isamu Yamamoto** is Associate Professor of Economics at the Faculty of Business and Commerce, Keio University.

# 1
# Demographic Challenges for Human Resource Management Practices and Labour Market Policies in Japan and Germany – an Overview

*Harald Conrad, Viktoria Heindorf and Franz Waldenberger*

In recent years, the rapid ageing of the Japanese and German populations has begun to catch the attention of both policymakers and company executives. In Japan, according to the official medium projections, the ratio of the population aged 65 and over is expected to rise from 21.7% in 2008 to 28.7% in 2025, and then to 35.7% in 2050 (NIPSSR 2002). In Germany, the ratio of those aged 65 and older is expected to rise from 19% (2005) to 30% in 2030, and then to 36% in 2050 (Statistisches Bundesamt 2006). Both countries will experience a marked decline in their populations coupled with an increase in the average age of their working populations. For example, predictions for Germany show that in 2020 almost 40% of the working population will be over 50 years old (Staudinger and Kühler 2006).

Longer life expectancy driving demographic change, and decline in population resulting from decreasing birthrates, are basically positive developments. A longer life is a blessing, and containment of population growth is necessary in view of increasingly scarce natural resources. In this respect, demographic change is associated with enormous welfare increases, albeit that most are not directly measurable in terms of money. The benefits of a longer life and the containment of population growth do not, however, come for free. On the cost side, demographic change necessitates severe social, cultural and economic adjustments. The purpose of this volume is to shed light on the burden of one major economic adjustment by focusing on how Japan and Germany are coping with the challenges that an older workforce poses for human resource management practices and labour market policies.

Japan and Germany have both been described as 'nonliberal' capitalist systems, as opposed to the 'liberal' capitalist systems of the Anglo-American variety (Streeck and Yamamura 2003). However, even among these nonliberal systems we can perceive substantial differences in nationally embedded institutions (Hall and Soskice 2001). In fact, as the discussion of policies and practices concerning the employment of older workers in this volume shows, the German and Japanese systems demonstrate a relatively high degree of institutional resilience. Although both countries are confronted with similar challenges, the way these challenges are dealt with depends very much on existing institutional settings. Changes are therefore very much path-dependent. In studying these different reactions, we not only learn about important developments in human resource management and labour market policies in both countries, but we also gain a deeper insight into the functioning of the respective socio-politico-economic systems.

## Employment of the elderly

Against the background of a declining younger population, longer life expectancy and limited productivity growth, Japan and Germany will only be able to preserve existing levels of per capita income if an increasingly higher proportion of the elderly population remains in employment. However, it is not only the level of income, but also its distribution that is affected by demographic change. As *Ohashi's* analysis of Japan in this volume shows, offering employment opportunities is important if one is to prevent elderly households from falling into poverty.

At present, Japan seems much better prepared than Germany to provide employment opportunities to older age groups. An international comparison between OECD (Organisation for Economic Co-operation and Development) countries shows that Japan fares quite well in terms of employment in older age groups. Employment ratios are well above OECD averages and unemployment rates well below. For Germany, the opposite holds true (Table 1.1).

Employment ratios and unemployment rates are labour market outcomes reflecting supply and demand. Such conditions are, in turn, influenced by a myriad of other direct and indirect factors. For Japan, *Ohashi's* contribution to this volume includes detailed statistical analyses on factors determining the labour participation of elderly people.

*Table 1.1* Employment ratios and unemployment rates by age group 2006

| | Employment ratios by age group | | | Unemployment rates by age group | | |
|---|---|---|---|---|---|---|
| | **15–64** | **55–59** | **60–64** | **15–64** | **55–59** | **60–64** |
| Germany | 67.2% | 64.6% | 30.1% | 10.4% | 12.9% | 10.9% |
| Japan | 70.0% | 73.9% | 52.6% | 4.3% | 3.5% | 4.5% |
| OECD | 66.1% | 62.8% | 40.4% | 6.3% | 4.6% | 3.9% |

*Source*: Data extracted on 2008/04/08 from OECD Stat.

It is not possible to provide a comprehensive explanation why the employment conditions of the elderly have been so much worse in Germany than in Japan. Nevertheless, the contributions collected in this volume are able to shed light on important factors that either directly or indirectly affect the supply of and demand for labour of older people.

## Compensation of older workers

With regard to the HRM (Human Resource Management) functions of appraisal and compensation, the most important issue relating to the ageing workforce is the prevailing seniority-orientation of the wage systems in Japan and Germany. Seniority-based wages have traditionally played an important role in Japan, and have been more pronounced than in Germany (Waldenberger 1999, chapter 6). However, a recent study by Zwick (2008) shows that Germany also has relatively strong seniority-oriented wage structures when compared with the United States, Great Britain, France, Portugal and Denmark.

As the average age of the workforce is rising in both countries, these seniority-based wage structures lead to an automatic increase in labour costs as more workers are concentrated in higher wage brackets. Japanese companies have on average been quite successful in flattening the age related wage curve so as to almost neutralise the demographic upward drift in the average wage level (Dirks et al. 2000). Nevertheless, as the analysis provided by *Higuchi* and *Yamamoto* in this volume shows, the proportion of elderly employees tends to be lower in companies that apply a steeper wage curve.

Many Japanese companies have moved away from seniority-based wage schemes to start experimenting with stronger performance-oriented wage systems (Conrad and Heindorf 2006; Conrad 2008). However, as

*Nakamura K.* discusses in this volume, this does not mean that the old wage systems are simply being replaced by performance-based wages linked to quantitative results. What we can witness instead is a change to wage systems that attempt to maintain the idea that workers are compensated for their abilities. However, in the past the wage systems tended to become seniority-oriented because workers were paid according to their *potential* abilities, which were assumed to increase with age, whereas the new systems try to focus on *proven* abilities. The effect of these reforms is expected to further flatten companies' wage curves, which in turn will induce companies to actively utilize older workers.

An important factor enhancing the employment of workers aged 55 and above in Japan is the possibility of renegotiating the terms of compensation, even if the employment relationship is continued. In 2006, male workers in the age group 55 to 59 earned on average 7% less than male workers in the age group 50 to 54, whereas those aged 60 to 64 earned 30% less (Kōseirōdōshō Daijin Kanbō Tōkei Jōhōbu 2008, table 4).[1] Such a practice is uncommon in Germany, as *Backes-Gellner* and *Stephan Veen* point out in their contribution to this volume.

## Work place adjustments and training

Three issues are of central importance in order to retain or attract qualified older workers. These are health, competence and motivation (Bellmann et al. 2007). Measures to keep older workers productive, such as lifelong learning programs, age-specific adjustments in the workplace and preventative health programmes – including ergonomic measures as discussed by *Luczak* and *Stemann* in this volume – will have to become standard procedures. As *Nakamura J.* shows in this volume, measures focused on labour safety and health care have a statistically significant effect on securing the employment of elderly people. Nevertheless, although the need for lifelong learning programmes and age-specific adjustments in the workplace might have been widely acknowleged, very few companies in both countries have so far addressed these issues systematically. In the case of Germany, a recent survey points to the fact that the percentage of companies that apply special measures for older workers, such as partial retirement, age-mixed groups, training, and workplace adjustments, decreased rather than increased from 19% to 17% between the years 2002 and 2006 (Bellman et al. 2007).

A basic factor in the qualification of the workforce is educational attainment. If we compare the educational attainment level of older workers in Japan and Germany, we find that Japan is currently lagging behind Germany, but that this situation will change dramatically by the year 2025 (see Figure 1.1). It is expected that in the year 2025 over 45% of Japanese workers will have a tertiary education, which will place Japan above its main competitors with regards to the proportion of highly educated elderly people (OECD 2004).

In Germany, the so-called dual system of vocational training aims to qualify workers in a specific profession and so provide them with marketable skills which enable them to switch employment more easily. However, as *Wolff, Gunkel* and *Wenzke* point out in this volume, the recruitment of workers over the age of 50 is extremely rare in Germany's one hundred largest companies, 86% of which state that they rarely recruit workers in this age group. In fact, in the first half of 2006, only 8% of newly employed workers in West Germany were over 50 years of age (Bellmann et al. 2007). *Backes-Gellner* and *Veen* expect that the already observable shortage of qualified workers will increase the recruitment of elderly workers in the near future.

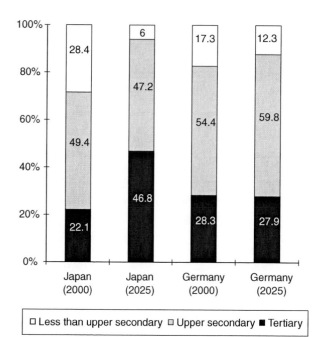

*Figure 1.1*   The educational level of older workers
*Source*: Adapted from OECD 2004.

While formal education and training is one important issue, changing job requirements mean that workers have to upgrade their skills and aquire new skills to remain competitive. In this regard the situation in Germany is currently unsatisfactory. For example, 59% of the largest companies state that they train employees aged over 50 only occasionally, whereas another 16% claim that they do so only rarely (Becker et al. 2006). As *Wolff, Gunkel* and *Wenzke* show in greater detail, the lack of public and private investment in human capital in Germany can be explained by the institutional framework, which at least until recently provided older workers with comparatively high public pensions and unemployment benefits, and made investment in human capital unattractive.

Unfortunately, there is no detailed and comparable data on the incidence of training for older workers. However, a comparison of the International Adult Literacy Survey and the Japanese Survey on Education and Training in the Private Sector undertaken by the OECD (2004) at least provides a broad picture. According to this data, Japan is at the top of OECD countries in terms of participation in job-related training (excluding on-the-job training), both in self-training and off-the-job training. Furthermore, the difference between older workers and mid-career (20 to 54) workers is relatively small in Japan compared to other OECD countries. Older Japanese workers therefore appear to be doing relatively well in terms of participation in training, although there is a wide gap between men and women.

## Mandatory retirement

Both Germany and Japan apply mandatory retirement ages in their public services. The practice is also very common in the private sector. In both countries mandatory retirement tends to be linked to the age of eligibility for public pensions. In Japan, the age limit for eligibilty for a public pension has until now been 60 years of age, and is being increased to 65. In Germany, the eligibility age has been 65, but is now being raised to 67. The difference between these countries is that the effective retirement age, that is, the age at which workers leave the labour market, has been around 69.6 in Japan, whereas it has been around 61.3 in Germany (OECD 2004). In other words, German workers have been leaving the workforce even before reaching the eligibility age for public pensions, whereas Japanese workers tend to work beyond the eligibility age for public pensions.

In Japan, mandatory retirement was used as a mechanism to cap seniority-based wage increases. By terminating the regular employment contract at a comparatively young age – the mandatory retirement age used to be only 55 in the mid 1960s – companies were able to control their wage costs. After mandatory retirement, many companies extended the employment to 'retired' workers (*kinmu enchō*) or re-employed (*saikoyō*) them at much lower salaries (Suzuki 2004). German companies never applied such an approach to control the labour costs of elderly workers. Instead, workers were offered attractive retirement packages. Public unemployment insurance benefits were systematically (mis)used to subsidize older unemployed workers until they became eligible for public pensions (see also the contribution by *Naegele* in this volume).

According to a 2004 survey by the Ministry of Health, Labour and Welfare, 91.5% of Japanese companies with more than 30 employees have a mandatory retirement system (Kōseirōdōshō Daijin Kanbō Tōkei Jōhōbu 2004). As *Shintani* discusses in this volume, Japanese labour unions have struggled for many years to increase the mandatory retirement age in order to close the gap between company retirement and the commencement of public pension payments. Legally, companies are now obliged to continue employing workers until the age of 65. They must either raise the mandatory retirement age from the current age of 60, adopt a continued employment scheme while leaving the mandatory retirement age at 60, or abolish the mandatory retirement age as such. Although employers have opposed the latest revision of the law, 80.4% of firms in a Nippon Keidanren survey replied that they would adopt or expand continued employment, with another 11.9% saying that they would not take any particular steps because they are already satisfied with the new requirements.

Continued employment will, in principle, be available for all workers who wish to continue working, but firms can use labour-management agreements to limit the range of eligible workers. For example, the agreements might contain abstract terms such as 'cooperative person' or 'person of good work behavior' (Yamashita 2007). Furthermore, until 2009, temporary measures make it possible for companies with more than 300 employees to limit the workers eligible for continued employment by stipulating conditions in working rules. Companies with less than 300 workers have an even longer grace period until 2011 (JILPT 2004). How these legal changes will impact employment and recruiting practices in the long run remains to be seen, but a survey by the Japan Institute for Labour Policy and Training from October 2006 showed that 43.6% of companies reacted by introducing a re-employment system, whereas 32.7% adjusted their existing re-employment systems (Nihon Rōdō Kenkyū Kikō 2007). Furthermore, 49.3% of companies answered that they planned to raise or had already raised their mandatory retirement age. Among those, 63.9% planned to raise the mandatory retirement age step-by-step with the increase of the age of eligibility for public pension insurance, whereas 32.8% answered that they had already raised their mandatory retirement age to 65.

The statistical analysis conducted by *Higuchi* and *Yamamoto* in this volume shows that mandatory retirement tends to stabilize employment up until the mandatory retirement age, but reduces stability after that. In his contribution to this volume, *Seike* presents similar evidence. The probability of employment for people in the age group 60 to 69 tends to be lower for those who have experienced mandatory retirement.

## Labour market policies for older workers

The efforts of companies to retain or re-employ older workers can be influenced by government policies. Both Japan and Germany have an extensive array of such measures, which are targeted at older workers and are usually paid for out of public unemployment insurance (for Japan see OECD 2004 and Conrad 2007).

In Japan, the so-called 'benefit for the continuous employment of older workers' (*Kōnenrei koyō keizoku kyūfu*) is one of the most important schemes. The scheme costs 4.1% of the total expenditure for unemployment benefits and covers 2.8% of the labour force aged 60 to 64 (OECD 2004). It was first introduced in 1995, and its explicit purpose is to support the employment of workers between the age of 60 and 65. Workers who continue to work after 60 and who earn at least 25% less than before are eligible. Currently, workers who earn less than 61% of their former salary receive a 15% subsidy. This subsidy shrinks step-by-step for those who earn more than 61% but less than 75% of their former salary. This arrangement becomes more complex if the worker is eligible for a public pension. In this case, a so-called earnings test is applied to the salary including the wage subsidy to reduce the pension (Shakai Keizai Seisansei Honbu 2005). As a result, the total income of many workers aged 60 to 65 consists of a salary, a reduced pension and a wage subsidy from unemployment insurance. An example of such a mix is provided by *Shintani* in this volume.

As well as this wage subsidy, there are a number of other policy measures that are aimed directly at employers who continue to employ older workers. Among these are, for example, subsidies for companies whose workers aged 60 to 64 make up at least 15% of the total workforce, subsidies for employers who have improved workplace facilities and equipment to facilitate the work of older employees, and subsidies to assist the job seeking activities of employees.

Unfortunately, there are few rigorous evaluations which allow a proper assessment of the effectiveness and efficiency of these schemes (OECD 2004). With regards to the 'benefit for the continuous employment of older workers', a study by *Higuchi and Yamamoto* (2002) suggests that its effect on full-time employment is not statistically significant. *Nakamura J.* in this volume, however, estimates a more significant positive contribution. He also discusses an intriguing difference between the results for older male and female workers. Whereas a relatively large number of public support measures seem to have a positive employment effect on elderly males, the results of his estimations suggest negative effects on female employment. Although the statistical data allows no definite assessement, it seems at least possible that the public measures have lead to the increased employment of older male workers at the expense of older female workers.

As *Naegele* discusses in this volume, labour market policies in Germany used to promote the early exit of older workers. To this end, the duration of the entitlement for unemployment benefits for elderly employees was expanded several times to finally reach 32 months for workers over 57. At the same time, long-term insured workers were able to draw early public pensions without reduced benefits.

These trends have recently been reversed by a comprehensive package of labour market and pension reforms. According to the so-called 'Hartz IV' reform, the duration of the maximum entitlement for unemployment benefits was cut in 2006 to a maximum of 18 months for workers over 55. Furthermore, public pension benefits for long-term insured people were reduced by 0.3% for each month of early retirement, and the age limit for the earliest possible entry into retirement following unemployment and partial retirement was raised from 60 to 63 in 2004. Furthermore, beginning in the year 2012, the regular pension age will be raised from 65 to 67.

As part of these reforms, a number of new measures were introduced to improve the integration of older employees and to increase their employment chances. Specifically, employers who hire employees over 50 can receive employment subsidies (*Eingliederungszuschuss*); in small and medium-sized companies with less than 100 employees training costs for employees over 50 are subsidized by the Federal Employment Agency (*Förderung der Weiterbildung*); employees over 50 can get an allowance amounting to 50% of the wage difference on the condition that they were entitled to unemployment benefits but choose instead to take up a lower-paid job (*Entgeltsicherung*); employers who hire a person over 55 are exempted from paying unemployment insurance contributions (*Befreiung des Arbeitgeberanteils zur Arbeitslosenversicherung*); and employees over 52 can be hired on repeated fixed-term contracts (*befristete Beschäftigung*).

However, recent evaluations of these programmes show that they are not very successful and that utilization is poor. For example, the programme which subsidizes training costs is only known about in around 50% of companies. Furthermore, almost 70% of companies who claim to know about the programme have not used it because they do not see any particular need (Lott and Spitznagel 2007).

In Japan, where early retirement was never seriously debated as a measure to improve youth employment, the incentive structure of public pensions has also had negative effects on labour supply. As *Seike* shows in this volume, the above mentioned earnings test of public pension schemes, according to which pension payments are reduced depending on simultaneous working income, has had a negative impact on the labour-supply decision of older workers. Although the earnings test has recently been reformed, it is still expected to have a negative influence on the labour supply of older workers in Japan.

All in all, labour market measures in Japan aim at the improvement of the employment situation for those who are 60 to 65, whereas the German debate focuses on workers over 50. This alone shows that expectations or goals are still quite different in both countries. Nevertheless, neither country has yet subscribed to completely 'age-free' pension and labour market policies.

## Conclusion

Human resource management practices and labour market policies in Japan and Germany have yet to fully meet the various challenges that ageing of their workforces poses. Systematic approaches towards the employment of older workers are still largely missing. In terms of recruitment and training, companies in both countries are still more or less following established patterns in which recruitment focuses on younger workers, and more effort is paid to the training of younger rather than older workers. In addition, policies to retain older workers and to increase their productivity through training programmes and workplace adjustments are not yet fully developed. In terms of public labour market policies, both countries have so far pursued the objective of 'employment until a certain age' rather than the more ambitious goal of 'age-free employment'. Both in Japan and Germany, many of the labour market measures to improve employment of the elderly are rather new. Although a proper evaluation is difficult, various studies indicate that the utilization and effectiveness of these schemes is currently rather low. In conclusion, labour market policies for the elderly need further improvement.

## Note

1. Earnings refer to contractual monthly income. For total earnings including overtime pay and bonuses the gaps between age groups are even more pronounced.

## References

Becker, F. G., R. Bobrichtchev and N. Henseler (2006) 'Ältere Arbeitnehmer und alternde Belegschaften. Eine empirische Studie bei den 100 größten deutschen Unternehmungen', *ZfM (Zeitschrift für Management)* 1, pp. 70–89.

Bellmann, L., E. Kistler and J. Wahse (2007) 'Betriebe müssen sich auf alternde Belegschaften einstellen', *IAB Kurzbericht*, 21.

Conrad, H. and V. Heindorf (2006) 'Recent changes in compensation practices of large Japanese companies: wages, bonuses and corporate pensions', in P. Matanle and W. Lunsing (eds), *Perspectives on Work, Employment, and Society in Contemporary Japan*. Houndmills and New York: Palgrave Macmillan, pp. 79–97.

Conrad, H. (2007) *Die Beschäftigung älterer Menschen in Japan – Ursachen und Rahmenbedingungen einer hohen Alterswerbsquote*, Expertise im Auftrag der Arbeitsgruppe 'Chancen und Probleme einer alternden Gesellschaft AG LeoTech Alter'.

Conrad, H. (2008) 'Human Resource Management Practices and the Ageing Workforce', in F. Coulmas, H. Conrad, A. Schad-Seifert, and G. Vogt (eds), *The Demographic Challenge – A Handbook about Japan*, Leiden and Boston: Brill, pp. 979–997.

Dirks, D., M. Hemmert, H. Meyer-Ohle and F. Waldenberger (2000) 'The Japanese Employment System in Transition', *International Business Review* 9, pp. 525–553.

Hall, P. A. and S. Soskice (eds) (2001) *Varieties of Capitalism – The Institutional Foundations of Comparative Advantage*, Oxford: Oxford University Press.

Higuchi, Y. and I. Yamamoto (2002) *Employment of Older Workers in Japan – Analysis on the Effectiveness of Employment Management, Employment Policies, and Pension Systems*, Proceedings of the Ninth EU-Japan Symposium, Brussels.

JILPT (Japan Institute for Labour Policy and Training) (2004) *Labour Situation in Japan and Analysis 2004/2005*, Tokyo: The Japan Institute for Labour Policy and Training.

Kōseirōdōshō Daijin Kanbō Tōkei Jōhōbu (2004) *Koyō kanri chōsa* (Survey on employment management), http://www.mhlw.go.jp/toukei/itiran/roudou/koyou/kanri/kanri04/07.html (last accessed 19/06/2006).

Kōseirōdōshō Daijin Kanbō Tōkei Jōhōbu (2008) *Heisei 18nen chingin kōzō kihon chōsa (zenkoku) kekka no gaikyō* (2006 Survey on Basic Wage Structure. Overview of Nationwide Results), http://www.mhlw.go.jp/toukei/itiran/roudou/chingin/kouzou/z06/dl/data.pdf (last accessed 09/04/2008).

Lott, M. and E. Spitznagel (2007) 'Wenig Betrieb auf neuen Wegen der beruflichen Weiterbildung', *IAB Kurzbericht*, 23.

National Institute of Population and Social Security Research (NIPSSR) (2002) *Population Projections for Japan: 2001–2050*, Tokyo: National Institute of Population and Social Security Research.

Nihon Rōdō Kenkyū Kikō (2007) *Kōnenreisha no keizoku koyō no jittai ni kan suru chōsa – Heisei 19-nen 4-gatsu* (Survey on the employment of older workers, April 2007), http://www.jil.go.jp/press/documents/20070402.pdf (last accessed 09/08/2007).

OECD (2004) *Ageing and Employment Policies Japan*, Paris: OECD.

Shakai Keizai Seisansei Honbu (2005) *Shakai hoken pointo kaisetsu 05/06* (Explanation of the Social Insurance 2005/2006), Tokyo: Shakai Keizai Seisansei Honbu.

Statistisches Bundesamt (2006) *Bevölkerung Deutschlands bis 2050 – Ergebnisse der 11. koordinierten Bevölkerungsvorausberechnung*, Wiesbaden: Statistisches Bundesamt.

Staudinger, U. M. and L. Kühler (2006) 'Das Ende der geistigen Frührente', *Personalwirtschaft*, February, pp. 10–13.

Streeck, W. and K. Yamamura (2003) 'Introduction: Convergence or Diversity? Stability and Change in German and Japanese Capitalism', in K. Yamamura and W. Streeck (eds), *The End of Diversity? Prospects for German and Japanese Capitalism*, Ithaca and London: Cornell University Press, pp. 1–50.

Suzuki, H. (2004) 'Dankai sedai to kigyō no jinkenhi futan' (The baby-boom generation and companies' personnel expenses), in Y. Higuchi et al. (eds), *Dankai seidai no teinen to nihon keizai*, Tokyo: Nihon Hyōronsha, pp. 149–166.

Waldenberger, Franz (1999) *Organisation und Evolution arbeitsteiliger Systeme. Erkenntnisse aus der japanischen Wirtschaftsentwicklung*, München: Iudicium.

Yamashita, Noboru (2007) Act Concerning Stabilization of Employment of Older Persons, *Japan Labor Review*, 4 (3), pp. 71–93.

Zwick, T. (2008) *Senioritätsentlohnung in Deutschland im internationalen Vergleich*, Mannheim: Zentrum für Europäische Wirtschaftsforschung.

# 2

# Ageing Workforces and Challenges to Human Resource Management in German Firms

*Uschi Backes-Gellner[1] and Stephan Veen*

The aim of this paper is to provide an overview of the main challenges imposed by demographic change on the human resource management (HRM) policies of German companies. Although many more aspects of business are affected by demographic change, such as changes in consumption or in savings and investment and therefore in capital costs, we concentrate on changes in personnel policies prompted by an ageing workforce. We cover a wide range of HRM policies, starting with recruitment problems, moving on to training issues, wages and incentives, and end with problems concerning innovation and technological change.

## Ageing workforces and human resource management

Due to demographic change, company workforces will on average be older in the future. Consequently, an age structure in which workers above 50 are the dominant group will no longer be an exception, but will instead become the rule (Buck and Schletz 2004: 9; Enquete-Kommission des Deutschen Bundestages 2003: 46–47). In this context, the actual share of older workers, as well as the optimal share, is partly determined by differences in firm characteristics in addition to external factors (Brussig 2005: 13).

## General challenges

Despite increasing public awareness of challenges arising from future demographic transitions, company awareness of problems resulting from an ageing workforce is still rather low. In fact, only 25% of firms expect that demographic change will cause serious problems in the long run (Schneider, Stein and Lorenzen 2006: 18–19). However, there is a growing literature on the challenges presented by ageing workforces and on prospective solutions. Busch (2004) presents a collection of studies analyzing the capabilities of older workers in general, and gives practical examples of HR policies that deal with older workers. Wächter and Sallet (2006) present a collection of papers studying company attitudes towards early retirement and attitudes towards an extension of working life. In those studies, the abilities of older workers are typically assumed to be different, not inferior, pointing to an optimal workforce age-mix that depends on the particular requirements of different companies (Bellman, Kistler and Wahse 2003: 30–31). In general, however, demographic change will generate increasing pressure on all kinds of personnel policies due to a growing lack of qualified employees (Astor and Jasper 2001: 31, 55–56).

In particular, small and medium-size companies without internal human resource departments, and thus with a lack of special infrastructure, face serious challenges. Contrary to their normal planning horizon of about two to five years, they will increasingly have to deal with long-term personnel problems and planning. On the other hand, it has been shown that medium-size enterprises are often more flexible with regard to older worker and family issues because they are able to deal with them more informally than larger firms. Within larger firms, an increasing number of pilot projects deal with the problems of an ageing workforce, highlighting important areas in need of consideration as well as the scope for organizing an ageing workforce. These areas include health management issues, adjusted promotion policies and career planning, changes in work designs, new personnel development strategies, changes in working time patterns and lifetime working arrangements (Altenbericht 2005: 104–113).

One of the main problems with the discussion so far is that it is focused on the potential benefits of such measures, whereas their costs are often neglected. Thus, cost-benefit analyses are often missing, and general conclusions are difficult to draw because results are dependent on companies' business strategies and on the markets in which they operate, meaning that optimal HR policies vary from company to company. In short, there is no 'one size fits all' solution.[2]

To evaluate age structures and respective problems, Köchling and Deimel (2006) make use of a practical tool for human resource managers based on detailed qualitative case studies in the electronics industry.

They study the problems that would arise if the present personnel strategy were retained. Initial results for the application of this tool can be found in Köchling and Deimel (2006). According to Bullinger, Buck and Schmidt (2003: 99), successful personnel policies need to focus on finding, binding, enhancing and deploying employees. These are the HR fields that we will study in more depth below.

## Recruiting

According to human capital theory, companies prefer younger job applicants in comparison to older job applicants because younger workers have more time to accumulate firm specific knowledge. In addition, their amortization period in the firm is longer, making investments more profitable. Signalling theory also holds that companies prefer younger applicants. Unemployed older workers represent a stronger negative signal for productivity than unemployed younger workers. This is because companies generally prefer to lay off younger workers as they possess less firm-specific human capital. Thus, if a company does nevertheless lay off older workers, these workers are stigmatized as being low performers. Furthermore, there is some prejudice regarding the flexibility, over-cautiousness and technical adaptability of older workers. Lower gain from training and a deficit in acquired skills and qualifications discourage the employment of older workers (Marshall and Taylor 2005: 576–577). A lack of foreign language skills and up-to-date training, and less flexibility and capacity for teamwork also discourage companies from hiring older workers (Höpflinger et al. 2006: 55).

On the other hand, German personnel managers also cultivate strong positive stereotypes of older workers, such as reliability, productivity and motivation (Marshall and Taylor 2005: 576–578). For Germany, Bellmann, Kistler and Wahse (2003) use the 2002 wave of the Institute for Employment Research (Institut für Arbeitsmarkt- und Berufsforschung, IAB) firm panel to analyze appreciation of older workers in companies. They found that in general 'classic virtues' like morale, discipline and quality consciousness are very important for firms, with experience and flexibility following close behind. These attributes, combined with loyalty, are exactly the same as those accredited to older workers.[3] Therefore, firms strongly value the abilities of older workers, but at the same time are deterred from employing older workers, which is somewhat puzzling. According to Bellman et al. (2003, *IAT* May/June 2005) and Brussig (2005: 14) the probability of finding employment is systematically lower for older workers than for younger workers.[4]

This puzzle is, however, easily resolved when one distinguishes between older workers who are employed, and older workers who are job applicants. Companies value the abilities of their own older employees, which they have been observing and fostering for a long time, but they cannot reliably assess the abilities of older workers in the external labour market which may be adversely selected (i.e. they are unemployed because they are not very good). Thus, when employers use unemployment as a signal for the unobserved productivity of an older job applicant, they can only use it as a negative signal, as mentioned above, and are thereby discouraged from hiring older applicants from the external labour market. In addition, one cannot discount the possibility that personnel managers are prejudiced against hiring older workers (Bellmann, Kistler and Wahse 2003: 33–34; Buck and Schletz 2004: 22). Whereas US managers judge their personnel to be fully productive up to the age of 60, German executives do so only up to the age of 51 (Enquete-Kommission des Deutschen Bundestages 2003: 47). Actual company and labour market cultures reflect these attitudes, and may in turn reinforce personnel policies which discourage the employment of older workers (Bellmann, Kistler and Wahse 2003: 34).

This situation may change once companies are faced with a severe lack of qualified job applicants from the external labour market due to demographic change. Today, about one third of German companies already have difficulties in filling managerial positions (Schneider, Stein and Lorenzen 2006: 18). In the long run, a continuous recruitment policy resulting in a mixed-age workforce seems to be advisable to avoid the occurrence of large demographically homogenous personnel clusters. One negative consequence of large homogeneous groups may be difficulties in integration and communication with employees who do not fit the dominant profile (Astor and Jasper 2001: 14), as homogeneity generally highlights differences. For example, the probability of young managers leaving a firm increases as the mean age rises and the homogeneity of the top management teams increases (Wiersema and Bird 1993: 1015–1019). In this respect, today's recruitment policies not only affect future workforce composition, but also cooperation and motivation, and therefore workforce productivity (Zenger and Lawrence 1989: 372–373).

To gain competitive advantages in thinner labour markets for younger qualified workers, firms have to make their personnel policies more attractive both to applicants and incumbent workers (Schneider, Stein and Lorenzen 2006: 20, 43).[5] Since in the long run only 80% of retired workers with a university degree can be replaced if nothing else changes

(Zwick 2007: 18), recruitment efforts and the training of incumbent employees will require increasing resources (Buck and Schletz 2004: 22). In this situation, small and medium-size companies will again face greater challenges. Compared to larger enterprises, they have a disadvantage when competing for skilled younger workers from the external labour market, and therefore have to consider older workers from the external and internal labour markets (Astor and Jasper 2001: 14–15; Buck and Schletz 2004: 13; Fuchs, Schnur and Zika 2005: 4; Köchling and Deimel 2006: 122–127; Schneider, Stein and Lorenzen 2006). Larger enterprises are able to offer better conditions regarding wages, career opportunities and prestige. In addition, they can more easily recruit skilled labour from international labour markets. Although recruiting foreigners for skilled staff and executive positions only plays a minor role, it will presumably become more important in the future as demographic change progresses. In summary, whereas large companies have recruitment advantages, small and medium-size enterprises have to deal with what is left, that is, they have to find ways to flexibly employ and hire older workers instead of younger workers. Consequently, small and medium-size companies already handle ageing workforces much more than large companies.

### Training and personnel development

Career planning as a personnel development task is supposed to balance individual age-specific capabilities and operative demands across entire individual careers. Personnel development has become more dynamic (Staudinger 2006: 695–696). For example, better incentives to keep human capital up-to-date, through internal career planning, mixed teams and inclusion in innovation processes, may ensure that older employees stay productive, especially in companies with modern production technologies (Boockmann and Zwick 2004: 61). Thus, age-friendly employment, qualified labour, as well as the motivation and suitable assignment of competences may be assured. However, this requires elaborate long-term personnel planning (Bullinger, Buck and Schmidt 2003: 100). Again, it is often small and medium companies which lack such a long range perspective (Altenbericht 2005: 109). Moreover, some of the observed age-specific HR policies, such as mixed teams and special workplace design, are not practicable in small firms (Bellmann, Kistler and Wahse 2003: 32). In particular, career planning and age specific training are generally rare in German companies (Höpflinger et al. 2006: 72–78). Systematic training is often limited to younger employees. This means that older workers face a relative disadvantage, not only in their stock of human capital, but also ivation and learning capabilities (Buck and Schletz 2004: 18ff; iger 2006: 694).

Bellmann and Leber (2004) use descriptive and multivariate analysis to gauge the determinants of participation for older employees in training. They use the 2002 wave from the IAB firm panel which focuses on training. Only a few firms offer special training for older workers, and just 6% of all companies include older employees in training. This rate is higher in firms involved in public administration, mining and energy, and credit and financing. Technological innovation and application of specific measures for older employees increase the probability of training for older workers. One should keep in mind that both the external selection of firms and self-selection by employees determine the training participation rate of older workers. Awareness of this and group specific measures are supposed to increase training participation rates (Bellmann and Leber 2004: 32–33).

Schröder and Gilberg (2005) also offer an empirical survey and forecasts of older worker training activity under demographic transition. They present recent data, figures and trends with explanations and prognoses. The official report on ageing (Altenbericht 2005) provides a short overview of general and specific training and potential benefits, and concludes by presenting policy measures to implement training and life-long learning programmes (Altenbericht 2005: 131–145, 174–181). Again, the cost of such training programmes for older workers is often not sufficiently taken into account. In addition, quality control does not meet professional standards and the pedagogic investigations are of poor scientific quality. Thus, company and learning culture may induce conditions that discourage learning (Staudinger 2006: 693–697).

To summarize the findings, the participation rate of older employees in training programmes is comparatively low. However, this is currently rational because the payoff period for investment in these programmes is comparatively short. On the other hand, this may alter when the number of younger workers shrinks dramatically due to demographic change. This will make younger workers more expensive, and in turn make it comparatively more profitable to train older employees and keep them on the payroll for longer.

A second aspect of the human capital of older employees is their implicit knowledge which may play a central role in an organization, and which has to be transferred to the next generation to keep the organization running smoothly. Layoffs of older employees lead to a considerable loss of implicit knowledge. Since this knowledge results from private networks and experience with inner organizational processes, companies often do not realize its importance until it is too late. Experience transfer requires a long period of working together which itself requires a minimum of personnel planning. Promotion of 'new seniors' has to be a long-term strategy with teamwork involving both new entrants and older workers; otherwise firms may lose the experience and knowledge of an entire generation of workers (Jasper 2004: 235–237; Staudinger 2006: 696).

For German firms, the problem is particularly severe due to early retirement regulations which set incentives for early and usually full-time retirement. Part-time retirement, or phasing out of the workforce, is very rare. As a result, companies reduce overlapping generations to a minimum because they cannot afford to simultaneously employ two full-time employees to do one job. This in turn makes knowledge transfer more complicated than in other countries where part-time retirement and phasing out is more common. At the same time, more formalized methods of competence and tacit knowledge transfer are becoming more important when retirement waves lead to a loss of experience, process knowledge and individual networks. Job rotation, tandem work, alumni networks and part-time transition into retirement are practical methods for experience transfers (Staudinger 2006: 696). Teams and workforces based on a diverse age range may also enable such a transferral of competences (Buck and Schletz 2004: 15–16).

## Wages and seniority-based pay

Seniority-based pay, that is, wages that rise with age, exist both in the public and private sector. Furthermore, older employees often qualify for more vacations and other non-monetary compensation (Hutchens 1989: 50). Bispinck (2006) investigates the manifold arrangements and different designs of seniority-based pay in collective wage agreements in Germany. Few seniority pay arrangements explicitly implement fixed wage rises. However, nearly all of them protect the status quo regarding income and non-monetary benefits for older employees (Bispinck and Tarifarchiv 2005; Bispinck 2006: 154).

Having said this, despite the obvious patterns of ever increasing compensation, it is important to distinguish between age-related and tenure-related wage increases, even though they are closely correlated. Wage increases based on tenure, that is, time spent in a company, are often implemented for economic reasons, and are assumed to pay off. Human capital theory, for example, predicts a rising wage with increasing tenure.[6] Investment in employee education and training increases productivity and therefore wages. Productivity gains from general training are fully paid out to the worker. When investing in firm-specific human capital, the employer may retain some of the returns since the productivity gains are realized only in the firm. This has implications for the financing of training. While costs for general training have to be completely paid by the worker, firms and employees share investments and returns from firm-specific training. But in both cases, wages always rise with seniority.

Contract theory provides an alternative theoretical explanation for seniority-based pay in seeing delayed payments as an incentive device (Hutchens 1989: 54–59). Part of the compensation is postponed towards the end of the employment contract to solve incentive problems. Lazear (1979) was the first to explain seniority-based pay. He showed that seniority-based pay is an instrument to bind employees and to set incentives against shirking in situations where the effort of employees is difficult to observe or tasks are ambiguous. Firms pay wages below productivity in early employment periods, and wages above productivity in later stages of employment. Workers only receive those wages above productivity and regain their early wage losses if they show sufficient effort and thereby avoid getting fired. Lazear explains the phenomenon of mandatory fixed retirement with his theory, arguing that once workers reach the stage where wages are above productivity they will no longer have an incentive to withdraw from the workforce voluntarily. Therefore, the retirement age has to be fixed in advance (Lazear 1998: 281, for Germany see also Schneider, Stein and Lorenzen 2006: 25; Bellmann and Leber 2004: 22).[7]

However, one precondition is necessary if this incentive mechanism is to be effective, namely that firms are ultimately able to fire employees that are caught shirking. Since firing is quite restricted in Germany, particularly for older employees and public sector employees, seniority-based wages are not likely to serve as an incentive for large parts of the workforce, that is those for whom strict employment protection laws are binding.

A few empirical studies have tried to directly compare age-related productivity and wage profiles. The results, however, indicate that older employees may on average be 'overpaid' in relation to their productivity. Crépon, Deniau and Pérez-Duarte (2002) find a 10% overpay rate for workers over 50 compared to workers aged between 35 and 49. Hellerstein and Neumark (2005) estimate that US workers over 55 are overpaid by approximately 20% compared to workers aged between 34 and 54. The estimated wage and productivity profiles are concave, with the wage profile being steeper than the productivity profile. Dostie (2006) also estimates age-earning and age-productivity profiles. Again both profiles are concave. The wages of younger workers are below their productivity rates, while the wages of those over 55 are above their productivity rates. Prinz (2004) compares different theories regarding age-earning profiles. His empirical results show that overall Lazear's model has the greatest explanatory power (Prinz 2004: 67–70, 203). In general, a large number of studies support a deferred compensation explanation for age-related wage increases (Dostie 2006; Prinz 2004).

However, these results have to be interpreted cautiously because precise firm data for individual wage-productivity differentials are missing, and the many econometric studies suffer from endogeneity and reverse causality problems. Wage-productivity differentials typically shrink once those problems are taken seriously. Aubert und Crépon (2003), for example, take into account the fact that less-productive firms stop hiring and therefore have an older work force. When controlling this, age-related wage effects disappear. Beffy et al. (2006) also find only small seniority-based wage effects for France, even though there is a seniority effect of about 2.5% for highly qualified workers. They explain that in comparison to the US, which has high seniority-based payments and high levels of worker mobility, French employees traditionally remain with one company and so do not have to be given extra incentives to stay. US firms, however, have to pay steep seniority-based wages to keep employees who are highly mobile. For Germany, it cannot be ruled out that seniority-based pay may play an important role in some industries, or among some groups of workers, and may thus discourage firms from employing older workers.

Another problem for age-related compensation policies is the increasing variety of productivity relevant determinants among older workers. As mentioned in the introduction, inter-individual productivity variance increases with age (Höpflinger et al. 2006: 41–42; Maintz 2004: 115). If companies are not able to adjust wages accordingly, this in turn creates another disincentive for employing older workers (Schneider, Stein and Lorenzen 2006: 23–26). Since wages in Germany are largely determined by collective agreements, the discretion available to make individual adjustments is rather low. Thus, as age increases, individual wages become less reflective of individual productivity. Consequently, there are more incentives to dismiss older workers than younger workers which lead to high rates of early retirement.

In Japan, by contrast, many employees are re-hired after retirement, typically at a lower level, with lower wages and less seniority benefits.

These employees are often re-employed by associated companies or by customers. Advisory occupations or project-oriented withdrawal from the original firm may also preserve the valuable experience of older workers (Schneider, Stein and Lorenzen 2006: 8). In such a second career, the wage variance is larger than before, and employees that find jobs with assistance from their former employers earn approximately 20% more (Clark and Ogawa 1997; Rebick 1995). In Germany, however, there is a bundle of labour market institutions and social security regulations that work against these alternatives.

## Innovation and technological change

Demographic change offers new markets for products and services for older people and is therefore also a chance for innovation (Cirkel, Hilbert and Schalk 2006; Weinkopf 2006; Prognos Trendletter January 2006: 12). These opportunities include housing, mobility, health, leisure and tourism. The 2005 age report dedicates a whole chapter to the opportunities to be found within a senior citizen economy (Altenbericht 2005: 227–250). An additional area of expertise analyzes new products, services and customer protection for older people (Deutsches Zentrum für Altersfragen 2006). Elderly people form a target group with substantial buying power. They have different lifestyles, needs and preferences, and may create new domains of demand. Of course, this is speculative, but it is obvious that the decline in today's dominant youth markets accompanies an expansion in senior citizen markets. This shift in markets and demand will require fast structural change as well as firm flexibility, and companies will have to adjust to these changes with an ageing workforce. However, companies are typically sceptical with respect to the innovative ability of older workers (Buck and Schletz 2004: 12). Innovation, dynamic behaviour and new ideas are characteristics typically attributed to younger workers.

If we look at the facts, however, several studies of computer use do not find any significant negative age effects. Older workers are able to learn and use new technology just as well as their younger colleagues (Borghans and ter Weel 2002; Spitz 2005).[8] Companies may stay innovative with older employees if their organization, personnel policy and work arrangements are designed accordingly (Astor and Jasper 2001: 36, 55). Having said this, there are a number of studies showing technological change is age-biased, at least to a certain degree. Weinberg (2004), for example, finds strong complementariness between older and younger workers using new technology, but it is mostly the young college graduates who profit. Beckmann (2007) finds that in Germany there is a lower demand for older workers in firms that use new technology and modern organizational structures. He concludes that technological and organizational innovation is age-biased since depreciation of qualifications and thereby dismissal increases with age (Beckmann 2007: 21–22). With accelerating technological diffusion, training needs are intensified and older workers need more intensive training to keep up (Boockmann and Zwick 2004: 17; Charness and Czaja 2005: 664–666). As a result, firms with modern technical equipment on average employ fewer older workers.[9]

For Germany, Spitz-Oener (2006) shows with BIBB/IAB data that job requirement profiles have become more complex. Today's jobs require more analytical and communicative skills, and less cognitive and routine manual tasks. Increased computer usage substitutes for manual and cognitive routines, while analytical and interactive tasks complement computer usage (Spitz-Oener 2006: 263–264). If skill profiles are dependent on education, they are therefore also dependent on age. When technological change alters job requirements, older generations are disadvantaged due to cohort effects in education and vocational training (Charness and Czaja 2005: 667). Ageing effects in human capital may lead to the inevitable substitution of older workers by younger ones despite continuous training. This is especially true in branches which use rapidly changing technology, as older employees may at some point have to be replaced by younger ones who possess an up-to-date stock of human capital (Jovanovic and Tse 2006).

Regarding restructuring and organizational change, younger managers and workers do seem to be more proactive. It is generally assumed that young management teams will be more likely to conduct strategic changes (Wiersema and Bantel 1992: 112).[10] This effect became obvious in many East German companies who had comparatively old and homogeneous workforces, and were only partially able to modernize their processes and organization (Lippert, Astor and Wessels 2001: 21–22). Thus, it seems that firms should maintain some younger managers to ensure that there is a sufficient willingness to take risks, be flexible and remain open to new ways of working. Older workers are generally more content with a given situation, while younger workers press for change (Astor and Jasper 2001: 53, 57). Demographic homogeneity skewed towards an older workforce may result in less experimental behaviour and may therefore hinder innovation (Astor and Jasper 2001: 25; Wiersema and Bird 1993: 1015–1019). Since the employment of older workers varies systematically between different branches and production regimes within firms, the capacity to innovate and the resulting cost and benefit of employing older workers and establishing age-friendly HRM policies can be expected to differ substantially between firms. Therefore, despite the general demographic trend of an ageing workforce, one can anticipate large inter-firm differences in age-related employment structures and growth.

## Summary and concluding remarks

Although it is well known that the workforce in Germany will age rapidly during the next decade, awareness of the problem at company level is still rather low. However, an increasing shortage of skilled labour coupled with increasing retirement will pressure companies into employing older workers. Small and medium-size enterprises may have more problem finding, binding and developing suitable and qualified employees, but they may be better suited to introducing flexible, active and innovative HR policies. One of the major challenges will be to get away from concentrating training on younger employees, which is still the dominant pattern today. Lifelong learning will be the key for companies and individuals alike, enabling both to meet future challenges resulting from demographic change. It is important for employees to realize that they may have to stay in the workforce longer, which makes training more profitable even later in life. For companies, it is important to realize that they will have to manage future challenges by employing an older workforce than they are used to. This of course will make the training of older workers more profitable in the future than it was in the past. Today, employing older workers is often viewed as being too expensive due to a variety of seniority rules. From an institutional perspective, it will thus be important to allow for more flexible and more individualized employment conditions for older workers, in order to allow companies to react to individual productivity differences and varying company requirements.

Finally, companies in Germany only recently started to realize that demographic change may even generate new product markets. Of course, companies need flexible and innovative employees to serve those new markets, which in turn may create incentives for companies to focus more on keeping their ageing workforce up-to-date in order to stay competitive in the long run. Thus, within an ageing German society, there will be push as well as pull factors working towards the greater employment of older workers.

## Notes

1. The author is member of The Joint Academy Initiative on Ageing in Germany. Its task is the analysis of the chances and problems of an ageing society with a focus on the world of work and lifelong learning. It is a project of the *German Academy of Sciences Leopoldina* and the *German Academy of Science and Engineering acatech* and funded by the *Jacobs Foundation*, Zurich.
2. Boockmann and Zwick (2004) analyze firm determinants for employment of older workers with the IAB firm panel. In particular, firms with wages above the general pay scale keep their older employees. Companies with a high proportion of women or apprentices have a lower employment rate for older workers (Boockmann and Zwick 2004: 17). Small firms and companies with a high proportion of older employees have a more positive valuation of the capabilities of their older workers (Bellman, Kistler and Wahse 2003: 30–32). This stresses the point that the appreciation and employment of older labour is endogenous.
3. Younger employees, on the other hand, are seen to have an advantage in physical capacity, learning aptitude, willingness to learn and creativity (Bellmann, Kistler and Wahse 2003: 30–31, 33).
4. All three sources refer to data and analyses from the IAB firm panel. Also see Bellmann, Kistler and Wahse (2003).
5. Schneider, Stein and Lorenzen (2006) analyze personnel policy strategies to cope with demographically determined recruiting shortages in German companies using data from the Institute for the Future of Labour (IZA).
6. Hutchens (1989) gives an initial comparison of human capital and agency or contract theory explanations for seniority-based pay.
7. In this context, the age of 65 is a completely normative but formative limit (Höpflinger et al. 2006: 65). Amongst others, Stern and Todd (2000) test various implications drawn from Lazear's model and find empirical evidence to support his approach.
8. Operationalization of individual innovative ability is not convincing. Most studies refer to technology application or transfer.
9. In this context, adoption of new technology is dependent on individual ability on the one hand, but is also affected by technical design on the other. Individual ability may be influenced by investment in training. Designing age-friendly technology is important for new consumer products, as well as for new production techniques (Charness and Czaja 2005: 662–665, 668). A completely age-friendly design, which is applicable without individual adaptation through training, is presumably never possible.
10. Regarding the probability of dismissal, older employees are less affected by organizational innovation and reorganisation (Aubert, Caroli and Roger 2006). It is likely that this is mainly due to legal protection.

## References

Altenbericht (2005) *Fünfter Bericht der Sachverständigenkommission zur Lage der älteren Generation in der Bundesrepublik Deutschland, Bundesministerium für Familie*, Senioren, Frauen und Jugend.

Astor, M. and G. Jasper (2001) Demographischer Wandel als Wachstumsbremse oder Chance? – Innovations – und Personalstrategien in den neuen Bundesländern, *Broschürenreihe: Demographie und Erwerbsarbeit*.

Aubert, P. and B. Crépon (2003) 'Âge, Salaire et Productivité: La Productivité des Salariés Décline-t-elle en Fin de Carrière?', Institute National de la Statistique et des Études Économiques, *Document de travail*, G 2003/06.

Aubert, P., E. Caroli and M. Roger (2006) 'New Technologies, Organisation and Age: Firm-Level Evidence', *The Economic Journal* 116 (509), pp. 73–93.

Beckmann, M. (2007) 'Age-Biased Technological and Organizational Change: Firm-Level Evidence and Management Implications', *WWZ Discussion Paper 05/07*.

Beffy, M., et al. (2006) 'The Returns to Seniority in France (and Why Are They Lower Than in the United States?)', *IZA Discussion Paper Series, C.E.P.R. Discussion Papers* (1935).

Bellmann, L. and U. Leber (2004) 'Ältere Arbeitnehmer und betriebliche Weiterbildung', in G. Schmid, M. Gangl, P. Kupka (eds), *Arbeitsmarktpolitik und Strukturwandel: Empirische Analysen*, Nürnberg: IAB, pp. 19–35.

Bellmann, L., E. Kistler and J. Wahse (2003) 'Betriebliche Sicht- und Verhaltensweisen gegenüber älteren Arbeitnehmern', *Das Parlament* 20 (12 May), pp. 25–34.

Bispinck, R. (2006) 'Senioritätsregeln in Tarifverträgen', *Beschäftigungssituation älterer Arbeitnehmer*, 1, Berlin: Lit Verlag, pp. 129–200.

Bispinck, R. and W. S. I. Tarifarchiv (2005) 'Senioritätsregeln in Tarifverträgen', *Expertise für den 5. Altenbericht im Auftrag des Deutschen Zentrums für Arbeitsfragen (DZA)*.

Boockmann, B. and T. Zwick (2004) 'Betriebliche Determinanten der Beschäftigung älterer Arbeitnehmer', *Zeitschrift für Arbeitsmarktforschung*, 37 (1), pp. 53–63.

Borghans, L. and B. T. Weel (2002) *Do Older Workers Have More Trouble Using a Computer Than Younger Workers?*, Maastricht: ROA.

Brussig, M. (2005) 'Die "Nachfrageseite des Arbeitsmarktes": Betriebe und die Beschäftigung Älterer im Lichte des IAB-Betriebspanels 2002', *Altersübergangs-Report*.

Buck, H. and A. Schletz (2004) 'Ergebnisse des Transferprojektes Demotrans', *Broschürenreihe: Demographie und Erwerbsarbeit*.

Bullinger, H. J., H. Buck and S. L. Schmidt (2003) 'Die Arbeitswelt von morgen; Alternde Belegschaften und Wissensintensivierung', *DSWR*, 4, pp. 98–100.

Busch, R. H. (2004) *Alternsmanagement im Betrieb ältere Arbeitnehmer – zwischen Frühverrentung und Verlängerung der Lebensarbeitszeit*, München: Rainer Hampp Verlag.

Charness, N. and S. J. Czaja (2005) 'Adaptation to New Technologies', in M. L. Johnson (ed.), *Cambridge Handbook of Age and Ageing*, Cambridge: Cambridge University Press, pp. 662–669.

Cirkel, M., J. Hilbert and C. Schalk (2006) 'Produkte und Dienstleistungen für mehr Lebensqualität im Alter', *Produkte, Dienstleistungen und Verbraucherschutz für ältere Menschen*, 4, Berlin: Lit-Verlag, pp. 7–154.

Clark, R. L. and N. Ogawa (1997) 'Transitions From Career Jobs to Retirement in Japan', *Industrial Relations*, 36 (2), pp. 255–270.

Crépon, B., N. Deniau and S. Pérez-Duarte (2002) 'Wages, Productivity, and Worker Characteristics: A French Perspective', *Série des documents de travail du CREST* (2003–04).

Deutsches Zentrum für Altersfragen (ed.) (2006) *Produkte, Dienstleistungen und Verbraucherschutz für ältere Menschen*, Berlin: Lit-Verlag.

Dostie, B. (2006) 'Wages, productivity and aging', *IZA Discussion Paper Series* (2496).

Enquete-Kommission des Deutschen Bundestages (2003) 'Demographischer Wandel – Herausforderungen unserer älter werdenden Gesellschaft an den Einzelnen und die Politik', *Das Parlament* 20 (12 May), pp. 43–54.

Fuchs, J., P. Schnur and G. Zika (2005) 'Arbeitsmarktbilanz bis 2020; Besserung langfristig möglich', *IAB Kurzbericht*, 19, pp. 1–4.

Hellerstein, J. K. and D. Neumark (2005) 'Production Function and Wage Equation Estimation with Heterogeneous Labor: Evidence from a New Matched Employer-Employee Data Set', *NBER Working Paper Series*.

Höpflinger, F., et al. (2006) *Arbeit und Karriere: Wie es nach 50 weitergeht. Eine Befragung von Personalverantwortlichen in 804 Schweizer Unternehmen*, Zürich: Avenir Suisse.

Hutchens, R. M. (1989) 'Seniority, Wages and Productivity: A Turbulent Decade', *The Journal of Economic Perspectives*, 3 (4), pp. 49–64.

IAT (2005) 'Altersübergangs-Report', *Infobrief* (May/June), pp. 1–2.

Jasper, G. (2004) 'Unterschiedliche Potentiale jüngerer und älterer Mitarbeiter erschliessen und nutzen', in R. Busch (ed.), *Alternsmanagement im Betrieb ältere Arbeitnehmer - zwischen Frühverrentung und Verlängerung der Lebensarbeitszeit*, München: Rainer Hampp Verlag, pp. 219–240.

Jovanovic, B. and C. Tse (2006) 'Creative Destruction in Industries', *NBER Working Paper Series* (W12520).

Köchling, A. and M. Deimel (2006) 'Ältere Beschäftigte und altersausgewogene Personalpolitik', in Deutsches Zentrum für Altersfragen (ed.), *Förderung der Beschäftigung älterer Arbeitnehmer; Voraussetzungen und Möglichkeiten*, vol. 2, Berlin: Lit Verlag, pp. 99–168.

Lazear, E. P. (1979) 'Why is there Mandatory Retirement?', *The Journal of Political Economy*, 87 (6), pp. 1261–1284.

Lazear, E. P. (1998) *Personnel Economics for Managers*, New York: Wiley.

Lippert, I., M. Astor and J. Wessels (2001) 'Demographischer Wandel und Wissenstransfer im Innovationsprozess', in M. Astor, G. Jasper (eds.), *Demographischer Wandel als Wachstumsbremse oder Chance? – Innovations- und Personalstrategien in den neuen Bundesländern*, Stuttgart: Öffentlichkeits- und Marketingstrategie demographischer Wandel, pp.10–34.

Maintz, G. (2004) 'Der ältere Arbeitnehmer im Spannungsfeld von Leistungsanforderung und Erwartung', in R. Busch (ed.), *Alternsmanagement im Betrieb ältere Arbeitnehmer - zwischen Frühverrentung und Verlängerung der Lebensarbeitszeit*, München: Rainer Hampp Verlag, pp. 113–122.

Marshall, V. W. and P. Taylor (2005) 'Restructuring the Lifecourse: Work and Retirement', in M. L. Johnson (ed.), *Cambridge Handbook of Age and Ageing*, Cambridge: Cambridge University Press, pp. 572–582.

Prinz, J. (2004) *Why Are Wages Upward Sloping with Tenure?*, München, Mering: Rainer Hampp Verlag.

Prognos Trendletter (2006) 'Die alternde Gesellschaft als Chance für Innovationen', *Zukunftschancen; Wege für Deutschland*, 1, p. 12.

Rebick, M. E. (1995) 'Rewards in the Afterlife: Late Career Job Placements as Incentives in the Japanese Firm', *Journal of the Japanese and International Economies*, 9 (1), pp. 1–28.

Schneider, H., D. Stein and O. Lorenzen (2006) 'Personalpolitische Strategien deutscher Unternehmen zur Bewältigung demografisch bedingter Rekrutierungsengpässe bei Führungskräften', *IZA Research Report*, 6.

Schröder, H. and R. Gilberg (2005) *Weiterbildung Älterer im demographischen Wandel empirische Bestandsaufnahme und Prognose*, Bielefeld: Bertelsmann.

Spitz, A. (2005) 'The Effects of Changes in the Unemployment Compensation System on the Adoption of IT by Older Workers', *ZEW Discussion Papers* (5–40).

Spitz-Oener, A. (2006) 'Technical Change, Job Tasks, and Rising Educational Demands: Looking Outside the Wage Structure', *Journal of Labor Economics*, 24 (2), pp. 235–270.

Staudinger, U. (2006) 'Konsequenzen des demographischen Wandels für betriebliche Handlungsfelder: Eine interdisziplinäre Perspektive', *ZFBF Schmalenbachs Business Review*, 58 (5), pp. 690–698.

Stern, S. and P. Todd (2000) 'A Test of Lazear's Mandatory Retirement Model', in S. W. Polachek (ed.), *Worker Well-Being*, vol. 19, Binghamton: Elsevier Science Inc., pp. 253–273.

Wächter, H. and D. Sallet (eds) (2006) *Personalpolitik bei alternder Belegschaft*, München, Mering: Rainer Hampp Verlag.

Weinberg, B. A. (2004) 'Experience and Technology Adoption', *IZA Discussion Papers* (1051).

Weinkopf, C. (2006) 'Haushaltsnahe Dienstleistungen für Ältere', *Produkte, Dienstleistungen und Verbraucherschutz für ältere Menschen*, vol. 4, Berlin: Lit-Verlag, pp. 155–219.

Wiersema, M. F. and A. Bird (1993) 'Organizational Demography in Japanese Firms: Group Heterogeneity, Individual Dissimilarity, and Top Management Team Turnover', *Academy of Management Journal*, 36 (5), pp. 996–1025.

Wiersema, M. F. and K. A. Bantel (1992) 'Top Management Team Demography and Corporate Strategic Change', *Academy of Management Journal*, 35 (1), pp. 91–121.

# 3
# Pensions and Labour Market Reforms for the Ageing Society

*Atsushi Seike*

Ageing populations are a common phenomenon among the world's advanced countries including Germany and Japan. Among the problems posed by population ageing, the financing of public pensions is one of the most difficult to cope with. It is therefore not surprising that the pension issue has been repeatedly placed high on the political agenda.

Under the pay-as-you-go system, which is widely used in most public pension schemes in advanced countries, an increase in the older population who are receiving pension benefits, coupled with a decrease in the younger population who are paying pension premiums, has in itself adversely affected the finances of public pensions. Of course, a fundamental solution to this problem would be to transform the pension scheme from a pay-as-you-go system to a fully funded system. However, a complete transformation to a fully funded system would be very difficult to achieve because of serious obstacles including the so-called double burden problem. With pension schemes having already matured in industrialized countries, there is a need to improve their financial situation using the existing pay-as-you-go system, though public pension funds can be increased to some extent and can be partially privatized.

One solution under the pay-as-you-go system would be to increase the premium. In Japan, the premium is scheduled to be increased by up to 18.3% in 2017, but it will increase even further if the population ages more rapidly. However, increasing the premium will result in lowering the living conditions of working generations while increasing the labour costs of employers.

Another possible solution would be to reduce the level of benefits. For example, the Japanese government decided to reduce future benefits when it revised the public pension law in 2000 and 2004. A drastic reduction in benefits would, however, lower the living standard of retired people, which would be inconsistent with a basic value held in advanced countries, namely the right to a stable retirement.

It is an undeniable fact that every time population forecasts changed, public pension schemes have repeatedly been revised so as to raise premiums and lower benefits, which has led to public scepticism over the veracity of these schemes. More positive and substantial solutions are now required to ensure the sustainability of public pension schemes.

One noteworthy scenario for coping with the problem is for older people who are willing and able to work to be allowed to continue working beyond the current retirement age. If, by staying in work, older people continue to be both tax and premium payers, it would significantly improve the financial situation of public pension systems. Such a scheme would be underpinned by an 'age-free active' scenario, whereby many older people would contribute to supporting the ageing society.

Based on the tenets of such a concept, Japan, the US and several European countries including Germany are now trying to promote the employment of older people. Japan in particular has a great advantage in promoting the employment of older people; that is, their intrinsically high motivation to participate in the labour force. Given the high motivation of its older workers, Japan might be considered to be the most promising country to develop an age-free active society (see Seike 2001 for details).

The purpose of this paper is to explore the possibility of an age-free active society by mainly examining the Japanese case, while referring to the US and Europe. In the process, it will examine the inherent influences of pension schemes and employment practices that could pose obstacles to promoting the employment of older people. Finally, it will offer some policy proposals toward the establishment of an age-free active society.

## Pension reform and employment policy toward promoting the employment of older people

In order to promote the employment of older people, pension reform and employment policy would play important roles. First of all, the pension scheme and the employment situation of older people are closely related. In particular, this is because their employment situation is influenced by the context in which the government regards the public pension system as having an effect on retirement inducements.

Observers have noted distinct trends in pension reforms and employment policies for older people in the US and Europe. In the late 1970s and the 1980s, European countries had policies that discouraged older people from continuing to work in favour of providing more job opportunities for younger people. By increasing early retirement and disability benefits, pension schemes were reformed to encourage the early retirement of older workers during that period. Partly as a result of that policy, the ratio of older worker participation in the labour force in Europe has declined to significantly lower levels compared to those of Japan and the US.

Even in Europe, however, there is of late a growing interest in promoting the employment of older people as a means of coping with rapidly ageing populations. In the 1990s, European pension policies were changed to encourage, not discourage, older people to continue working. A raise in the age of entitlement for pensions and a reduction in benefits are also being considered by some European countries.

Regarding employment policy, the German government has, for example, implemented a new policy package called 'Campaign 50 Plus', which provides wage subsidies to employers who employ people over 50 and assists in the retraining of such workers. In the Netherlands, employment policy promotes part-time jobs as a means of expanding job opportunities, including opportunities for older people. It is apparent from such examples that European countries have begun moving towards the promotion of employment for older people.

On the other hand, the US government has had a policy of promoting the employment of older people for several decades. Its most salient aspect was the introduction of the Age Discrimination in Employment Act. This law was first enacted in 1967 and then revised in 1978 and 1986. It first aimed at eliminating age discrimination against people up to 65. The age limit was raised to 70 in the first revision, and then lifted altogether in the second revision. This has created an employment environment where there is no mandatory retirement or age limit for hiring, with a few exceptions.

With regard to public pensions, called social security in the US, the US government has recently got rid of one work-discouraging effect associated with its pension system. In January 2001, it eliminated its 'earnings test' scheme for social security eligibility in order to remove the negative effect it had on the labour supply of those eligible for pensions. This earnings test scheme was considered to have discouraged people who were eligible for pensions from working, or to have induced them to reduce their working hours. This problem attracted particular attention in the US, where there has been much discussion about the introduction of the so-called negative income tax to avoid the work-discouraging effect of income maintenance programs, which have an effect similar to the social security earnings test.

In Japan, older people have been more motivated to work as shown in the labour force participation rate. Government policies have acted to expand job opportunities for older people, making full use of their motivation. The main measures taken have been to lift the mandatory retirement age and to prompt the re-hiring, by the same employer, of workers who have been subjected to mandatory retirement. The law that has played the central role in this area is the Employment Stabilization Act for the Elderly, which was first enacted in 1986 and has since been revised several times. Mandatory retirement under the age of 60 is illegal under the 1998 revision. Raising the mandatory retirement age, and other measures, has prompted employers to continue the employment of workers up to 65.

Thus, the advanced countries in Europe, North America and Japan are all adopting policies to promote the employment of older people. At least in general terms, a consensus now appears to be forming over the creation of an age-free active society. However, the devil is in the details, in particular public pension schemes and the employment practices of private firms still contain many obstacles.

## The impact of the public pension on the labour supply of older people

Public pension benefits act to reduce the labour supply of people eligible for pensions. Table 3.1 shows the labour supply elasticity of public pensions among Japanese men aged 60 to 69 in the 1980s and 1990s.

*Table 3.1*   The negative effect of public pension benefits on labour force participation (Japanese men aged 60–69 in the 1980s and 1990s)

| Year | Elasticity |
|------|-----------|
| 1980 | −0.258 |
| 1983 | −0.280 |
| 1988 | −0.435 |
| 1992 | −0.424 |
| 1996 | −0.436 |

*Source:* Seike and Suga 2001.

The coefficients representing elasticity have constantly been estimated as negative to a statistically significant degree.

There are two ways that public pension schemes have an effect on reducing the labour supply. One is the income effect. People eligible for pensions are able to retire on their pension benefits, which they receive as non-earned income. The other is the effect of the earnings test of public pension schemes. Under it, pension benefits may be reduced or stopped according to the level of earnings of those eligible for pensions who continue to work and earn income. Consequently, workers eligible for pensions tend to reduce their labour supply to avoid having their benefits reduced or cut. Of these two effects, the income effect has an impact irrespective of the type of public pension scheme.

With regard to the earnings test for pension benefits, it poses a problem because it levies a kind of penalty on the work of people eligible for pensions. Figure 3.1 shows the effect of the earnings test on labour

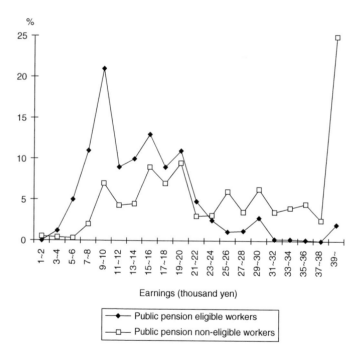

*Figure 3.1*   Earnings distribution for public pension eligible workers and non-eligible workers

*Source*: Seike 1995.

supply by tracking the earnings distribution of Japanese workers eligible to collect public pension benefits. In the year of the collected data, workers eligible for pensions were eligible to receive 80% of their full benefits if their earnings were lower than 95,000 yen.

As seen in Figure 3.1, 21% of people eligible for pensions worked just to the point where their monthly earnings were about 95,000 yen, while people who were not eligible for public pensions did not show such an earnings distribution. Many workers eligible for pensions reduce their labour supply, because if they do not exceed the ceiling of the earnings test they can receive 80% of their pension benefits.

In addition to the negative impact of public pension schemes on the labour supply of people eligible for pensions, these schemes can also

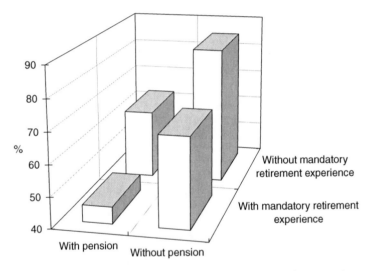

*Figure 3.2* Proportions of workers by pension and mandatory retirement experience who have the same occupations as at the age of 55

*Note*: The figure shows the percentage of male workers aged 60 to 69 who are working in the same occupation as at the age of 55 by pension status and mandatory retirement experience. Among workers who are collecting pensions and have mandatory retirement experience, 45.4% are working in the same occupation as at the age of 55. Among workers who are not collecting pensions but have undergone mandatory retirement, 68.9% are working in the same occupation as at the age of 55. For workers who are collecting pensions but do not have mandatory retirement experience, 62.5% are working in the same occupation as at the age of 55. For workers who are not collecting pensions and do not have mandatory retirement experience, 84.9% are working in the same occupation as at the age of 55.

*Source*: Seike and Yamada 1998b.

obstruct the full utilization of the skills and abilities of these older workers. That is, they may affect whether the person is able to continue working in the same occupation.

Figure 3.2 shows the ratio of workers aged 60 to 69 working in the same occupation as they had been at age 55.

Because the possibility of working in the same occupation is correlated with mandatory retirement experience, and there is a high correlation between public pension eligibility and mandatory retirement experience, the observation sample is divided between those with mandatory retirement experience and those without. In both cases, workers who receive public pension benefits have a statistically lower possibility of being in the same occupation as they were at age 55, and therefore a lower possibility of being in a workplace where their abilities are fully utilized.

## The impact of mandatory retirement and age limits in hiring on the employment of older people

Obstacles to the employment of older people in companies include employment practices that rely upon the age of workers. The most serious of these practices is mandatory retirement (see also Seike and Yamada 2004).

According to the Survey on Employment Management by Japan's Ministry of Health, Labour and Welfare, 95.3% of Japanese firms with 30 or more employees practiced mandatory retirement in 2005. Under the Employment Stabilization Act for the Elderly, the mandatory retirement age should not be set below 60; and again according to the Survey on Employment Management, 91.1% of firms with mandatory retirement set the minimum age at 60.

As mandatory retirement is a practice that requires severance simply because of age, it impacts in two ways on the utilization of an older workforce. One is by reducing the motivation of older people to continue working. In Japan, mandatory retirement from primary employers does not necessarily mean complete retirement from the workforce. Many older workers go on to secondary jobs. However, mandatory retirement is also a major determinant of complete retirement from the labour market. Many researchers have estimated the labour supply functions of older people and found that the experience of mandatory retirement significantly reduces the labour force

*Table 3.2*   The negative effect of mandatory retirement on labour force participation

| Research Papers | Observation Year Estimation Sample | Coefficients on the Probability of Labour Participation |
|---|---|---|
| Seike (1993) | 1983 – men aged 60~69 | −0.1774*** |
| Abe (1998) | 1983, 1998, 1992 – men aged 60~69 | −0.227*** |
| Ogawa (1997) | 1980, 1983, 1988, 1992 – men aged 60~64 | −0.1283*** |
| Seike and Yamada (2004) | 2000 – men aged 60~69 | −0.180*** |

***Statistically significant at the respective level of 1%.

participation propensity of these people. Table 3.2 provides estimated parameters that represent the impact of mandatory retirement on labour force participation.

As seen in the table, mandatory retirement experience exerts a significantly negative impact on the labour force participation of older people. Though the degree of this impact, that is, the size of the parameters, varies depending on the data vintage and the age group of the data samples, mandatory retirement reduces the probability of labour force participation in men aged 60 to 69 by about 20 percentage points, *ceteris paribus*.

The other negative impact of mandatory retirement is that it reduces the utilization of older workers' potential abilities. This is seen when comparing the probability of workers with and without mandatory retirement experience being able to work in the same occupation as their primary jobs. This comparison is made in Figure 3.2. In both the cases of workers receiving and not receiving public pensions, those having experienced mandatory retirement have a statistically lower possibility of working in the same occupation as they did at age 55. Again, this means that workers subjected to mandatory retirement are less likely to work in a workplace where their abilities are fully utilized.

Another problem associated with age-based employment practices is the setting of age limits by employers when hiring. Particularly for workers seeking new employment after mandatory retirement, or even before the age of mandatory retirement for those who become unemployed in mid-career, such age limits in hiring seriously constrain their job opportunities.

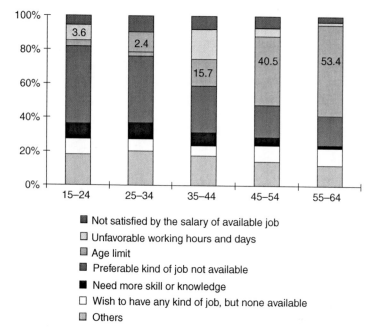

- ■ Not satisfied by the salary of available job
- ☐ Unfavorable working hours and days
- ■ Age limit
- ■ Preferable kind of job not available
- ■ Need more skill or knowledge
- ☐ Wish to have any kind of job, but none available
- ■ Others

*Figure 3.3*   Proportion of unemployed persons by reasons of failure to find a job due to age

*Source*: Statistics Bureau, Ministry of Management and Coordination, Report on the Special Survey of the Labour Force Survey, February 2005.

Partly because of these age limits, the ratio of applicants to job openings significantly drops in the age range of 45 to 49 and higher.

Figure 3.3 shows the results of the Special Survey of the Labour Force Survey by the Statistics Bureau of the Management and Coordination Agency conducted in February 2000, in which unemployed persons were asked their reasons for not being able to find work.

The top reason for those over 45 has always been 'age limits'. In the case of unemployed persons over 45, about 40% of those between 45 and 54, about 50% of those between 55 and 64, and about 60% of those aged 65 and over answered 'age limits' as their reason.

Thus, it is obvious that age-based employment practices such as mandatory retirement and age limits in hiring pose serious obstacles to the employment of older workers. Of course, there are good reasons for employers to want to use such practices, particularly their desire to eliminate wage and promotion systems that increase employees' rank and wage in line with age and seniority. Thus in order to reduce the use of mandatory retirement and age limits in hiring, substantial reform will need to be done to the seniority-based wage and promotion systems in Japan.

## The necessity of human capital investment

So far this paper has discussed the influence of public pension schemes and employment practices on promoting the employment of older people. I would now like to shift focus to the influence of individual choice on later working life, especially on personal investment in 'human capital'.

Among the aspects of human capital, of particular importance are one's physical condition and professional skills. In conducting econometric analyses on the labour supply of older people, physical condition is one of the most significant and influential variables affecting the probability of labour force participation. Skill levels, extrapolated from educational levels, are also very significant variables affecting the probability of labour force participation among older

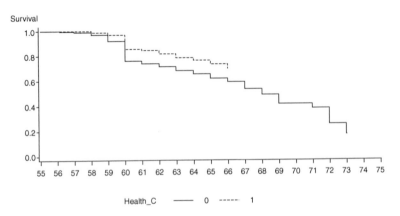

*Figure 3.4*   The impact of health condition on the survival curve of the labour force

-------- Good health condition ------ Not so good health condition

*Note*: The line for the good health condition breaks after the age of 66 because there were not enough samples available.

*Source*: Seike and Yamada 1998a.

people. Figures 3.4. and 3.5 verify, using the so-called Hazard Model, the effects of human capital variables on older people's survival rate within the labour force.

The Hazard Model gives the survival ratio until the end, namely 'life expectancy', of a given event. Here, the duration of labour force participation until retirement is measured as life expectancy for the sake of analysis. Comparison is made among the survival ratios until complete retirement from the labour force based on different variables of health condition and educational level.

Figure 3.4 shows the influence of health condition on the retirement process. The survival ratio curve of those who are in good health is statistically significantly higher than that of those who are not.

Figure 3.5 clearly shows the influence of educational attainment on the retirement process, in particular the survival ratio curve of those who have a college education is significantly higher than that of those who do not. People with a higher education have a higher probability of surviving in the labour force.

Education is the most typical form of human capital investment. Good health is at least to some extent the result of good health maintenance and physical fitness, which are regarded as human capital investment. This being the case, the results of the analyses in Figures 3.4 and 3.5

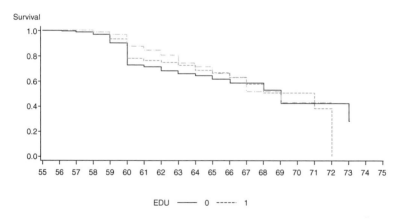

*Figure 3.5* The impact of educational attainment on the survival curve of the labour force

– · – · –College graduates – – – – – High School graduates
——— Compulsory education only

*Source*: Seike and Yamada 1998a.

clearly show that human capital investment has a positive impact on older people's survival in the labour force.

## Policy proposals

From the points of view discussed, I would like to make four policy proposals with regard to establishing an 'age-free active society'.

Proposal I: 'Reform public pension schemes in such a way that they do not discourage older people from continuing to work'. Because public pensions affect income in a way that induces retirement, it is important to lift the eligible age to avoid discouraging the continuation of work. In fact, governments in Europe, the US and Japan have already started in this direction, though it will be necessary for them to accelerate the timing of their reforms and to reconsider their final target age for pension eligibility. Of course, in lifting the pension age on the one hand, it will, on the other, be necessary to guarantee the right to receive an early but reduced pension for those who want to retire before reaching the age of eligibility for full benefits.

To avoid the discouraging effect of the earnings test on the labour supply of people eligible for pensions, it will be necessary to substantially revise the earnings test for public pensions. When sustaining the public pension system requires promoting the employment of older people, it is inconsistent for the public pension scheme itself to discourage older people's participation in the labour market. As the US government has done, the earnings test should eventually be eliminated on the one hand, and favourable treatment of pension benefits should be abolished in the income tax system on the other hand. Income redistribution from older people with high earnings to others should be done not through the pension system but through the tax system.

Proposal II: 'Reform employment practices in such a way that they do not pose an obstacle to the promotion of the employment of older people'. To avoid the serious negative impact of mandatory retirement on the employment of older people, it will eventually be necessary to eliminate the practice itself. It will also be necessary to substantially remove age limits in hiring so as to provide more job opportunities for older and middle-aged people. For these purposes, the introduction of an anti-age discrimination rule should be seriously considered.

Because seniority-based wage and promotion systems are the major reason why employers adopt practices of mandatory retirement and age limits in hiring, it will also be important to reform these systems. In this sense, workers and labour unions will need to be willing to accept compromises that move away from seniority-based to more merit-based wage and promotion systems.

Proposal III: 'Develop a life-long human capital investment scheme'. The most important thing for individuals in an age-free active society will be to invest in their own human capital so as to have valuable skills and a good physical condition when they become older. To support such individual effort, the government should improve its programmes of professional training and recurrent education. It will also be necessary for it to provide financial support to help individuals cover the cost of human capital investment. Because it is an investment, this financial support should not take the form of a subsidy, but should be a loan – one applied to a program that will give the individual the best return on the investment, thus allowing them to pay the loan back.

Proposal IV: 'Learn from each other in establishing age-free active societies'. As mentioned at the beginning of this report, population ageing is a common problem among advanced countries. However, the socio-economic background factors of each country differ, as do the specific policies employed by their governments.

European countries have developed mutually supportive societies in which older people are still able to enjoy a comfortable retirement, though a system of gradual retirement is being used to have them share some of the burden of supporting an ageing population. In the US, anti-age discrimination law and public pension reform have been implemented to promote the employment of older people through the labour market.

Japan is a country where older people are already highly motivated to work. By taking advantage of this motivation while applying lessons garnered from the examples of other countries, Japan should work to realize its propensity, possibly the highest among the advanced countries, to establish an age-free active society. If Japan takes the necessary measures, including those proposed above, it could set global standards for creating an age-free active society.

## References

Abe, Y. (1998) 'Labor Supply of the Japanese Elderly in the 1980s to the 1990s and the Employee's Pension Benefits', *JCER Economic Journal*, 36, July, pp. 50–82.

Ogawa, H. (1997) 'Pensions and the Labor Supply of Men', in the Japan Institute of Labor (ed.), *An Analysis of the Effect of the Revision of Public Pension System on the Labour Force Participation Behavior of Older People*, Tokyo: The Japan Institute of Labour, pp. 17–49.

Seike, A. (1993) *Kōreika shakai no rōdō shijō (The labour market in the aging society)*, Tokyo: Tōyōkeizai Shinpōsha.

Seike, A. (1995) 'The Impact of the Earnings Test', in *Report on the Analysis of Utilization of Human Capital and Structural Change in the Labor Market*, Japan Center for Economic Research.

Seike, A. (2001) 'Beyond Lifetime Employment', *The Geneva Papers*, 26 (4), pp. 642–655.

Seike, A. and M. Suga (2001) 'An Analysis of the Impact of the Employees' Public Pension on the Labor Supply of Older Men by the Employment Status Survey of the Elderly in 1988, 1992 and 1996', *Paper for the Labour Market Committee of the Statistical Research Institute.*

Seike, A. and A. Yamada (1998a) 'A Hazard Analysis of Retirement Behavior', *Mita Business Review*, 41(4), pp. 115–144.

Seike, A. and A. Yamada (1998b) 'The Impact of Mandatory Retirement and the Public Pension System on Human Capital Loss', *The Economic Analysis*, No. 155, Economic Research Institute, Economic Planning Agency.

Seike, A. and A. Yamada (2004) *Kōreisha shugyō no keizaigaku (The Economics of the employment of older workers)*, Tokyo: Nihon Keizai Shinbunsha.

# 4
# Effects of Institutions on Human Capital Investment: A Comparison of Policies in Japan, Germany and the USA

*Birgitta Wolff, Marjaana Gunkel and Sebastian Wenzke*

In Germany, as almost everywhere in the industrialized world, the working population is ageing. It is predicted that in the year 2020 almost 40% of the working population will be over 50 years old (*Economist* 2006; Staudinger and Kühler 2006: 10). This demographic change in the labour force calls for action. The ageing workforce needs to be kept up to date with modern technologies and developments. Investments in human capital have become an unavoidable expense, and lifelong learning will be inevitable. This seems to present governments, firms and employees with challenges which, at least in Germany, are not yet being met. According to Eurostat statistics, the participation rate of German employees in training is one of the lowest in Europe, only 42% of 25 to 64 year olds in the German workforce participated in training of any kind, whereas the participation rate, for example, in Scandinavian countries was over 70% (Eurostat 2005: 2). Moreover, in comparison with other OECD countries, the percentage of German 25 to 64 year olds in the workforce who participate in non-formal job-related education and training is low. In the United States, for instance, over 40% of the workforce participate in such training, whereas in Germany the participation rate is under 15% (OECD 2005: 50). OECD statistics show that public and private investment in education at all levels is low in Germany, although lifelong learning seems to be one of the key factors for future competitiveness under demographic change. We suggest that possible reasons for the low investment in human capital can be found in the German institutional framework (North 1990; Williamson 1996), namely relatively high unemployment benefits and early retirement. We will approach our topic empirically by analyzing and comparing human capital investments and the institutional frameworks of Germany, Japan and the USA. The data will be interpreted by using simple personnel economics models.

Section two will provide an overview of human capital investment and other relevant labour market data. Section three will compare the regulatory frameworks, and section four will conclude by pointing to a need for action in Germany. Low investment in human capital, especially among older workers, and poor workforce participation among older people do seem to some extent to be caused by Germany's institutional framework. With different rules for mandatory retirement and unemployment income there would most likely be more human capital investment in Germany's older workforce and a higher participation rate.

## Workforce participation and spending on education and jobs

In order to compare the levels of human capital investment in Japan, Germany, and the USA, we will provide some data on labour force participation and expenditure on education in the three countries.

### Labour force participation by age

As can be seen from OECD data summarized in Tables 4.1 and 4.2 (OECD 2005: 241–243), people in the 25 to 54 age group have by far a larger workforce participation rate than those over 54. In all three countries, the rate lies above the OECD average which is slightly above 80%. Out of the three countries we are comparing, Japan, with an almost constant rate of about 82%, has the lowest rates for the time period 2001 to 2004. Germany's rate is the highest among the three, increasing to 87.7% in 2004. In contrast, participation in the USA, while still

*Table 4.1* Labour force participation by selected age groups (25–54), both sexes

|            | 2001 | 2002 | 2003 | 2004 |
|------------|------|------|------|------|
| Japan      | 82.2 | 82.0 | 82.1 | 82.2 |
| Germany    | 85.5 | 85.8 | 86.0 | 87.7 |
| USA        | 83.7 | 83.3 | 83.0 | 82.8 |
| Total OECD | 80.2 | 80.3 | 80.2 | 80.6 |

*Source*: OECD 2005: 241–243.

*Table 4.2* Labour force participation by selected age groups (55–64), both sexes

|  | **2001** | **2002** | **2003** | **2004** |
|---|---|---|---|---|
| Japan | 65.8 | 65.4 | 65.8 | 66.0 |
| Germany | 42.9 | 43.3 | 43.1 | 44.2 |
| USA | 60.4 | 61.9 | 62.4 | 62.3 |
| Total OECD | 50.6 | 51.7 | 52.6 | 53.1 |

*Source*: OECD 2005: 241–243.

above the OECD average, steadily declined from 83.7% in 2001 to 82.8% in 2004.

Investigation of the participation rates in the 55 to 64 age group reveals an entirely different picture (Table 4.2). Labour force participation is clearly lower in this age group compared to younger employees between 25 and 54. Ranging from 65.4% in 2002 to 66.0% in 2004, Japan has the highest rate among the three countries. The data for the USA represents a gradual increase within the time period starting at 60.4% in the year 2001, increasing to 62.3% in 2004. Germany has by far the lowest participation rates, from 42.9% in 2001 to 44.2% in 2004. These rates are not only far below those in the other two countries, they also lie clearly below the OECD average, which increased from 50.6% in 2001 to 53.1% in 2004.

Result: Compared to Japan and the USA, Germany has a slight lead in labour force participation in the 24 to 54 age group, but is well behind Japan and the USA in the over 54 age group. This data seems to provide a puzzle that deserves some more analysis. Why is labour force participation among older people particularly low in Germany?

One standard argument in labour market and personnel economics is that employment is related to education (Backes-Gellner, Lazear and Wolff 2001: 1–47). The higher the level of an individual's education, the more likely it is that they will be active in the workforce as their opportunity cost of not participating will be higher.

## Impact of education on labour force participation

In the second step of our analysis we investigated the effect that educational achievement has on labour market participation. As can again be drawn from comparative OECD statistics from the year 2003, achievements in education, and qualifications, do have a positive impact on participation. In all three countries, labour force participation clearly increases with the level of education attained (OECD 2005: 250–252).

Again, there are also clear differences between the three countries. Table 4.3 shows that people who attained less than upper secondary education have a participation rate of 71.3% in Japan, but only 64.1% in the USA. Germany's rate is even lower at 61.2% and thus below the OECD average of 63.0%. Labour force participation in the group with upper secondary education is below the OECD average of 78.1% in all three countries, Germany again displays the lowest rate at 77.7%. In the group of people who completed tertiary education, however, Germany has the highest labour force participation rate with 87.5%. This lies above both the OECD level and the USA, with participation rates of 85.2% and 85.1%, respectively. Japan, with only 82.3%, has the lowest rate in this group. Japan also reveals the lowest increase in labour force participation depending on level of education. There is a difference of only 11 percentage points from less than upper secondary education to tertiary education. The biggest difference in labour force participation between the lowest and the highest educational level can be found in Germany at 26.3 percentage points.

Result: Participation rates increase with the level of education in all three countries. Germany has the lowest participation rate among people with less than tertiary education, while it has the highest rate among people with tertiary education. A question that we will have to answer in this paper is why labour force participation in Germany is so low among people with a low level of education. We will propose an institutional answer to this question later on.

The German labour market seems to react particularly strongly to education. It appears that education improves individual employment prospects as well as employment rates in all countries, but this trend is much stronger in Germany than in Japan and the USA. If it is true that the German labour market reacts so positively to education, one might wonder why Germany does not simply increase its investment in

*Table 4.3*   Labour force participation by educational achievement, both sexes in 2003

|  | Less than up. sec. education | Upper secondary education | Tertiary education |
|---|---|---|---|
| Japan | 71.3 | 77.8 | 82.3 |
| Germany | 61.2 | 77.7 | 87.5 |
| USA | 64.1 | 78.0 | 85.1 |
| Total OECD | 63.0 | 78.1 | 85.2 |

*Source*: OECD 2005: 250–252.

education in order to increase workforce participation, especially among older people.

Let us now turn our attention to differences in public and private expenditure between the three countries. Data on spending as a percentage of Gross Domestic Product (GDP), and public expenditure for education as a percentage of total public spending will be provided.

## Public spending

As a matter of fact, total public expenditure as a percentage of GDP has increased in each of the three countries between 2001 and 2003 for all levels of education combined. While Japan had the lowest percentage, at 3.64% in 2001, and still remained the lowest in 2004 at 3.71%, the USA had the highest with a steady increase from 4.94% in 2000 up to 5.43% in 2004. The data for Germany reveals expenditure of 4.45% in 2000 and 4.71% in 2004. This lies below the level of the USA and also below the EU15 average as can be seen in Table 4.4 (Eurostat 2006a).

Public expenditure on education as a percentage of total public expenditure is highest in the USA. Also, as shown in Table 4.5, shares of 15.49% in 2000 and 15.69% in 2003 of public spending were dedicated

*Table 4.4* Total public expenditure on education as a percentage of GDP (all levels of education)

|         | 2000 | 2001 | 2002 | 2003 |
|---------|------|------|------|------|
| Japan   | 3.82 | 3.64 | 3.66 | 3.71 |
| Germany | 4.45 | 4.49 | 4.70 | 4.71 |
| USA     | 4.94 | 5.08 | 5.36 | 5.43 |
| EU 15*  | 4.73 | 5.01 | 5.13 | 5.21 |

*Note:* *Data for EU15 are Eurostat estimates.
*Source:* Eurostat 2006a.

*Table 4.5* Total public expenditure on education as a percentage of total public expenditure (all levels of education)

|         | 2000  | 2001  | 2002  | 2003  |
|---------|-------|-------|-------|-------|
| Japan   | 10.49 | 10.54 | n/a   | 10.64 |
| Germany | 9.88  | 9.43  | 9.77  | 9.72  |
| USA     | 15.49 | 17.15 | n/a   | 15.68 |
| EU 15*  | 10.45 | 10.81 | 10.95 | 10.98 |

*Note:* *Data for EU15 are Eurostat estimates.
*Source:* Eurostat 2006a.

to education. This is much higher than the share in Japan with 10.49% in the year 2000 and 10.64% in 2003. Germany's share, with 9.88% and 9.72% for the respective periods, lies below every reference group. This is clearly below the USA and Japan, and also below the steadily rising EU15 average of 10.45% in 2000 and 10.98% in 2003 (Eurostat 2006a).

Result: Germany ranks between Japan and the USA with respect to public expenditure on education as a percentage of GDP, while at the same time Germany ranks lowest in the list of public spending on education as a percentage of total public spending. This might suggest two interpretations. First, Germany's share of government spending as a percentage of GDP is higher than elsewhere. Second, within German public spending, education seems to have a lower priority than it has in Japan and the USA. In other words, the governmental share of GDP in the USA might be smaller than in Germany, however, among the things governments spend money on, education ranks much higher in the priority list of the American and Japanese governments than of the German government.

### Private spending

When looking at the expenditure on educational institutions from private sources as a percentage of GDP, the USA is in the lead (Table 4.6). With 2.23% in the year 2000 and 2.06% in 2003, the ratio was more than twice as high as in Germany in the same period. With a decline from 0.97% in 2000 to 0.92% of GDP in 2003, Germany has the lowest percentage of the three countries. However, the EU15 average of 0.6% looks even worse (Eurostat 2006a).

The data for private expenditure on education as a percentage of total expenditure on education in Table 4.7 reveals once more that the level of private involvement seems to be lower in Germany than in Japan and the USA. In the USA, 31.8% of educational funds in 2000, and 27.7% in 2003, came from private sources. Although this represents a slightly

*Table 4.6*   Expenditure on educational institutions from private sources as a percentage of GDP (all levels of education)

|           | 2000 | 2001 | 2002 | 2003 |
|-----------|------|------|------|------|
| Japan     | 1.23 | 1.16 | 1.22 | 1.26 |
| Germany   | 0.97 | 0.96 | 0.87 | 0.92 |
| USA       | 2.23 | 2.26 | 1.90 | 2.06 |
| EU 15*    | 0.60 | 0.58 | 0.58 | 0.63 |

*Note*: *Data for EU15 are Eurostat estimates.
*Source*: Eurostat 2006a.

*Table 4.7* Expenditure of private sources of funds for educational institutions as a percentage of public and private sources of funds for educational institutions (all levels of education)

|         | 2000 | 2001 | 2002 | 2003 |
|---------|------|------|------|------|
| Japan   | 24.8 | 25.0 | 25.5 | 25.9 |
| Germany | 18.9 | 18.6 | 16.7 | 17.4 |
| USA     | 31.8 | 30.8 | 26.2 | 27.7 |
| EU 15*  | 11.5 | 10.9 | 10.8 | 11.4 |

*Note*: * Data for EU15 are Eurostat estimates.
*Source*: Eurostat 2006b.

negative trend, it nevertheless remains far above a quarter. Japan has the second highest share of private funding at an increasing rate from 24.8% in 2000 up to 25.9% in 2003. This implies that less than three quarters of expenditure on education comes from public sources in both the USA and Japan. In Germany, only 18.9% and 17.4% came from private sources during the same period (Eurostat 2006b). That means that far below one fifth of spending on education comes from private sources.

Result: Germany is lagging behind Japan and the USA in the share of spending on education as a share of public spending, and Germany has by far the lowest share of private spending in the educational sector. It appears that neither the government nor private individuals or firms invest enough in human capital in Germany. This is even more surprising considering how sensitive the German labour market seems to be to increases in education levels (Table 4.3).

If not improving education, what does the German government do in order to improve workforce participation, especially among older workers?

## Public expenditure in labour market programmes

Germany is commonly known as a social market economy. This implies that the German government spends substantial amounts of money on securing a relatively high minimum standard of living for those at the bottom of the economic spectrum (Wolff 1996). Social expenditure such as unemployment benefits provides a certain amount of income to people that fall into the social security net. OECD statistics for expenditures in labour market programmes show that Germany is indeed the leading country compared to Japan and the USA with respect to subsidies that flow into post-educational programmes. Spending on start-up incentives, direct job creation, employment incentives and out-of-work income maintenance, for example, are significantly higher than in Japan and the United States (OECD 2005: 266–275).

## Subsidizing the creation of jobs

Expenditures on start-up incentives were ten times higher in Germany than in Japan and the USA. At the same time, less than 0.005% of GDP was spent on direct job creation in Japan and only 0.01% of GDP in the USA, whereas 0.17% and 0.12% of GDP was spent in Germany, in the years 2002 and 2003 respectively. Moreover, expenditures on employment incentives, which include recruitment and employment maintenance incentives, amounted to 0.11% of GDP in Germany. Only 0.02% was spent in Japan and less than 0.005% of GDP was spent in the USA for the same purpose (OECD 2005: 266–275).

Result: German policies seem to set a relatively firm emphasis on creating and maintaining jobs through direct subsidies, while Japan and the USA place greater importance on education when deciding about public spending. This suggests that Germany might be curing the symptoms of low workforce participation rates rather than its causes.

## Unemployment benefits

In relation to GDP, Germany spent more than four times as much on unemployment benefits in the years 2002 and 2003 than Japan or the USA. It dedicated 2.14% in 2002 and 2.27% of GDP in 2003 to economically inactive people, as can be seen in Table 4.8. Japan spent

*Table 4.8* Out-of-work income maintenance and support as a percentage of GDP

|  | 2002–03 | 2003–04 |
|---|---|---|
| Japan | 0.48 | 0.46 |
| Germany* | 2.14 | 2.27 |
| USA | 0.51 | 0.37 |

*Note:* *Fiscal years 2002 and 2003 respectively.
*Source:* OECD 2005: 266–275.

0.48% and 0.46% and the USA 0.51% and 0.37% for the fiscal years of 2002/03 and 2003/4 respectively (OECD 2005: 266–275).

Further analysis of the composition of out-of-work income maintenance and support reveals that most of it originates from full unemployment benefits. In Germany, full unemployment benefits make up 94% of income maintenance, of which almost a 100% come from unemployment insurance. In the USA, total expenditure presented in Table 4.8 stems from unemployment insurance exclusively (OECD 2005: 266–275). In Germany, however, other payments within this category exist. Partial and part-time benefits make up 0.03% and 0.04% of GDP in the same two years, and redundancy and bankruptcy compensation accounted for 0.09% and 0.08% respectively.

Result: It again appears as if German institutions address the symptoms rather than the causes of low workforce participation among certain groups of people. In addition, the German system of unemployment support seems to be not only more generous but also more complex than in Japan and the USA.

Let us now analyze why Germany has particularly severe problems employing people of low educational background as well as older workers, while in Japan and the USA the situation appears to be less severe.

## Institutional frameworks and investment in human capital

### Unemployment benefits

The OECD data reveals a very high level of spending on labour market programmes in Germany in comparison to Japan and the USA. Moreover, out-of-work income maintenance and support is comparatively high in Germany (Table 4.8). The data reveals that the higher the education level of employees, the higher the workforce participation rate, particularly in Germany (Table 4.3). This suggests that it pays to invest in human capital in Germany. There should be strong incentives for individuals to invest in their education in order to get into or stay in the workforce. Having said this, private spending on education is also strikingly low in Germany (Table 4.7). The comparatively generous unemployment benefit system, which prevailed in Germany until the recent introduction of substantial labour market reforms in 2006, might help to explain this puzzle. Table 4.9 summarizes the unemployment payment systems in the three countries up to the year 2005.[1]

*Table 4.9*   Unemployment benefits in Germany, Japan and the USA up to the year 2005

| Germany | Japan | USA |
|---|---|---|
| Depending on social status, about 60 % of earnings for an individual without children for up to a maximum of 32 months. After that a monthly lump sum payment varying from € 331 to € 345 per month. | Between 50% and 80% of the average daily wage for six months. Additional days of unemployment benefit are possible for special cases, such as unemployment from an industry in recession, mental or physical illness, or the employee undergoing training. | According to different state regulations, about 50% of earnings for on average 20 weeks. |

*Sources*: Gunkel 2006: 85; Social Security Programs throughout the World 2005b: 100.

Unlike in Japan and the USA, German employees were until 2006 eligible for continuous unemployment support for an unlimited period of time. Since the possibility of unemployment did not lead to as substantial a loss of income in Germany, unlike in Japan and the USA, the incentive to invest in human capital was lower in Germany. In other words, in Germany individuals had a guaranteed income, even if they remained unemployed for the rest of their lives. For people with a very low education and, thus, productivity, the level of the government's out-of-work-support (often in combination with unofficial jobs) might actually be more attractive than accepting a regular job at their productivity and pay-level (Figure 4.1). This applies in particular to people who have been out of the workforce for a long time.[2]

One can plausibly assume an upward sloping curve with decreasing marginal returns to education because from the first units of education, for example, learning how to read and write, the benefits will be much higher than from learning, for instance, a twenty-seventh foreign language.

Result: The de facto minimum wage that was provided through Germany's unemployment benefits made it unattractive for people at the very lowest educational level to invest in their education. They will rather accept alternative sources of income.

Let us now see if this argument also helps to explain the low workforce participation rate among older people in Germany. It is possible

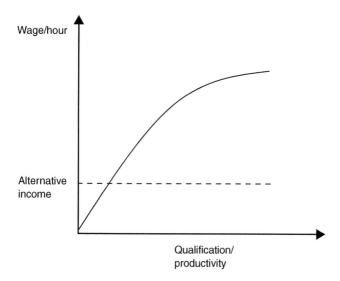

*Figure 4.1* Out-of-work income as a de facto minimum wage

that there is a disproportionately high rate of poorly qualified people among those who are older than 54.

## Lack of incentives to invest

As discussed above, low skilled labour does not have any incentive to invest in human capital because of the relatively attractive outside options provided by non-labour market income. However, private spending in human capital does not only come from individuals, it can also come from firms. Thus, in order to understand the low level of private investment in education, it will be interesting to analyze the perspective of employees as well as the perspective of employers. Whom do corporations invest in? A study of the employment of older workers among Germany's 100 biggest corporations revealed that 86% of those corporations hardly ever recruit workers older than 50, and that 14% do so 'occasionally' (Becker, Bobrichtchev and Henseler 2006: 80). No-one reports that they are recruiting from this age group 'often'. Table 4.10 summarizes the results for the different age groups. It shows that 95% of corporations seem to recruit the absolute majority of their workforce from the younger age group, with all companies recruiting from that group.

*Table 4.10*   Recruiting at Germany's 100 biggest firms

| Age group | Often | Occasionally | Rarely |
| --- | --- | --- | --- |
| <30 | 95% | 5% | – |
| 30–50 | 62% | 36% | 3% |
| >50 | – | 14% | 86% |

*Source:* Becker, Bobrichtchev and Henseler 2006: 80.

*Table 4.11*   Training of employees by age group

| Age group | Often | Occasionally | Rarely |
| --- | --- | --- | --- |
| <30 | 86% | 14% | – |
| 30–50 | 89% | 11% | – |
| >50 | 25% | 59% | 16% |

*Source:* Becker, Bobrichtchev and Henseler 2006: 81.

Another revelation is provided by the responses regarding training practices (Becker, Bobrichtchev and Henseler 2006: 81). Table 4.11 summarizes the data. While 86% and 89% respectively report that they often have the younger or the middle age group participating in training programmes, only 25% say this for the over 50 age group. All companies train the younger and the middle age groups. However, 16% report that they rarely have workers older than 50 participating in training programmes.

In addition, 86% of firms state that they do not have any specific training programmes for older employees, and only 14% report to be planning such programmes (Becker, Bobrichtchev and Henseler 2006: 82). At the same time, 59% of corporations state that these programmes will mainly be offered to managerial employees, that is, a workforce that is already at a high skill level. Other studies provide a similar picture and conclude that German corporations are simply not prepared to handle the upcoming demographic challenges (i.e. IZA 2006: 6).

Does the German government with all their existing subsidy programmes also subsidize training programmes for the older work-force? For instance, the public old age pension insurance can, in principle, subsidize training measures for people who are unemployed. However, a German court recently ruled that the standard practice of not granting such retraining to people older than 45 is illegal

(Sozialgericht Koblenz, AZ S 3 RI 131/04). Instead, there has to be an individual assessment of how much a proposed retraining program will actually increase a person's chance to get back into the labour market. The logic behind this is interesting. First, there seems to be the general assumption that investment in older people's human capital does not pay off. Second, even if practices based on this general assumption have been outlawed, investment in older people still requires special scrutiny and proof that they actually do have some positive effect.

Results: It seems to be common practice to only reluctantly invest in older people's human capital in Germany. This applies to all involved, namely the individuals themselves, corporations and governmental organizations.

The question now is: Why is everybody so reluctant to invest in older people's skills? A comparison of institutional rules might provide an answer.

## Mandatory and early retirement

In all three countries an official retirement age for employees exists. That means that after reaching a certain age, employees are eligible for a full public pension or a minimum guaranteed pension. In Germany, Japan,[3] and the USA[4] (Social Security Programs throughout the World 2005c: 179) the standard retirement age is 65 years (Social Security Programs throughout the World 2005a: 89, 2005b: 94 and 2005c: 179). However, the official retirement age does not give the full picture of the situation in the three countries. Unlike in Japan and the USA, there are comprehensive, publicly subsidized early retirement schemes in Germany. Such schemes were introduced to fight increasing unemployment, especially among young people. These early retirement schemes provide employees with an opportunity to retire from their jobs earlier than the official retirement age. In addition, the schemes provide unemployed individuals aged 58 and over with the option not to search for new employment opportunities and not to accept job offers anymore. In the year 2004, 75% (392,000 individuals) of unemployed individuals aged 58 years and older used this option (OECD 2006: 60–62). Such institutional practices might help to explain the low level of employment of older individuals in Germany and, at the same time, explain why older employees in particular do not have many incentives to invest in their human capital. For them the de facto alternative income is particularly high (see Figure 4.1). Nor do firms have strong incentives to invest in older workers' human capital. The closer retirement is, the more unlikely the amortization of given investment costs.

This is illustrated by the equation below that describes the returns of higher education (Backes-Gellner, Lazear and Wolff 2001). *R* is the discounted return on the human capital investment, *K* describes the income on a better educational level, and *J* the income on the existing skill level. *K–J* is, thus, the income difference between with and without training. *r* describes the interest rate, and *T* the time horizon, that is, the time that is left in the person's working life to capture the returns from the investment.

$$R = \sum_{t=1}^{T} \frac{K_t - J_t}{(1+r)^t}$$

The equation explains why, *ceteris paribus*, investments will be less likely if there is not much work time left. But why is the situation in Japan and the USA different from what we observe in Germany?

In Japan, exactly the opposite is subsidized from that in Germany. The Japanese government provides wage subsidy schemes for hiring and retaining workers between the ages of 60 and 64. Moreover, even though German firms are now subsidized for hiring older workers, the age limit for the subsidy is substantially lower than in Japan, that is, 50 years and older (OECD 2006: 111). In addition, strict employment protection regulations prevail in Germany, which are a major barrier to hiring any employee (OECD 2006: 64). If dismissing employees is costly, employers think twice before they sign an employment contract. And if employees are considered unlikely to retrain and adjust their skills to changing conditions, they will think harder still.

Figure 4.2 shows that the effective retirement age in Japan, for both female and male, is substantially higher than the official retirement age.[5] In the USA, the workforce seems to retire just a bit earlier than the official retirement age, whereas German employees retire substantially earlier than the official retirement age. Neither Japan nor the USA applies the rigid practice of virtually forcing people older than the official retirement age out of the labour market. In Japan as well as in the USA, people may still accept legal employment, even if they are older than 65. In Germany, this occurs only under very restrictive, exceptional rules and at a loss of income from the government pension plan. In Japan and the USA, many older people actually remain in the workforce because they still want to improve their income and/or pension entitlements. In Germany, this is legally impossible for most of the workforce. Over all, Germans retire far earlier than both Japanese and Americans.

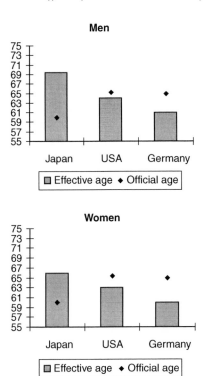

*Figure 4.2*   Official and effective retirement ages for males and females in OECD countries

*Source*: Adapted from OECD 2006: 32.

Alternative income options can, once more, help to explain different decisions in different countries. The level of retirement payments can be assumed to influence the desire to retire. If the retirement payments are relatively high, the incentive to keep working – or retraining – past the official retirement age decreases. Figure 4.3 presents the net pension benefits in OECD countries as a percentage of net pre-retirement earnings at the level of 100% of average production worker earnings.

The pensions from mandatory retirement plans are higher in Germany than the OECD average. Employees in Japan and the United States receive lower retirement benefits from public pension plans than do employees in Germany. However, in the USA there is substantial additional income from voluntary pension plans, which lifts the total pension entitlements close to the German level, although these private

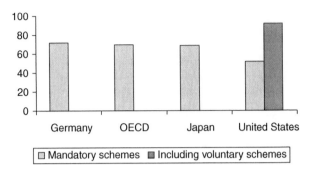

*Figure 4.3* Net pension replacement rates (%) in OECD countries
*Source*: Adapted from OECD 2006: 58.

pension plans are typically not held by low skilled workers. Thus, for a large group of workers, retirement can be assumed to be a more desirable state in Germany than in Japan and the USA with respect to alternative income.

Result: The German labour force appears to retire earlier and with higher pensions than employees in Japan and the USA. In addition, there is mandatory retirement in the sense that continuing to work is usually not an option. The effective retirement age in Germany is clearly below those in Japan and the USA (Figure 4.2). Combined with relatively high pensions, this leads to reduced incentives to invest in older workers' human capital at an even earlier age than in other countries. Neither the prospective retiree, nor his/her (potential) employer has an interest in investing if there is no time left to recover some adequate return on the investment, and pensions are acceptable anyway.

## Conclusion and outlook

According to our analysis, it does not seem to be true that individuals and firms harm themselves by 'under investing' in older workers' human capital. From their utility maximizing perspective, it might be perfectly rational to do exactly what they are doing – given the institutional framework they are embedded in. The low level of private investment in education in Germany seems to be influenced by the German institutional framework. In particular, the regulations relating to the retirement of employees, as well as unemployment benefits, seem to have an influence on the willingness to invest in human capital, especially for low skilled workers. Even though the data show that investment in human capital has positive effects in the form of higher workforce participation rates, private as well as public spending on education remain lower in Germany than in Japan and the USA. The data reveals that, particularly in Germany, more investment in education could greatly increase workforce participation in general, while there are few incentives to invest in older people's skills.

The discussion presented is, at this stage, exploratory, and further research is still required. However, to draw a preliminary conclusion, it would appear that the German institutional framework does not seem to offer enough incentives for lifelong learning. In some cases, it actually seems to provide disincentives to firms and individuals for investing in human capital, for example, in the form of relatively generous retirement and, at least until recently, high unemployment benefit systems. Providing better incentives for lifelong learning to the ageing population in Germany will require further institutional change.

## Notes

1. As part of a substantial package of labour market reforms (often referred to as the so-called *Hartz-reforms*), unemployment benefits were curtailed quite significantly in 2006. More specifically, the prevailing period for drawing unemployment insurance (*Arbeitslosengeld*) was curtailed from a maximum of 32 months to 18 months for workers over 55. Once these benefits run out, unemployed workers can no longer draw monthly lump sum payments as part of *Arbeitslosenhilfe*. Instead, they may only be eligible for benefits (Arbeitslosengeld II) which are generally as high as social assistance benefits.
2. In Germany, long-term unemployment is substantially higher than in the US and Japan.
3. There are some exceptions for women and individuals with the right to an early pension. The pension can also be deferred up to the age of 69.
4. The pension can be deferred up to the age of 70.
5. Note that here the official retirement age is the earliest age at which the employees are entitled to full public pensions.

## References

Backes-Gellner, U., E. P. Lazear and B. Wolff (2001) *Personalökonomik. Fortgeschrittene Anwendungen für das Management,* Stuttgart: Schäffer-Poeschel.
Becker, F. G., R. Bobrichtchev and N. Henseler (2006) 'Ältere Arbeitnehmer und alternde Belegschaften. Eine empirische Studie bei den 100 größten deutschen Unternehmungen', *ZfM (Zeitschrift für Management),* 1, pp. 70–89.
*The Economist* (2006) 'Special Report: The Ageing Workforce', *The Economist* 2/18/06, pp. 52–54.

Eurostat (2005) *Lifelong learning in Europe 2003*, http://epp.eurostat.ec.europa.eu/pls/portal/docs/PAGE/PGP_PRD_CAT_PREREL/PGE_CAT_PREREL_YEAR_2005/PGE_CAT_PREREL_YEAR_2005_MONTH_09/3-06092005-EN-BP.PDF (last accessed 13/06/06).

Eurostat (2006a) *Data Collection: Expenditure on Education as % of GDP or Public Expenditure*, http://epp.eurostat.ec.europa.eu/portal/page?_pageid=1996,4532 3734&_dad=portal&_schema=PORTAL&screen=welcomeref&open=/edtr/ educ/educ_finance&language=en&product=EU_MASTER_education_ training&root=EU_MASTER_education_training&scrollto=0 (last accessed 26/05/06).

Eurostat (2006b) *Data Collection: Funding of Education*, http://epp.eurostat.ec. europa.eu/portal/page?_pageid=1996,45323734&_dad=portal&_schema= PORTAL&screen=welcomeref&open=/edtr/educ/educ_finance &language=en&product=EU_MASTER_education_training&root=EU_ MASTER_education_training&scrollto=0 (last accessed 26/05/06).

Gunkel, M. (2006) *Country-Compatible Incentive Design – a Comparison of Employees' Performance Reward Preferences in Germany and the USA*, Wiesbaden: Deutscher Universitäts-Verlag.

IZA Compact (2006) Personalpolitische Strategien deutscher Unternehmen – Auf den demographischen Wandel nur bedingt vorbereitet, April/May, pp. 5–7.

North, D. C. (1990) *Institutions, Institutional Change and Economic Performance*, Cambridge: Cambridge University Press.

OECD (2005) *OECD Employment Outlook 2005*, http://www.oecd.org/ dataoecd/36/30/35024561.pdf (last accessed 13/06/06).

OECD (2006) *Aging and Employment Policies – Live Longer, Work Longer*, Paris: OECD Publishing.

Social Security Programs throughout the World (2005a) *Social Security Programs in Germany*, http://www.ssa.gov/policy/docs/progdesc/ssptw/2004-2005/europe/ germany.pdf (last accessed 14/06/06).

Social Security Programs throughout the World (2005b) *Social Security Programs in Japan*, http://www.ssa.gov/policy/docs/progdesc/ssptw/2004-2005/asia/japan. pdf (last accessed 14/06/06).

Social Security Programs throughout the World (2005c) *Social Security Programmes in the U.S.A.*, http://www.ssa.gov/policy/docs/progdesc/ssptw/2004-2005/ americas/unitedstates.pdf (last accessed 14/06/06).

Sozialgericht Koblenz, AZ S 3 RI 131/04.

Staudinger, U. M. and L. Kühler (2006) 'Das Ende der geistigen Frührente', *Personalwirtschaft*, February, pp. 10–13.

Williamson, O. E. (1996) *The Mechanisms of Governance*, Oxford: Oxford University Press.

Wolff, B. (1996) 'Incentive-Compatible Change Management in a Welfare State: Asking the Right Questions in the German Standort-Debate', *Working Paper No.6.4/1996*, Center for European Studies, Harvard University.

# 5

# Labour, Income and Poverty among Elderly Japanese

*Isao Ohashi*

The ageing of a country's population has a variety of effects on its society and economy. Of most serious concern is the impact on public finances for pensions and medical care. But ageing not only increases the burden on the younger generation, it also depletes the resources necessary to drive strong economic growth. In this respect, Japan is confronted with a difficult situation.[1] As an illustration, it would be worthwhile to point out that, as of 2004, the percentage of the total population that was 60 years old or over was 19.5%, the highest in the world, while the total fertility rate was 1.29, close to the lowest in the world. Furthermore, the situation is rapidly becoming more serious.

One effective solution to the problem of ageing is to promote the employment of elderly people. In fact, the Diet passed the Revised Law concerning the Stabilization of Employment of Older Persons in 2005, thereby making it compulsory for companies to continue to employ elderly people until the age of 65. While such measures are indeed conducive to promoting the employment of aged people, it gives rise to a number of ancillary problems that remain to be solved. For example, in Japan, where the percentage of elderly people in the workforce is already among the highest in the world, can they continue to work longer? What about the economic conditions under which they work? Are those conditions attractive enough to give them the incentive to work? What kind of work is available? What about the working hours? The main purpose of this paper is to clarify the basic facts concerning these issues.

The problem of the ageing of society is often addressed together with that of the dwindling number of children. Such an approach, however, obscures the nature of the problem because these two issues are not totally dependent on each other. Suffice it to say that, regardless of whether the number of children decreases, the population will continue to age as the average life expectancy increases. It should be noted that according to the *White Paper on Labour and Welfare* (Kōseirōdōshō 2003), the average life expectancy was 69.3 years for men and 74.7 years for women in 1970, when the mandatory retirement age was generally 55. In 2001, it was 78.1 years for men and 84.9 years for women, showing in both cases an increase of approximately 10 years over a period of about 30 years. This means that to support themselves, the Japanese now have to work 10 years longer than in 1970. Moreover, the WHO *World Health Report 2005* predicts a further increase of 6.4 years in average life expectancy by 2050. Even these simple calculations indicate that, regardless of the dwindling number of children, the average Japanese will need to continue to work until the age of 70 or so in order not to increase the economic burden on other people.

From the above perspective, this paper will discuss a number of issues, such as whether it is possible for many elderly people to continue to work until about 70 years of age; what obstacles, if any, exist; what economic foundation they should have; how they can escape poverty; and what preconditions are necessary for them to work comfortably while getting satisfaction from working. In particular, this paper will outline the current status of, and trends in, the employment of elderly people (Section 2); shed light on the configuration and distribution of their income (Section 3); discuss the causes of poverty (Section 4); and analyze the relationship between their economic situation, mode of work, and level of satisfaction (Section 5). Finally, Section 6 will conclude the paper.

## Status of labour force participation among elderly people

This section outlines the status of employment of people in their 60s, based on a series of surveys titled *Survey of Employment Conditions of Older Persons* published by the former Ministry of Labour and the current Ministry of Health, Labour and Welfare (hereafter abbreviated to 'the Surveys'). These Surveys have been conducted every four years since 1988 among people in the age bracket of 55 to 69 (inclusive) (approximately 30,000 individuals) and establishments employing five or more full-time employees (approximately 12,000 establishments). The Surveys on individuals, which are linked to the National Census (conducted by the Ministry of Internal Affairs and Communications), provide the most detailed information available concerning the current status of employment of elderly people in Japan and their economic circumstances such as home environment, pension, earned income and desire to work. For the present study, the author attempted to obtain values as close as possible to the actual status of the total population of elderly Japanese by using the sampling weights.

It is a well-known fact[2] that Japan has a significantly higher labour force participation ratio of people in their 60s than other advanced nations. Figure 5.1 presents the trends in different forms of labour force participation for people in their 60s. In the Surveys, a 'person participating in the labour force' is defined as anybody who did work that generated income in September of the year of that survey.

The Surveys reveal that the percentage of people in this age bracket who participated in the labour force rose from 48.7% in 1988 to 49.5% in 1992, a very slight increase of 0.8 percentage points, just after the bursting of the Bubble Economy. Thereafter the percentage dropped by

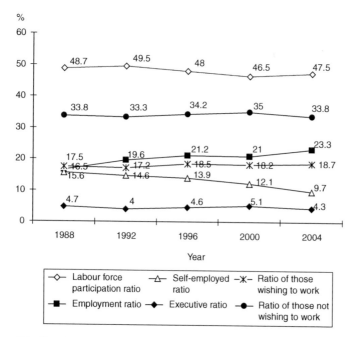

*Figure 5.1*  Trends in status of employment of people in their 60s

*Note*: The figures for 2004 are the author's estimates.

*Source*: Ministry of Health, Labour and Welfare, Survey of Employment Conditions of Older Persons, various years.

three points toward the year 2000 as the lingering economic slowdown adversely impacted the employment of elderly people.[3] The ratio is, however, now seeing a gradual upturn, reflecting the recent economic recovery. Interestingly, of the different forms of labour force participation, the percentage of self-employed people (self-employment ratio) has been dropping significantly, while that of employed people (employment ratio) has generally increased. This trend is in line with general trends in the Japanese economy.

Another trend to be noted is that, of those not in the labour force, the percentage of elderly people who do not wish to work has remained constant, whereas the percentage of those wishing to work has been on the rise. For example, the ratio of those wishing to work increased by 1.2 points from 17.5% in 1988 to 18.7% in 2004. As a result, today, 35.6% of those not in the labour force, who make up 52.5% of all elderly people, wish to re-enter the labour force. As the economy recovers, the percentage of elderly people in the labour force is likely to increase. Tables 5.1 and 5.2 illustrate the trends in the labour participation ratio of elderly people by gender and by age group (lower 60s and upper 60s).

The tables reveal a number of interesting facts. First, there is a big gap in the labour force participation ratio between those in their lower 60s and those in their upper 60s. In 2004, the difference was nearly 20 percentage points for men: the ratio for men in their lower 60s was close to 70%, whereas that for men in their upper 60s was slightly less than 50%. On the other hand, the difference for women was slightly less than 14 percentage points: the ratio for women in their lower 60s was 42.3%, as opposed to 28.5% of women in their upper 60s. It should be noted, however, that the rate of decrease in the labour force participation ratio due to age was greater for women than for men.

Second, for both men and women, the employment ratio increased more significantly for those in their lower 60s than for those in their upper 60s. Taking the period of 1988 to 2004, for example, this employment ratio increased nearly 10 percentage points for those in their lower 60s, as opposed to 3 and 4 points for those in their upper 60s, again for both men and women. Third, little change was seen in the self-employment ratio between those in their lower 60s and those in their upper 60, for both men and women. In particular, there was practically no difference in 2004 between these two age groups. The self-employment ratio, however, dropped greatly (as much as 10 to 11 percentage points) during the period of 1988 to 2004 for men in both age groups (lower and upper 60s). In light of the fact that self-employment is a relatively easy way for elderly people to remain in

*Table 5.1*  Trends in labour participation ratio among elderly males (unit: %)

| | Lower 60s | | | | | Upper 60s | | | | |
|---|---|---|---|---|---|---|---|---|---|---|
| | 1988 | 1992 | 1996 | 2000 | 2004 | 1988 | 1992 | 1996 | 2000 | 2004 |
| In labour force | 70.3 | 70.9 | 69.9 | 66.5 | 68.8 | 53.8 | 58.5 | 53.1 | 51.6 | 49.4 |
| Employed | 29.7 | 35.8 | 37.2 | 35.4 | 39.3 | 17.3 | 22.0 | 22.8 | 20.7 | 21.1 |
| Self-employed | 24.3 | 21.4 | 18.9 | 17.0 | 13.7 | 23.7 | 21.5 | 18.1 | 17.6 | 13.7 |
| Executives | 9.2 | 8.0 | 9.4 | 9.1 | 9.0 | 6.8 | 5.5 | 5.7 | 7.1 | 5.5 |
| Other | 7.1 | 5.7 | 4.3 | 5.0 | 6.8 | 6.0 | 9.5 | 6.5 | 6.2 | 9.1 |
| Not in labour force | 29.7 | 29.1 | 30.1 | 33.5 | 31.2 | 44.2 | 41.5 | 46.9 | 48.4 | 50.6 |
| Wishing to work | 16.9 | 15.6 | 19.7 | 18.5 | 16.1 | 17.5 | 15.5 | 18.7 | 18.2 | 21.1 |
| Not wishing to work | 12.9 | 13.5 | 10.4 | 15.0 | 15.1 | 26.7 | 26.0 | 28.2 | 30.2 | 29.5 |
| Total | 100 | 100 | 100 | 100 | 100 | 100 | 100 | 100 | 100 | 100 |

*Note*: 'other' includes those who 'worked arbitrarily at the request of a neighbour or a company', who 'worked at home on a part-time basis', and who 'assisted a self-employed person'.

*Source*: Ministry of Health, Labour and Welfare, Survey of Employment Conditions of Older Persons, various years.

*Table 5.2*  Trends in labour participation ratio among elderly females (unit: %)

| | Lower 60s | | | | | Upper 60s | | | | |
|---|---|---|---|---|---|---|---|---|---|---|
| | 1988 | 1992 | 1996 | 2000 | 2004 | 1988 | 1992 | 1996 | 2000 | 2004 |
| In labour force | 41.0 | 38.2 | 40.9 | 41.5 | 42.3 | 28.7 | 31.8 | 27.8 | 28.7 | 28.5 |
| Employed | 12.1 | 14.1 | 16.4 | 19.2 | 21.9 | 6.5 | 6.6 | 8.1 | 8.7 | 9.7 |
| Self-employed | 9.6 | 7.6 | 10.8 | 7.7 | 6.1 | 7.4 | 9.5 | 8.4 | 7.1 | 6.0 |
| Executives | 1.7 | 1.6 | 1.8 | 2.6 | 1.6 | 1.9 | 1.1 | 1.4 | 1.8 | 1.1 |
| Other | 17.6 | 14.9 | 11.9 | 12.0 | 12.7 | 12.9 | 14.6 | 9.9 | 11.1 | 11.7 |
| Not in labour force | 59.0 | 61.8 | 59.0 | 58.5 | 57.7 | 71.3 | 68.2 | 72.2 | 71.3 | 71.5 |
| Wishing to work | 19.0 | 20.4 | 19.5 | 20.4 | 19.7 | 16.4 | 16.9 | 16.1 | 15.3 | 18.3 |
| Not wishing to work | 40.0 | 41.4 | 39.5 | 38.1 | 38.0 | 54.9 | 51.3 | 56.1 | 56.0 | 53.2 |
| Total | 100 | 100 | 100 | 100 | 100 | 100 | 100 | 100 | 100 | 100 |

*Source*: Ministry of Health, Labour and Welfare, Survey of Employment Conditions of Older Persons, various years.

the labour force, this downward trend is not desirable in terms of providing working opportunities.

Table 5.3 lists a breakdown of the reason why those wishing to work were unable to participate in the labour force, from the 2000 Survey.[4]

According to this table, the ratio of those saying 'Could not find an appropriate job' was 53.4% overall, but was extremely high (70.7%) for men in their lower 60s. The ratio was 56% for men in their upper 60s and just under 50% for women in their lower 60s. The second most often cited reason was 'Own health concerns'. This accounted for about 23% of both men and women, with higher ratios among those in their upper 60s. Another noteworthy trend was that a higher percentage of women than men mentioned 'Family member's health (nursing care, etc.)' and 'Household matters (chores)'. These two reasons were mentioned by 24.4% of women, with a higher percentage for those in their upper 60s. Thus, more women cited one or other of these reasons than concerns for their own health.

The survey further asked those responding with 'Could not find an appropriate job' about their reasons. The results are summarized in

*Table 5.3*   Reasons why those wishing to work could not work (2000) (unit: %)

| | | Male | | Female | |
|---|---|---|---|---|---|
| Reason | Total | Lower 60s | Upper 60s | Lower 60s | Upper 60s |
| Could not find an appropriate job | 53.4 | 70.7 | 56.0 | 48.4 | 36.8 |
| Own health concerns | 22.9 | 18.5 | 27.8 | 20.8 | 26.2 |
| Family member's health (nursing care, etc.) | 6.6 | 3.2 | 4.0 | 8.4 | 11.1 |
| Household matters (chores) | 8.6 | 0.7 | 3.6 | 13.6 | 16.6 |
| Other | 8.5 | 6.9 | 8.6 | 8.8 | 9.3 |
| Total | 100 | 100 | 100 | 100 | 100 |

*Note*: 'other' included 'preparing to start a new business', and 'did not receive orders on a contract or part-time job'.

*Source*: Ministry of Health, Labour and Welfare, Survey of Employment Conditions of Older Persons, 2000.

Table 5.4. The most often cited reason was 'Could not find a job commensurate with my skills or experience', scoring about 68% among men and 46.5% among women. Concerning the working conditions, relatively large numbers of women cited time-related reasons such as 'Working hours did not suit me' and 'Commuting time did not suit me', constituting about 19% of the total.

As has already been mentioned, many of those wishing to work but not in the labour force cited 'Could not find an appropriate job'. This trend also applies to those not in the labour force who did not wish to work. Table 5.5 lists the main reasons cited by those not in the labour force who said 'Did not wish to work'.

According to the table, 6.1% responded with 'My skills or experience was no longer of any use' or 'Could not find an appropriate employer'. In particular, the ratio of such men in their lower 60s was over 15%. There is no major difference between the number of elderly people who did not participate in the labour force for these reasons and those wishing to work but not in the labour force who 'could not find an appropriate job'. Thus, the number of men in their lower 60s who were not in the labour force because they could not find a job which suited them, including both those wishing and those not wishing to work, was as high as 45.9% of all those who were not in the labour force.

*Table 5.4* Reasons for not finding an appropriate job (2000) (unit: %)

| Reason | Male | Female |
|---|---|---|
| Could not find a job commensurate with my skills or experience | 67.9 | 46.5 |
| Working hours did not suit me | 8.2 | 13.9 |
| Salary did not suit me | 4.2 | 2.0 |
| Commuting time did not suit me | 1.1 | 4.9 |
| Other | 18.5 | 32.8 |
| Total | 100 | 100 |

*Source*: Ministry of Health, Labour and Welfare, Survey of Employment Conditions of Older Persons, 2000.

*Table 5.5* Reasons for not wishing to work (2000) (unit: %)

| Reason | Total | Male | | Female | |
|---|---|---|---|---|---|
| | | Lower 60s | Upper 60s | Lower 60s | Upper 60s |
| Economic reasons | 9.2 | 14.9 | 14.3 | 6.7 | 6.9 |
| My skills or experience was no longer of any use | 1.8 | 4.9 | 3.1 | 0.7 | 1.1 |
| Could not find an appropriate employer | 4.3 | 10.5 | 6.9 | 3.8 | 1.7 |
| Own health concerns | 35.5 | 33.2 | 44.8 | 28.1 | 36.9 |
| Family member's health (nursing care, etc.) | 6.5 | 8.4 | 3.2 | 8.0 | 6.5 |
| Wishing to concentrate on hobbies or volunteer activities | 11.8 | 18.6 | 16.4 | 10.8 | 8.6 |
| Wishing to concentrate on household chores, etc. | 25.0 | 3.4 | 3.3 | 36.8 | 32.6 |
| Other | 6.0 | 6.1 | 7.9 | 5.1 | 5.7 |
| Total | 100 | 100 | 100 | 100 | 100 |

*Source:* Ministry of Health, Labour and Welfare, Survey of Employment Conditions of Older Persons, 2000.

'Health concerns' were another major reason for not being in the labour force. Table 5.3 indicates that 23% of all the respondents were not working because of concerns about their own health although they wished to. The percentage was somewhat higher among those in their lower 60s than among those in their upper 60s. There was only a small difference in the ratios between men and women. Among those who did not wish to work, the percentage of those who cited health concerns as the main reason was higher. Table 5.5 puts this ratio at 35.5% with men and women combined, while the ratio among men was higher than among women. As many as 44.8% of men in their upper 60s who did not wish to work cited 'health concerns' as the main reason.

Figure 5.2 shows trends in the percentages of those not in the labour force citing 'health concerns' as the main reason among those wishing to work and also among those not wishing to work (retirees).

This figure indicates that the percentage of those not in the labour force citing 'health concerns' as the main reason has been decreasing steadily both among retirees (since 1988) and among those wishing to work (since 1992).[5] More specifically, the ratio for retirees in their lower 60s dropped from 53.9% to 29.5%, a 24.4 points decrease, and that for those in their upper 60s dropped from 59.2% to 39.5%, a nearly 20 points decrease. The ratio for those wishing to work dropped more sharply (by slightly more than 20 points) among those in their upper 60s than among those in their lower 60s. It is to be expected that advances in medical technology and the proliferation of higher education will further reduce the percentage of people in their 60s not wishing to work for health reasons,[6] thereby increasing the supply of elderly workers.

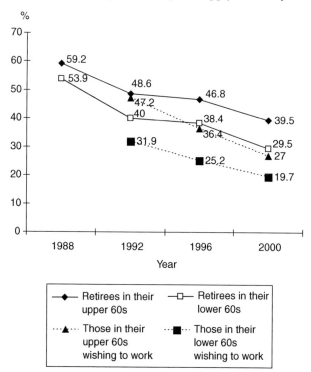

*Figure 5.2* Percentages of those not working for health reasons

*Source:* Ministry of Health, Labour and Welfare, Survey of Employment Conditions of Older Persons, various years.

## Distribution of personal income

In recent years, the widening income disparity has become such a major issue as to be taken up and debated by the National Diet. However, no general consensus has yet been reached among scholars and policy-makers on how to interpret the current situation. Tachibanaki (1998), for example, maintains that the income disparity in Japan widened during the 1980s and the 1990s, and that Japan has now become a society of inequality comparable to major countries in Europe. On the other hand, Ohtake and Saito (1999) and Ohtake (2005) argue that since the gaps in income and spending tend to increase with age, the ageing of society itself has caused an apparent overall income disparity to widen. Meanwhile, a number of other scholars have also been studying this issue and how to interpret the data, with the majority of arguments gradually converging toward the conclusion that the income disparity in Japan is still smaller than in the US and Europe. How these arguments have evolved over time is documented in detail by Funaoka (2001) and Ohtake (2005) and also analyzed in depth from an international perspective by Shirahase (2002) and Seike and Yamada (2004).[7]

What the wide income disparity means from the viewpoint of policy-making greatly depends on individual values. However, many would support the notion that some political measures need to be taken for those who cannot maintain the standard of living guaranteed by the Japanese Constitution. From this perspective, this section sheds light on the distribution pattern of elderly people's personal income, and the next section will discuss what factors cause poverty among elderly people, and analyze the income of households with one or more elderly members.

Table 5.6 summarizes the average values and distribution of elderly people's personal income in 1996 and 2000 by age group: upper 50s, lower 60s, and upper 60s.

In the table, the term 'earned income' means the income (including taxes, i.e. before source deduction of taxes) earned from work during September of the year of survey, and the term 'non-earned income' means the income (including taxes) obtained from sources other than work during the same month. Further, the suffix 0 is appended (e.g. 'Income 0') where the data for elderly people with no income are included in the calculation, while the suffix 1 is appended (e.g. 'Income 1') where it is excluded. While a variety of indices such as Gini's coefficient are used to express the distribution or spread of income, this paper

Table 5.6  Distribution of personal income of elderly people (unit: ¥1,000)

| Type of income | | 2000 | | | 1992 | | |
|---|---|---|---|---|---|---|---|
| | | Upper 50s | Lower 60s | Upper 60s | Upper 50s | Lower 60s | Upper 60s |
| Earned Income 1 | Average | 309 | 228 | 186 | 277 | 212 | 178 |
| | SCV | 0.65 | 1.12 | 1.76 | 0.73 | 1.32 | 2.24 |
| | MLD | 0.31 | 0.41 | 0.52 | 0.30 | 0.38 | 0.48 |
| Non-Earned Income 1 (including pension) | Average | 136 | 133 | 135 | 131 | 121 | 112 |
| | SCV | 0.89 | 0.70 | 0.57 | 1.01 | 0.92 | 0.96 |
| | MLD | 0.36 | 0.35 | 0.26 | 0.30 | 0.39 | 0.37 |
| Pension 1 | Average | 104 | 121 | 126 | 113 | 109 | 103 |
| | SCV | 0.36 | 0.56 | 0.46 | 0.28 | 0.61 | 0.65 |
| | MLD | 0.18 | 0.34 | 0.24 | 0.16 | 0.35 | 0.34 |
| Total Income 1 | Average | 311 | 234 | 199 | 278 | 215 | 177 |
| | SCV | 0.68 | 0.93 | 1.12 | 0.72 | 1.02 | 1.43 |
| | MLD | 0.31 | 0.38 | 0.36 | 0.31 | 0.40 | 0.47 |
| Earned Income 1 | Component contribution | 95 | 83 | 68 | 94 | 73 | 59 |
| Non-Earned Income 1 | Ratio to disparity (%) | 5 | 17 | 32 | 6 | 27 | 41 |

Continued

Table 5.6  Continued

| Type of income | | 2000 | | | 1992 | | |
|---|---|---|---|---|---|---|---|
| | | Upper 50s | Lower 60s | Upper 60s | Upper 50s | Lower 60s | Upper 60s |
| Earned Income 0 | Average | 237 | 120 | 66 | 200 | 104 | 65 |
| | SCV | 1.16 | 3.03 | 6.72 | 1.28 | 3.34 | 6.56 |
| Non-Earned Income 0 (including pension) | Average | 19 | 89 | 129 | 25 | 82 | 105 |
| | SCV | 12.89 | 1.52 | 0.64 | 10.00 | 1.84 | 1.10 |
| Total Income 0 | Average | 255 | 209 | 195 | 224 | 186 | 170 |
| | SCV | 1.06 | 1.16 | 1.17 | 1.15 | 1.30 | 1.52 |
| Earned Income 0 | Component contribution | 95 | 80 | 68 | 89 | 76 | 70 |
| Non-Earned Income 0 | Ratio to disparity (%) | 5 | 20 | 32 | 11 | 24 | 30 |
| Pension Take-up Ratio | % | 4.8 | 59.9 | 94.7 | 10.6 | 63.7 | 92.6 |
| Labour Force Participation Ratio | % | 74.6 | 53.6 | 39.5 | 73.6 | 54.1 | 44.0 |

*Notes:* 'Income 0' includes, in its statistical calculation, elderly persons with the income in question (pension) being zero, whereas 'Income 1' includes, in its statistical calculation, only elderly persons with the income in question (pension) being non-zero. The element contribution ratio to disparity has been calculated from SCV using the element decomposition method proposed by Sharrocks (1982).

*Source:* Ministry of Health, Labour and Welfare, Survey of Employment Conditions of Older Persons, 1992 and 2000.

uses the squared coefficient of variation (SCV) and mean log deviation (MLD).[8]

Let us first study earned income. Table 5.6 indicates that in both 1992 and 2000, Average Earned Income 1 decreased with age, apparently reflecting a decline in earning power. A closer look, however, reveals that the average earned income of those in their upper 60s was still ¥186,000, higher than the average non-earned income of ¥135,000. This means that the income of elderly people heavily depended on whether or not they had earned income. Average Earned Income 0 (the calculation of which includes those with no earned income) also decreases with age, and to a greater degree than Average Earned Income 1, both in terms of absolute value and in terms of rate of decrease. For example, for people in their upper 60s, Average Earned Income 1 was ¥66,000, lower than the average non-earned income of ¥129,000. This was clearly because the amount of pension increased with age, while the labour force participation ratio decreased with age.[9]

Table 5.6 reveals that in both 1992 and 2000, both the SCV and MLD for Income 1 of those with earned income increased with age. It further shows that the SCV for Income 0 also increased with age,[10] but that the values were smaller than for Income 1 in all the age groups. The direct reasons why SCV had greater values for the group including those with no income are that zero is the smallest value and that the inclusion of those with no income significantly reduces the overall average.

Why does the gap in Earned Income 1 increase with age? For example, in 2000, the MLD for Income 1 increased with age from 0.31 for the youngest group through 0.41 to 0.50 for the oldest group. Let us note here that the distribution of earned income varies significantly with the type of job. Table 5.7 shows how MLD varied with job type in 2000. The following three points emerge out of this data. First, for all job types, MLD increases with age, meaning that the higher the age, the greater the gap in earning power. Especially noteworthy is the increase in MLD for corporate executives and self-employed people. For example, the MLD for corporate executives in their upper 60s was 1.86 times as high as for those in their upper 50s, and the MLD for self-employed people in their upper 60s was 1.48 times as high as for those in their upper 50s. Second, MLD was generally high for self-employed and 'other' ancillary job types, and the percentages of the population with these job types increased significantly with age.

As shown in Table 5.7, from the upper 50s to the upper 60s, the relative population of self-employed people grew from 14.9% to 30.7%, an increase of 15.8 percentage points, and that of other job types grew

*Table 5.7*   Mean log deviation of earned income by job type (2000)

| Job type | Upper 50s | Lower 60s | Upper 60s |
|---|---|---|---|
| Employed MLD | 0.238(67.9%) | 0.249(50.7%) | 0.264(36.6%) |
| Self-employed MLD | 0.312(14.9%) | 0.403(22.9%) | 0.462(30.7%) |
| Executive MLD | 0.219( 8.7%) | 0.290(10.8%) | 0.408(10.9%) |
| Other MLD | 0.359( 8.5%) | 0.373(15.6%) | 0.406(21.8%) |
| Total MLD | 0.312(100%) | 0.408(100%) | 0.495(100%) |
| Intra-Job MLD | 0.255(81.7%) | 0.305(74.8%) | 0.365(73.7%) |
| Inter-Job MLD | 0.057(18.3%) | 0.103(25.2%) | 0.135(26.3%) |

*Note:* Numbers in parentheses are percentages.

*Source:* Ministry of Health, Labour and Welfare, Survey of Employment Conditions of Older Persons, 2000.

from 8.5% to 21.8%, an increase of 13.3 percentage points. To take a closer look at the situation, let us break down the overall MLD into the deviation within a job type ('Within-Job MLD') and the deviation between job types ('Between-Job MLD'). In Table 5.7, the increase in MLD within each job type and the increase in the relative population of people in job types with a high MLD now manifest themselves in a combined form as an increase in Within-Job MLD.[11] Third, the deviation between job types also tended to increase with age. Table 5.7 shows that, again from the upper 50s to the upper 60s, the Between-Job MLD grew from 0.057 to 0.135, at a higher rate than the Within-Job MLD, in terms of relative increase.

Variance in non-earned income, of which pensions make up a significant portion, is affected significantly by the amount of pension received. In general, the variance for people who are eligible for a pension was smaller among those in their upper 60s than those in their lower 60s. More precisely, the SCV for Non-Earned Income 0 is 1.52 among the former and 0.64 among the latter in 2000. This is attributable to the increase in the number of people receiving pensions. Similarly, both the SCV and the MLD for Non-Earned Income 1 (only for people with some non-earned income) were lower among those in their upper 60s than those in their lower 60s. One of the reasons was an increase in the percentage of people receiving only the national pension, which does not have a portion linked to salaries. It should be noted that of all the people receiving pensions, 13.3% received only the national pension in their lower 60s, but this ratio increased to 29.3% for the people in their upper 60s.

Table 5.6 also indicates that the average total income, which is the sum of earned income and non-earned income, decreased with age for both Income 0 and Income 1. This is attributable mainly to the decrease in earned income, since the average of non-earned income increased for Income 0 and remained constant for Income 1. It should be pointed out that the average Total Income 0, which includes those without any income, showed a smaller decrease. This is because non-earned income such as pensions made up for the decrease in earned income. In fact, for both Income 0 and Income 1, the ratio of non-earned income including pensions to the total income on average increased steadily with age. As can easily be inferred from the trends in the average amount of Pension 1 and in the pension take-up ratio given in Table 5.6, the ratio of pension income to total income increased from less than half for those in their lower 60s to more than half for those in their upper 60s.

Let us now analyze the gap in total income for all elderly people including those without any income. Table 5.6 shows that the SCV for Total Income 0 increased slightly from 1.06 for those in their upper 50s to 1.16 for those in their lower 60s and then stayed almost flat, at 1.17, for those in their upper 60s. Two factors contribute to this pattern of shift in total income disparity. One is the change in the gap in the two components of total income: earned income and non-earned income. According to Table 5.6, the SCV for Earned Income 0 increased significantly with age, whereas the SCV for Non-Earned Income 0 dropped sharply. An important question here is which variance contributed more to the gap in total income. Table 5.6 also shows the component contribution ratio defined by Sharrocks (1982). The component contribution ratios for earned income were 95%, 80%, and 68% for the three age groups in ascending order, much higher than the ratios for non-earned income. Thus, one can presume that the gap in total income reflects that in earned income. It should be noted, however, that as the ratio of non-earned income such as pensions increases with age, the SCV for Total Income 0 remains constant for people in their retirement ages, that is, 60s.

Under a pension system such as an employee's pension and a mutual aid pension, where the amount received is linked to salary, those who had high earned income while in the labour force receive higher pensions. This often gives rise to the argument that the pension system widens income disparity. This argument is invalid if it aims to imply that income disparity while in the labour force is amplified at the time of retirement. It should be obvious that, according to Table 5.6, the SCV and MLD of Pension 1 are the lowest among all types of income. It would be fair, however, to take this argument to mean that the gap in earning power is reflected in the amount of pension received, and that the two sources of income together contribute to the widening income disparity. Let us examine the correlation coefficient between the earned income and the amount of pension received by elderly people in the labour force in 2000. It was 0.036 for those in their lower 60s and 0.158 for those in their upper 60s, when the amount of pension received is fixed. Further, the SCV for only those who have earned income increased with age, from 0.65 through 0.76 to 0.81, which indicates that elderly people with higher earning power were receiving higher pensions.[12] Many previous studies have revealed that pensions have a negative income effect on the supply of elderly labour.[13] Therefore, if pensions have a large negative income effect on working hours, the correlation coefficient between earned income and the amount of pension received can be negative. Nonetheless, the data in this study has produced a positive correlation coefficient as shown above. This can be attributed to the fact that under the salary-linked pension system, the positive effect of earning power outweighed the negative income effect of the pension.[14] One cannot, however, argue that pensions widen income disparity in the entire elderly population, including those who had high earning power while in the labour force but whose sole income after retirement is their pension, and those who were full-time home-makers and now receive a pension. Indeed, the correlation coefficient between earned income (across the entire group of elderly people including those without earned income) and the amount of pension was −0.019 for those in their lower 60s and 0.093 for those in their upper 60s, and further, as shown in Table 5.6, the income disparity in terms of Total Income 0 was relatively stable between the different age groups.

Finally, let us check whether income disparity increased between 1992 and 2000. First, as for disparity in Total Income 1, which deals with only those having some income, SCV and MLD were smaller for all the age groups in 2000, except that MLD remained the same (0.31) for those in their upper 50s between the two years. Furthermore, as for disparity in Total Income 0, which covers also those having no income, SCV was smaller in 2000 for all the age groups. Therefore, it should be concluded that there was no sign of growing income disparity between elderly individuals.

## Analysis of poverty among elderly households

Rather than income disparity itself, what would probably be of greater interest from the perspective of policy-making is how many elderly people are needy in daily life and what has driven them to poverty. This section, therefore, will analyze the income of households with one or more elderly persons ('elderly households'), instead of the income of elderly individuals. The 2000 Survey first asked about the number of members in each elderly household and whether there was another household member participating in the labour force. If an elderly household had another member with a regular income, they were then asked about their gross income (with taxes included) for the month of September, 2000.[15] For elderly households with no members participating in the labour force and elderly households without a family (i.e. single elderly households), the present study uses the total income data that were used in previous analyses. The total income was recorded in ¥100,000 brackets, from less than ¥100,000 to ¥1,000,000 or more. Those with zero personal income were classified into the bracket of less than ¥100,000.

Figure 5.3 illustrates the distribution of the personal (individual's) income and household income of elderly households in their 60s. Whereas personal income decreased uniformly, household income showed a log-normal distribution pattern. It is worth noting that up to the bracket of ¥200,000–¥300,000, personal income exceeded household income, whereas for all the income brackets beyond this level, it was smaller. This implies that elderly people with low income were transferred into higher income brackets thanks to the additional income earned by another household member. In particular, the fact that this difference was greatest for the lowest income bracket (less than ¥100,000) indicates that the greatest transfer took place in this income bracket. This finding suggests that one of the best ways for an elderly person to avoid poverty is to live together with a household member who has some income. Recent reports, however, have pointed out that the ratio of elderly couples living together with other household members has been on the decline.[16]

One of the indices used to evaluate the level of elderly people's living conditions is the 'adjusted individualized household income', that is, the per-capita income adjusted by the equivalent scale (taking the family size into consideration), which is often used in international comparative studies by the OECD. In the present study, the author also uses this index, choosing 0.5 as the equivalent scale and taking the household income divided by the square root of the number of household members as the adjusted individualized household income. For those households whose

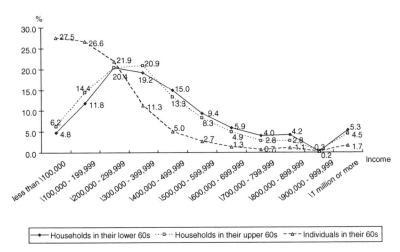

*Figure 5.3*　Distribution of elderly people's income: individual vs. household

*Source*: Ministry of Health, Labour and Welfare, Survey of Employment Conditions of Older Persons, 2000.

income could not be identified beyond the level of income bracket (because there was another household member with some income), the author assumes (for the purpose of calculation) the household income for the income bracket of less than ¥100,000 to be ¥90,000, that for the income bracket of ¥1,000,000 or more to be ¥1,000,000, and that for other income brackets to be the median value of the bracket. These assumptions for the sake of calculation would not pose a major problem.

As a result, the median value of the total equivalent income was calculated to be 196.2 thousand yen, while 50% and 40% of the median value were 98.1 thousand yen and 78.5 thousand yen, respectively. These values are referred to as relative poverty lines. Let us call the former Poverty Line 1, and the latter Poverty Line 2.

For those elderly households whose income could not be identified except for the level of income bracket (because there was another household member with some income), the criteria for these poverty lines can be summarized as follows:

| Income bracket: | Less than ¥100,000 | ¥100,000–¥200,000 | ¥200,000–¥300,000 |
|---|---|---|---|
| Poverty 1 | All households | 3 or more members | 6 or more members |
| Poverty 2 | 2 or more members | 4 or more members | 10 or more members |

Thus, it should be concluded that 7.6% of elderly households fell below Poverty Line 1 and 4.6% fell below Poverty Line 2. Note that the threshold for livelihood assistance for 2003 was ¥80,980 for Tokyo and ¥62,760 for rural districts for single elderly households (age of 68), and ¥122,180 and ¥94,690 for married elderly households (ages of 68 and 65). Considering that Poverty Line 2 was far below these numbers, the remainder of this section makes no further analysis of that group.

Table 5.8 summarizes the results of a probit analysis with the explained variable being a dummy variable which takes a value of '1' when an elderly household is classified below Poverty Line 1 and a value of '0' otherwise.[17] The table lists, for each explaining variable, the estimated coefficient, the asymptotic t-value, and its marginal effect.

First, let us take a look at elderly women living alone (single elderly females), who are often regarded as a poverty-prone group. Here we introduce several dummy variables combining gender and marital status, with the status of an elderly female living with other household members taken as the basis of comparison. The dummy variable 'male_m' takes a value of '1' for an elderly male living with other household members, 'male_s' takes a value of '1' for an elderly male living alone (single elderly male), and 'female_s' takes a value of '1' for an elderly female living alone (single elderly female); all these dummy variables take a value of '0' otherwise. The 'Equation 1' columns in Table 5.8 show that the coefficients for 'male_m', 'male_s', and 'female_s' were all positive and that these effects were statistically significant with a significance level of 10%. These data signify that elderly males and single elderly females (elderly females living alone) were more likely to fall into poverty than elderly females living with other household members. In particular, elderly females living alone were 6.8 percentage points more likely to face poverty than elderly females living with other household members. Also, living alone (being single) increased the probability of poverty by 0.7 points (= 1.9–1.2) for males. Further, it should be kept in mind that such effects tend to be underestimated. To illustrate the point, it would be worthwhile to note that 'other_earner', or the number of other earners living together as household members with the elderly person, had a marginal effect of –3.5%; in other words, it had a positive effect with a significance level of 1%. As a result, since living alone (being single) means that there are no other earners in the household, the probability of elderly females living alone falling into poverty was actually 10.3 (= 6.8+3.5) percentage points higher than that of elderly females living with one earner. Similarly, the probability of elderly males

*Table 5.8*   Probit analysis of poverty groups among elderly people

| Equation | Equation 1 | | | Equation 2 | | |
|---|---|---|---|---|---|---|
| | Coef. | *t*-value | Marginal E. | Coef. | *t*-value | Marginal E. |
| male_m | 0.143 | 3.01 | 0.012 | −0.045 | −1.01 | −0.004 |
| male_s | 0.197 | 1.82 | 0.019 | 0.368 | 3.81 | 0.047 |
| female_s | 0.543 | 6.82 | 0.068 | 0.678 | 9.44 | 0.105 |
| other_earner | −0.419 | −13.92 | −0.035 | −0.272 | −10.40 | −0.026 |
| early_sixties | 0.093 | 2.12 | 0.008 | 0.041 | 0.97 | 0.004 |
| high_sch | −0.484 | −11.15 | −0.038 | −0.452 | −10.93 | −0.042 |
| univ_sch | −0.664 | −5.78 | −0.035 | −0.583 | −5.93 | −0.038 |
| illness | 0.141 | 3.33 | 0.012 | 0.305 | 7.88 | 0.032 |
| work | −0.774 | −10.82 | −0.066 | | | |
| executive | −0.927 | −3.48 | −0.038 | | | |
| self_emp | 0.325 | 4.24 | 0.033 | | | |
| help_w | 0.295 | 2.78 | 0.031 | | | |
| free_w | 0.396 | 3.75 | 0.045 | | | |
| n55_work | 0.402 | 4.41 | 0.045 | | | |
| want_job | 0.256 | 4.05 | 0.025 | | | |
| n_right_job | −0.076 | −0.77 | −0.006 | | | |
| m_retire | −0.359 | −2.91 | −0.022 | | | |
| pension | −0.197 | −3.66 | −0.018 | −0.128 | −2.52 | −0.013 |
| national_p | 0.589 | 11.56 | 0.068 | 0.508 | 10.62 | 0.065 |
| mutual_p | −0.865 | −5.48 | −0.040 | −1.007 | −5.55 | −0.050 |
| _cons | −0.674 | −8.17 | | −1.110 | −16.10 | |
| Log Likelihood | −2536 | | | −2663 | | |
| Pseudo R2 | 0.202 | | | 0.160 | | |
| Number of Observations | 11.763 | | | 11.845 | | |

*Note*: 'Coef.' stands for 'coefficient', 'z' means the asymptotic t_value, and 'Marginal E' means the marginal effect.

*Source*: Own calculations based on data from Ministry of Health, Labour and Welfare, Survey of Employment Conditions of Older Persons, 2000.

living alone falling into poverty turned out to be 5.4 (= 1.9 + 3.5) percentage points, much higher than the marginal effect (1.2) of elderly males living with other household members.

As has been illustrated above, one of the major reasons why elderly females living alone are more likely to fall into poverty is that nobody supports them financially. Even so, if they can work or get a sufficient pension, they should be able to avoid poverty. In the 'Equation 1' columns in Table 5.8, however, the effects of these factors are controlled in general. More specifically, the values for a number of dummy variables such as 'work' (indicating whether the elderly person is in the labour force or not), and, assuming the value to be '1', several subordinate dummy variables indicating the type of job, for example, 'executive' (corporate executive), 'self_emp' (self-employed), 'help_w' (assistant to a self-employed person), and 'free_w' (freelance job, part-time job at home), as well as 'want_job' (indicating that the elderly person was willing to work but was not working because he/she could not find an appropriate job), 'pension' (indicating whether the elderly person was receiving a certain pension), and its subordinate dummy variables (for those answering 'yes' to the above question) such as 'national_p' (receiving national pension) and 'mutual_p' (receiving pension from mutual aid association for public service personnel, etc.) were controlled.[18] Thus, it would be only fair to say that the effects of living alone (being single) revealed by the present analysis are only partially explained by this method of analysis. In other words, the use of dummy variables such as these is not yet powerful enough to clearly characterize the population of elderly females living alone.

Are elderly females living alone handicapped in any way with regard to working? If, for example, a full-time female homemaker is bereaved or divorced from her husband, then her vocational capability would be considered low. If, as a result, she finds it difficult to find a job, or gets only a low salary when employed, she would be likely to fall into poverty. Let us consider two cases. The first is the case where an elderly female living alone cannot find a job. The dummy variable 'want_job', which takes a value of '1' when the person wishes to work but cannot find a job and takes a value of '0' otherwise, takes a value of '1' in this case and, from the marginal effect shown in Table 5.8, increases the probability of poverty by 2.5 points.[19] Therefore, the probability of this elderly female living alone falling into poverty is higher than that of an elderly female not wishing to work who lives with a household member by a total of 12.8 (= 6.8 + 3.5 + 2.5) points. The second is the case where an elderly female living alone has indeed found a job but does only an insubstantial job such as freelance work subcontracted from a neighbour or a part-time job at home. The marginal effect of 'work' is –6.6, whereas that of 'free_w' is +4.5; the net effect, therefore, is that the probability of falling into poverty is reduced by 2.1 points. As a result, the probability of poverty for this elderly female living alone is only 8.2 (= 6.8 + 3.5 – 2.1) points higher than that for an elderly female not wishing to work who lives with a household member.

Next, let us make estimates while eliminating all the dummy variables concerning employment and job type, as shown in the 'Equation 2' columns in Table 5.8. The marginal effect for elderly females living alone increases to 10.5%. When combined with the marginal effect of 'other_earner' (2.6%), it rises to as high as 13.1%, close to the value for the case of an elderly female living alone who cannot find a job. This observation leads us to conclude from Table 5.8 that the situation of elderly females cannot be summarized by one value of 'female_s' simply because it does not shed enough light on the real characteristics of the vocational capability of single females, taking into consideration the relationship between being single and getting a job.[20]

Seike and Yamada (2004) argue that the fall of single elderly households into poverty is triggered by the combination of 'pension and work'. This argument is true because either one of them, if sufficient, would prevent poverty. To further explore the relationship, the author made an estimate by eliminating the three dummy variables 'pension', 'national_p', and 'mutual_p', in the same way as with work. The result, although not shown in the table, yielded a marginal effect of 5.7 for elderly females living alone, which was only slightly lower than the effects exhibited in the 'Equation 1' columns. This means that falling into poverty as a result of receiving an insufficient pension is a widespread phenomenon and not that elderly females living alone were receiving particularly small pensions. In fact, according to the Surveys, the statistics for only those who were receiving some pension indicated that the average amount of pension received was ¥80,000 for all females in their 60s, as opposed to ¥108,000 for single females in their 60s. Also, the statistics including those who did not receive any pension put these values at ¥58,000 and ¥90,000, respectively, indicating that elderly females living alone were receiving larger pensions than elderly females living with a household member. On the other hand, the average pension received was higher for the entire elderly population including males than for elderly females living alone, as shown in Table 5.6. Thus, the observation that elderly females living alone are more likely to fall into poverty can be explained by the fact that they are not provided with sufficient job opportunities or they are not living with someone whose income they can depend upon, while they receive smaller pensions than males.

'Early_sixties' is a dummy variable which takes a value of '1' for the age bracket of the lower 60s and a value of '0' for the age bracket of the upper 60s. The 'Equation 1' columns in Table 5.8 show a statistically significant positive effect of this dummy variable with a significance level of 1%, while its marginal value was as small as 0.8. One of the reasons for the higher probability of poverty among people in their lower 60s than those in their upper 60s can be attributed to the fact that the starting age for receiving the national pension and that of receiving employee pensions are both 65 in principle. In practice, however, people usually start receiving a pension before reaching the age of 65, by requesting an early start in the case of the former, or by getting a special old age welfare annuity in the case of the latter. Whereas the existence or absence of a pension itself is controlled by dummy variables such as 'pension', there seems to be a very significant variation from individual to individual as to when those in their lower 60s start to receive a pension. In other words, the lower 60s is a transition period during which the main source of income changes from salary (earned income) to pension, or elderly people become dependent household members. For many, the transition is not smooth, involving problems such as an insufficient length of premium payment period, or a need to delay the start date for receiving the pension in order to avoid a reduction in the future.

'Illness' is a dummy variable which takes a value of '1' when the person generally 'does not feel very well' or 'is, or tends to be, ill' and a value of '0' when he/she generally feels 'well'. Table 5.8 shows that Illness has a statistically significant positive effect with a significance level of 1%, while its marginal effect was only 1.2. This means that elderly people in poor health were 1.2 percentage points more likely to fall into poverty than healthy elderly people. This coefficient appears to be much lower than generally expected; it can be attributed to the fact that illness correlates with a number of explaining variables such as gender, age, education level, and the status of employment. For example, it is generally the case that the higher a person's level of education is, the better his or her health will be; and, the worse a person's health is, the more difficult it will be for him or her to get a job. Thus, if we eliminate the variables related to level of education and status of employment, the marginal effect of 'illness' goes up to 4.0, more than three times as high. Therefore, one can conclude that poverty and health have a very close correlation.

If we are to presume that the impact of health, as revealed by Equation 1, does not stem from the differences in level of education or status of employment of elderly people, then where do they come from? A number of answers can be thought of. First, as Ohashi (2005) pointed out, people in poor health, if employed, tend not to be able to work long hours and tend to have lower hourly rates. Second, unless they became prone to illness in their 60s for the first time, they are likely to have already been in poor employment conditions in their earlier years, and therefore their non-earned income, such as pensions, is likely to be lower. According to the surveys, among those with some non-earned income, the average non-earned income was ¥143,000 for healthy elderly people, but only ¥118,000 for those in poor health. Third, if the elderly person is ill and needs nursing care from family members, the earning power of the entire household decreases.

In Table 5.8, both 'work' and 'want_job' exhibit positive and statistically significant effects with a significance level of 1%. However, the marginal effect, which indicates the difference in the probability of falling into poverty between those who were working or wanted to work but were not actually working and those who did not want to work was negative (−6.6) for the former and positive (+2.5) for the latter. It is interesting to note that, even among those in the labour force, the probability of poverty varies significantly with the type of job. Table 5.8 indicates that the probability of poverty among self-employed elderly people was higher than among elderly employees.[21] As has been pointed out, among the self-employed, although income varied greatly, the average was relatively high. Thus, the probability of a self-employed elderly person falling into poverty was as much as 3.3 points higher than that of employees. Also, the probability of poverty for those engaged in insubstantial jobs, such as assistants to a self-employed person and part-time jobs at home, was between 3% and 4%, which is relatively high. Assuming that these elderly people were not employed by a company or other organization at the age of 55 (i.e. 'n55_work' was '1'), its marginal effect was 4.5, and the sum of this marginal effect and the effects caused by engaging in insubstantial jobs exceeded 6.6, which was the negative effect of 'work'. For example, the marginal effect of doing freelance work subcontracted from a neighbour or a part-time job at home was 4.5, and the sum of this marginal effect and that of 'n55_work' came to

9. This more than offset the negative marginal effect of 'work' and even increased the probability of poverty by 2.4 points, which was comparable to the effect of 'want_job' (2.5). In other words, working itself does not necessarily cure the problem: if the job is insubstantial, it hardly helps reduce the probability of poverty.

As has already been observed, there are various types of elderly people who wish to work but cannot find a job. Let us take a look at 'n_right_job', a dummy variable which takes a value of '1' when no appropriate job can be found and a value of '0' otherwise. Whereas the marginal effect of 'n_right_job' was negative, it was not statistically significant with an ordinary significance level. On the other hand, the marginal effect of 'm_retire', representing elderly people who had taken mandatory retirement but could not find an appropriate job, was negative with a statistical significance. It was –2.2, which almost offset the effect of 'want_job'. This means that those who had taken retirement but were not working because they could not find an appropriate job were almost as prone to poverty as those who were not working because they did not want to work.

Table 5.8 shows that 'pension', a dummy variable indicating that the person is receiving some pension, had a negative marginal effect which is statistically significant with a significance level of 1%. Its value, however, was –1.8%, not particularly great in absolute terms. The marginal effect of 'pension' indicates how much lower the probability of poverty is for those receiving some pension (e.g. national pension, employee pension, mutual aid benefit, or private pension) than for those who are not receiving any pension. This effect serves as the basis for evaluating the relationship between pension and poverty, and is supplemented by 'national_p', which represents the effect on recipients of national pensions, and 'mutual_p', which represents the effect on those who received a pension from a mutual aid association, such as public service personnel.[22] Interestingly, the effect varies greatly between pension systems. For example, the marginal effect of 'national_p' was +6.8, as opposed to –4.0 for 'mutual_p'. This means that elderly people receiving only the national pension were as much as 5.0 (= 6.8 – 1.8) percentage points more likely to fall into poverty than those who did not receive any pension.[23] As has been pointed out, if a national pension recipient can work as an employee, then it has a marginal effect of +6.6, whereas if he/she works as a self-employed person, it has a marginal effect of –3.3% (=–6.6 + 3.3), offsetting the effect of 'national_p' completely in the former case and partially in the latter case. Incidentally, of all national pension recipients who did not have anybody else having any income in their household, 63.6% were working, of whom 28.6% were employed by a company or other organization and 47.2% were self-employed. Further, those who received an employee pension or a mutual aid pension actually received an earnings-related component in addition to the basic old-age pension which recipients of the national pension received, and were therefore less likely to fall into poverty.

In summary, whether there is somebody else with income in the household or whether the amount of pension received is sufficient is beyond each elderly person's control. Under such circumstances, the only way to avoid poverty is to get a job. The problem, however, is that such a way out is closed to those unlucky elderly people who have poor health, who are not provided with job opportunities, or who have some-body in the household requiring nursing care.[24]

## Mode of work and level of satisfaction

As has been discussed in the previous section, elderly people who do not work are likely to fall into financially troubled situations. Does this imply then that elderly people who work do not have major problems? As one grows older, one's physical strength, eye sight, memory, and gen-eral health deteriorate; therefore, elderly people need to change the way they work. If they cannot work in ways that suit their ability, they will find themselves in a difficult situation and will be greatly dissatisfied. This section will analyze the way elderly people work and how satisfied they are.

First, let us take a look at the distribution of working hours of males and females in their 60s. As shown in Figure 5.4, which also includes the distribution of working hours for people in their upper 50s for com-parison, the working hours of people in their 60s, particularly females, are significantly short. More specifically, the average and standard deviation of monthly working hours were 169 hours and 64 hours for those in their upper 50s, 126 hours and 74 hours for females in their 60s, and 154 hours and 72 hours for males in their 60s. Also, the longer the working hours are, the smaller the standard deviation. It should be noted that most of those who work for less than 160 hours a month are likely to be part-timers and other non-regular employees. The ratio of such people was 44.4% for males in their 60s and 65.5% for females in their 60s, much higher than the average (31.1%) for those in their upper 50s.

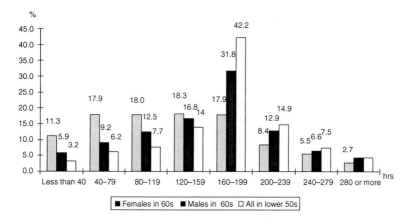

*Figure 5.4* Distribution of monthly working hours

*Source:* Ministry of Health, Labour and Welfare, Survey of Employment Conditions of Older Persons, 2000.

The *Survey of Employment Conditions of Older Persons, 2000* (carried out by the former Ministry of Labour) asked working elderly people how satisfied they were with their wages, hours worked, work circumstances, use of experience, and the worth (challenge) of the job, in addition to their basic working conditions. For the level of satisfaction, it gave a choice of five levels: 'very satisfied', 'somewhat satisfied', 'neutral', 'somewhat dissatisfied', and 'very dissatisfied'. Here we would like to introduce a dummy variable, which takes a value of '1' for 'very satisfied' and 'somewhat satisfied' and a value of '0' otherwise, and conduct a probit analysis. Table 5.9 summarizes the results.[25] What follows are some of the intriguing findings.

First, let us examine the effect of illness. In all the estimation equations in Table 5.9, 'illness' has negative effects that are statistically significant with a significance level of 1%, which means that elderly people with a health problem had a strong tendency to be dissatisfied with their work circumstances, use of their experience, and the worth of the job, as well as their wages and hours worked.

The 2000 Survey indicates that the percentage of working elderly people in their 60s with a health problem was 18.3% for males and 23.9% for females. In other words, more working elderly females had a health problem. These people were particularly dissatisfied with wages, with 44.3% saying 'very dissatisfied' or 'somewhat dissatisfied', which was higher than the 35.7% for healthy elderly people. Another point to be

Table 5.9 Probit analysis of satisfaction with work

| Equation | Equation 3 | | Equation 4 | | Equation 5 | | Equation 6 | | Equation 7 | |
|---|---|---|---|---|---|---|---|---|---|---|
| Satisfaction with | Wages | | Hours worked | | Circumstances | | Use of experience | | Worth of the job | |
| | Coef. | z | Coef. | z | Coef. | z | Coef. | z | Coef. | z |
| male | 0.054 | 0.97 | -0.086 | -1.54 | -0.074 | -1.40 | 0.131 | 2.79 | -0.029 | -0.64 |
| early_sixt-s | 0.041 | 0.82 | 0.043 | 0.87 | 0.077 | 1.63 | 0.036 | 0.86 | -0.038 | -0.93 |
| illness1 | -0.223 | -3.56 | -0.177 | -2.83 | -0.240 | -4.03 | -0.275 | -5.33 | -0.346 | -6.93 |
| high_sch | 0.045 | 0.86 | 0.111 | 2.10 | 0.154 | 3.10 | 0.194 | 4.43 | 0.265 | 6.28 |
| univ_sch | 0.250 | 3.23 | 0.223 | 2.81 | 0.316 | 4.22 | 0.443 | 6.45 | 0.474 | 7.01 |
| small_scale | -0.011 | -0.13 | -0.010 | -0.12 | -0.251 | -3.38 | -0.136 | -1.93 | -0.126 | -1.84 |
| executive | 0.634 | 6.98 | 0.342 | 3.68 | 0.233 | 2.71 | 0.258 | 3.13 | 0.277 | 3.41 |
| self_emp | -0.146 | -1.55 | -0.222 | -2.31 | -0.362 | -4.16 | -0.027 | -0.34 | -0.020 | -0.26 |
| help_w | -0.012 | -0.10 | -0.097 | -0.84 | -0.287 | -2.67 | -0.045 | -0.47 | -0.014 | -0.16 |
| free_w | -0.033 | -0.31 | 0.014 | 0.13 | -0.252 | -2.51 | -0.052 | -0.57 | 0.049 | 0.55 |
| home_loan | -0.149 | -1.68 | -0.135 | -1.49 | -0.157 | -1.83 | -0.099 | -1.35 | 0.116 | 1.68 |
| other_income | 0.006 | 3.23 | 0.010 | 5.06 | 0.010 | 5.42 | 0.007 | 3.96 | 0.007 | 3.94 |
| other_earner | 0.052 | 2.04 | 0.088 | 3.40 | 0.043 | 1.74 | 0.030 | 1.36 | 0.031 | 1.44 |
| Log Likelihood | -1914 | | -1870 | | -2154 | | -2818 | | -3046 | |
| Pseudo R2 | 0.074 | | 0.061 | | 0.073 | | 0.053 | | 0.051 | |
| Number of Observations | 5154 | | 5128 | | 5102 | | 5109 | | 5131 | |

Note: For notations and abbreviations, refer to Note on Table 5.8. In the estimations, industry dummies are controlled for, although the respective coefficients are not listed.

Source: Own calculations based on data from Ministry of Health, Labour and Welfare, Survey of Employment Conditions of Older Persons, 2000.

noted is that working elderly people were not necessarily less likely to fall into poverty. The probability of poverty was 7.4% for working elderly people, only slightly lower than that for the overall elderly population including those not working (7.6%).

'Home_loan' is a dummy variable which represents an elderly person whose home loan repayment per year exceeds 20% of his/her own annual income. Table 5.9 shows that 'home_loan' had a negative effect on the levels of satisfaction with wages, hours worked, work circumstances, and use of experience. Of these, the negative effects on the satisfaction levels of wages and work circumstances were statistically significant with a significance level of 10%. A person who still has an outstanding home loan naturally needs a higher wage and may need to work longer hours,[26] and therefore tends to have little freedom to choose a job according to work circumstances or use of experience. Interestingly, unlike 'illness', 'home_loan' had a positive effect on 'worth of the job' which was statistically significant with an ordinary significance level.

Table 5.9 shows that both 'other_income', which is the non-earned income such as the pension an elderly person receives, and 'other_ earner', which represents the existence of other earners in the household, had a positive effect on all the items. All the effects other than the effects of the latter on 'use of experience' and 'worth of the job' were statistically significant with a significance level of 10%. This means that elderly people who enjoyed financially favourable circumstances were not very concerned about wages and thus found it relatively easy to get a job which met their expectations in terms of hours worked, work circumstances, and type of work. Conversely, if they could not find an appropriate job, they tended to choose not to work at all. Ohashi (2005) regards this behaviour of elderly people as a kind of investment in their job and attributes to such behaviour the higher level of satisfaction among financially unstressed elderly people.[27]

Education level has an impact on a number of indices. In the analysis of Table 5.9, since health, job type, and non-earned income such as pension are controlled as explaining variables, education level can be considered a proxy variable for other variables, especially earned income. Table 5.9 shows that the higher the education level, the higher the level of satisfaction with most indices. Furthermore, all the effects except that of high school graduates or equivalent on wages were statistically significant with a significance level of 1%. This effect can be interpreted in the same way as the effect of 'other_income' or 'other_earner': people with higher earning power are in a better position to choose a job in old age.

It is generally accepted in Japan that the larger a company is, the higher the wages and the shorter the working hours will be. Table 5.9, however, demonstrates a trend which seems to go against this general perception. In Table 5.9, 'small_scale' is a dummy variable which indicates that the company or organization elderly people work for has less than 100 employees.[28] While it is clear that in terms of work circumstances, use of experience, and worth of the job, larger companies were more attractive to elderly people, 'small_scale' did not have statistically significant effects on wages and hours worked with an ordinary significance level. Regarding this phenomenon, two points should be noted. First, in 2000, more than 90% of companies and governmental or other public offices with 100 or more employees set the retirement age at 60, allowing few people to continue to work beyond this age. According to the survey, the percentage of elderly people working for a company or public office with 100 or more employees was 14.9%. Second, most people continuing to work for a large company or a public office are downgraded in status to that of a non-regular staff member or an employee on a short-term contract, work shorter hours, and receive significantly lower wages. These two points are thus considered the main reasons why the size of the employer (company or organization) does not have a statistically significant effect on wages or hours worked. It should be reiterated, however, that in terms of work circumstances, use of experience, and worth of the job, continuing to work for a large company or a public office seems to offer better levels of satisfaction.

Another phenomenon of interest is that the level of satisfaction was higher for three out of five indices among females than among males and also decreased for almost all indices as people got older. This seems to mean that they were satisfied with the very fact that they could work, while their deterioration in physical strength and the tighter situations at their employers were making it increasingly difficult to find a job.

For dummy variables representing job type, employees of companies and other organizations are taken as the norm. According to Table 5.9, 'executive' had a positive effect on all the indices which was statistically significant with a significance level of 1%. This was only to be expected since executives are considered successful among employees. What is interesting is that 'self_emp', which represents a self-employed person, had a negative effect on all the indices. In particular, its effects on hours worked and work circumstances were both statistically significant with a significance level of 1%. The number of hours worked was an average of 170 hours for self-employed elderly people, as opposed to an average of 136 hours for employed elderly people. The standard deviation for the former was 78 hours, considerably larger than the 58 hours for the latter. While self-employed people can manage their own time, they may need to work longer hours depending on the results of their business, and hence the number of hours worked tends to vary widely.

Although not shown in Table 5.9, the analysis also uses dummy variables representing industry, with the manufacturing industry taken as the norm. The major findings are as follows. The wholesale/retail industry and eating/drinking establishments had a negative effect on all the satisfaction indices which was statistically significant with a significance level of 1%. According to the Survey, the ratio of the population working in these sectors to the total working population was 16.4%, the third largest after the service industry (24.1%) and agriculture (16.7%). People working in agriculture also had generally low satisfaction levels with a significance level of 10%, except that the effect on work circumstances was statistically insignificant. Further, the transportation and telecommunications industries had generally negative effects, although only on wages was the effect statistically significant with a significance level of 10%. The service industry, which was the most populous, showed generally positive effects. In particular, the effects on hours worked, work circumstances, and worth of the job were statistically significant with a significance level of 10%. The construction industry, which was somewhat similar to the manufacturing industry in mode of work, did not show effects that were statistically significant with ordinary significance levels on any indices. For reference, the ratio of population working in the construction industry to the total working population was 10.9% and that for the manufacturing industry was 15.8%.[29]

Let us summarize the findings in this section. Those elderly people who were in financially better situations as a result of pensions and the existence of other earners in their households found it relatively easy to get a job which met their expectation in terms of hours worked, worth of the job, and work circumstances; taking advantage of these conditions, they invested in the job and thus were generally satisfied with the job itself despite the low wages. In other words, their pension and the income earned by other household members tended to supplement their wages, thereby making the working life of elderly people less stressful. In contrast, those who had a health problem and yet had to work and those who still had the burden of home loans tended to be dissatisfied not only with wages and hours worked, but also with work circumstances and the worth of the job. Further, many self-employed elderly people were dissatisfied with the mode of work.

## Summary

For many elderly people, the main sources of income from which they pay their expenses are basically earned income, pension, income earned by other household members, and assets. Of these, earned income is said to have a relatively high weight in Japan, which has a high labour force participation ratio. Indeed, according to the materials used in this study the ratio of earned income to the total personal income was over 50% on average among people in their lower 60s. Also, the disparity indices (SCV and MLD) among those in their lower 60s were greater for earned income than for non-earned income. For those in their upper 60s, however, the ratio of non-earned income, particularly pensions, to the total income was over 60%, if we are to include elderly people with a total income of zero. If we are to take only those with a non-zero total income, however, the ratio of earned income to the total income was still over 50% for people in their upper 60s as well. We can thus conclude that staying in the labour force is important to sustain life in old age. At the same time, however, it should be noted that more than 18% of elderly people could not work although they wished to work because they could not find an appropriate job, were ill, or had someone in their household who needed nursing care. On a positive note, the number of elderly people who could not work for health reasons has been declining significantly in recent years.

While average earned income decreases with age, the average non-earned income such as pension increases with age, and as a result, the decrease in total personal income is very small. The study reveals that the disparity in earned income among individuals was greater in the upper 60s than in the lower 60s. This phenomenon is attributable to two factors. First, the disparity increased with age within each job category. Second, the ratio of the number of self-employed persons and those engaged in insubstantial jobs, which had relatively greater income disparities, to the total number of working elderly people increased with age, while the ratio of employed elderly people, among whom the income disparity was relatively small, decreased. Further, the disparity in non-earned income such as pensions decreased among those in the age group with a high pension take-up ratio.

Under an earnings-related pension system such as the employee pension system, elderly people with higher earning power receive greater amounts of pension. Therefore, if we are to think only of working elderly people, we would need to realize that the pension system tends to widen income disparity. If, however, we consider the entire population including those who had high earning power while at work but now have a pension as their only source of income and those full-time homemakers who have never worked but now receive a pension, then we cannot conclude that pensions increase income disparity.

The standard of living of retired elderly people depends greatly on the income of the members of their household as well as on their own income. In analyzing the lifestyle of elderly people, it is therefore necessary to analyze the total income of their household. This paper first defined the poverty group by the relative poverty line that is often used in international comparative studies and then analyzed what factors cause elderly households to fall into poverty. The factor which contributes most to the probability of poverty has turned out to be being an elderly female living alone (single elderly female), which increases the risk of poverty by about 10 percentage points over the average for the total elderly population. If she can find a job, she may be able to stay out of poverty; nevertheless, many females who have lost a working husband seem to face difficulties in finding a good opportunity in the job market. Other factors which affect the probability of poverty were the existence of a job, health, education level, job type, and the type of pension. Worth particular attention is the fact that elderly households receiving only a national pension, which were typically those of self-employed people, were more likely to fall into poverty than elderly households not receiving any pension.

Working, or participating in the labour force, is likely to keep elderly people out of poverty. If, however, elderly people with a health problem have no choice but to work for financial reasons, they then tend to find themselves in a difficult situation because they cannot choose the working hours and mode of work that best suit their physical strength, experience, or expertise. This was the case more with self-employed elderly people, who received only a national pension, than with company employees and public service personnel.

## Appendix

*Table 5.10*   Appendix – basic statistics

| Variables | | Column A | | Column B | |
|---|:--:|:--:|:--:|:--:|:--:|
| | | Average | Standard deviation | Average | Standard deviation |
| poverty1 | * | 0.076 | 0.265 | | |
| satisfy_wage | * | | | 0.140 | 0.347 |
| satisfy_hours | * | | | 0.129 | 0.336 |
| satisfy circum. | * | | | 0.163 | 0.369 |
| satisfy skill use | * | | | 0.267 | 0.442 |
| satisfy job | * | | | 0.312 | 0.463 |
| male | * | | | 0.607 | 0.488 |
| male_m | * | 0.449 | 0.496 | | |
| male_s | * | 0.034 | 0.181 | | |
| female_m | | 0.448 | 0.447 | | |
| female_s | * | 0.070 | 0.255 | | |
| other_earner | | 1.42 | 0.99 | 1.06 | 0.90 |
| other_income | | | | 10.16 | 11.39 |
| home_loan | * | | | 0.079 | 0.270 |
| early_sixties | * | 0.521 | 0.499 | 0.596 | 0.491 |
| high_sch | * | 0.429 | 0.495 | 0.424 | 0.494 |
| univ_sch | * | 0.093 | 0.290 | 0.111 | 0.314 |
| illness | * | 0.352 | 0.478 | 0.205 | 0.404 |
| work | * | 0.465 | 0.499 | | |
| executive | * | 0.051 | 0.219 | 0.108 | 0.311 |
| self_emp | * | 0.122 | 0.327 | 0.260 | 0.439 |
| help_w | * | 0.045 | 0.207 | 0.096 | 0.295 |
| free_w | * | 0.039 | 0.195 | 0.080 | 0.279 |
| n55_work | * | 0.074 | 0.262 | | |
| want_job | * | 0.180 | 0.385 | | |
| n_right_job | * | 0.096 | 0.295 | | |
| m_retire | * | 0.054 | 0.226 | | |
| pension | * | 0.766 | 0.423 | | |
| national_p | * | 0.175 | 0.379 | | |
| mutual_p | * | 0.085 | 0.279 | | |
| small_scale | * | | | 0.317 | 0.465 |

*Note*: Column A includes all elderly people in their 60s, whereas Column B includes only elderly people in their 60s who were working. An '*' means that this is a dummy variable.

*Source*: Own calculations based on data from Ministry of Health, Labour and Welfare, Survey of Employment Conditions of Older Persons, 2000.

## Notes

1. See Iwamoto (2004) for an overview of the financial burden of medical care in Japan.
2. Refer to OECD (2004), for example.
3. Compared with the data obtained from the *Labour Force Survey* (Ministry of Internal Affairs and Communications), which checks the status of labour force participation during the last week of each month, and the *Employment Status Survey* (Ministry of Internal Affairs and Communications), which checks the normal state in October every five years, the results of the *Survey of Employment Conditions of Older Persons* (Ministry of Health, Labour and Welfare) tend to show labour force participation ratios about 3% higher; however, they all tend to exhibit more or less the same trends.
4. Since the Survey for the year 2004 showed data only in summary form without breakdowns, the analysis and discussion in this paper is based on the data for 2000.
5. The 1988 Survey did not ask those wishing to work about why they did not find a job.
6. It is widely known that there is some correlation between health and level of education. The 2000 Survey also endorses this fact. On a related note, the ratio of people rating their general health condition as 'not very good' or 'sick or often sick' was 42.5% among people with only a junior high school level of education, 30.4% among high school or junior college graduates, and 19.4% among university/college graduates (here, 'graduates' include those with equivalent levels).
7. While many research reports define an 'elderly person' as anybody aged 65 and above, this paper defines it as anybody aged 60 and above. Further, while many research reports focus only on the gap in household income, this paper also studies the gap in elderly people's personal income. Another study focusing on individuals' income disparity was made by Kojima (2001).
8. Each sample includes some individuals with extremely high income. To avoid abnormal data and to prevent the income of a small number of elderly people from overly affecting the overall distribution, this paper modified the scope of analysis as follows: From the calculation of Income 1, those with income deviating from the average by more than four sigmas (standard deviations) were excluded, and from the calculation of Income 0, those with an income of over ¥3 million were excluded. After these eliminations, the present study covers more than 99% of the sample for the former, and more than 99.5% for the latter.
9. Disney, Mira and Scherer (1998) point out, based on an international comparative study, that the significance of earned income at the time of retirement is greater in Japan than in Europe. Fukawa (1995) makes the same observation in a comparison with the US.
10. Note that MLD for Income 0 cannot be calculated because the logarithm for zero (0) cannot be defined.
11. For the breakdown of MLD by layer among the employed, refer to Mookherjee and Sharrocks (1982).

12. Here, the author focuses on the SCV for only those with an earned income, whereas the SCV for Total Income 1 in Table 5.6 covers everybody who had either earned income or non-earned income.

13. To mention one recent example, Ohashi (2005).

14. The correlation coefficient was significantly smaller for those in their lower 60s than for those in their upper 60s. This can be explained by the pension reduction system whereby the amount of pension received is reduced in accordance with earned income and the practice of extending the period of pension premium payments so as to secure a higher amount of pension.

15. If no payment was received in September, it was averaged out over the respective period to produce an equivalent monthly payment.

16. A number of researchers have discussed the effect of the income of members of the same household on income disparity. In particular, Iwata (1996) and Funaoka (2001) analyzed the effects of the income of other members of elderly households. Regrettably, the Survey quoted in the paper did not specify whether these other household members were the spouses.

17. The descriptive statistics values of the variables discussed in this section are summarized in Column A of Appendix.

18. Each of the dummy variables introduced here takes a value of '1' when the notion it represents is true, and a value of '0' otherwise. For the dummy variables concerning job types, the case of being employed is taken as the norm; for the dummy variables concerning pension, people receiving pensions are taken as the norm.

19. 'want_job' and 'work' are dummy variables which take a person not wishing to work as the norm.

20. While inclined to take this issue as one of endogeneity, the author has been unable to secure a sufficient number of appropriate instrumental variables since there are many variables concerning job and employment.

21. Note that the norm for the job type dummy variable is employees.

22. Here, a 'national pension recipient' means anybody who receives only the national pension including the basic old-age pension, basic disability pension, survivor's pension, and/or widow's pension, without receiving an employee pension. Some of 'those receiving a pension from a mutual aid association' receive other pensions in addition to the pension from the mutual aid association.

23. The basic old-age pension, which in general is paid as the national pension, is about ¥66,000/month on average, even if the premium has been paid to the fullest (a maximum of 40 years). Recipients of this amount alone will fall into poverty.

24. Iwata (1996) breaks down households with elderly people aged 65 or above into single and married, and into a further three categories: 'working households', in which the head of the household works; 'general households', in which the head of the household is self-employed; and 'jobless households', in which the members of the household live mainly on pensions. Focusing on relatively poor households in each category, she points out that the 'jobless' category has the highest ratio of poor households and concludes that presently the 'independence' of elderly people can rarely be achieved with a pension alone; rather, it can be achieved only by participating in the labour force.

25. Column B of the Appendix lists the descriptive statistical values of the variables discussed in this section.
26. In fact, according to the 2000 Survey, the average income from a job was ¥186,000 and the average monthly working hours were 154 hours for the group with 'home_loan' being '1', as opposed to ¥100,000 and 140 hours, respectively, for the group with 'home_loan' being '0'.
27. Ohashi (2005) argues that elderly people bargain with their employers over wages, hours worked, and investment in the job. As examples of investment in jobs, he lists work improvement using a robot, relocation to a less stressful section, and reductions in quotas, which usually result in a reduction in hourly rate.
28. For those working for a governmental or other public office, 'small_scale' is given a value of '0'.
29. The ratios of the population working in the mining, utility (electricity, gas, heating, water supply), transportation/telecommunications, and financing/banking/insurance/real estate industries and the public services were 0.6%, 2.1%, 4.7%, 2.9%, and 4.2%, respectively.

# References

Disney, R., M. Mira and P. Scherer (1998) 'Maintaining Prosperity in an Aging Society: The OECD Study on the Policy Implications of Aging Resources during Retirement', *OECD Working Papers*, Paris.

Fukawa, T. (1995) 'Kōreisha no keizai jōkyō – nichibei hikaku (Economic Circumstances of Elderly People: A Comparison between Japan and the US)', *Kikan Nenkin to Koyō*, 14 (2), pp. 44–53.

Funaoka, F. (2001) 'Nihon no shotoku kakusa no kentō (Study of Income Disparity in Japan)', *Keizai Kenkyō*, 52 (2), pp. 117–131.

Iwamoto, Y. (2004) 'Issues in Japanese Health Policy and Medical Expenditure', in T. Tachibanaki (ed.), *The Economics of Social Security in Japan*, Cheltenham: Edward Elgar, pp. 219–232.

Iwata, M. (1996) 'Kōreisha no "jitatsu" to hinkon, fubyōdō no kakudai ("Independence" and Poverty among Elderly People: Widening of Inequality)', *Ohara Shakai Mondai Kenkyō Zasshi*, 477, pp. 15–25.

Kojima, K. (2001) 'Kōreisha no shotoku kakusa (Income Disparity among the Elderly)', *Jinkōgaku Kenkyō*, 29, pp. 43–52.

Kōseirōdōshō (2003) *Ksōeōirōdō hakusho* (*White Paper on Labour and Welfare*), Tokyo: Gyōsei.

Mookherjee, D. and A. Sharrocks (1982) 'A Decomposition Analysis of the Trend in UK Income Inequality', *The Economic Journal*, 92 (368), pp. 886–902.

OECD (2004) *The OECD Employment Outlook*, Paris: OECD.

Ohashi, I. (2005) 'Wages, Hours of Work and Job Satisfaction of Retirement-Age Workers', *The Japanese Economic Review*, 56 (2), June, pp. 188–209.

Ohtake, F. and M. Saito (1999) 'Shotoku fubyōdōka no haikei to sono seisakuteki gain: nenrei kaisōnaiteki kōka, nenreikaisōkan kōka, jinkō kōreika kōka (The Background of Widening Income Disparity and Its Implication for Policy Making: Effects Inside and Across Age Groups, and Effects of Aging of Population)', *Kikan Shakai Hoshō Kenkyō*, 35 (1), pp. 65–76.

Ohtake, F. (2005) *Nihon no fubyōdō – kakusa shakai gensō to mirai* (Japan's Inequality: Illusion and Future of Disparity Society), Tokyo: Nihon Keizai Shinbunsha.

Seike, A. and A. Yamada (2004) *Kōreisha shōgaku no keizaigaku* (*Economics of the Education of Elderly Persons*), Tokyo: Nihon Keizai Shinbunsha.

Sharrocks, A. F. (1982) 'Inequality Decomposition by Factor Components', *Econometrica*, 50 (1), pp: 193–211.

Shirahase, S. (2002) 'Nihon no shotoku kakusa to kōreisha settai – kokusai hikaku no kanten kara' (A Study of Income Inequality and Households with Elderly Members in Japan), *Nihon Rōdō Kenkyū Zasshi*, 500, pp. 72–85.

# 6

# The Employment of Older Workers in Japanese Firms: Empirical Evidence from Micro Data

*Yoshio Higuchi and Isamu Yamamoto*

The willingness of older people to work is generally said to be low in Europe. Thus, in order to raise the European labour force participation rate, it is important both to motivate older people to work and to encourage firms to utilize older workers. In Japan, however, older people are relatively willing to work, so that the key determinant for the employment of older workers is the nature of company employment practices.

The Japanese labour force participation rate for men in their early 60s was 71% in 2003, which is much higher than the 15% in France and the 33% in Germany. Nevertheless, it is not clear that the high willingness to work amongst older Japanese is being effectively utilized in firms, especially after workers reach the mandatory retirement age.

According to the 2004 'Survey on Employment Conditions of Older Persons' (Ministry of Health, Labour and Welfare), 74.4% of companies with five or more employees implement a mandatory retirement system, and 88.3% of those firms set the mandatory retirement age at 60. Among the workers who reach this mandatory retirement age, 31.8% either move to other firms or retire. The remaining 68.8%, who stay in their firms through employment extension or the re-hiring system, change their employment status, to 'entrusted employee' and 'part-time employee'. Based on the 2004 'Labour Force Survey' (Ministry of Internal Affairs and Communications), the ratio of regular male workers (including executives) in their late 50s is 64%, but declines to 31% when workers reach their early 60s, whereas the ratio of non-regular workers increases from 7% to 20%.

As for large firms with 1,000 or more employees, the number of older workers who remain in regular positions also decreases. All large firms adopt a mandatory retirement system, 97% of which set the mandatory retirement age at 60. Only 2% of workers who experience mandatory retirement remain in their firms under the employment extension system. If we include those who are continuously employed in their firms via the re-hiring system, this figure only rises to 27%. Therefore, the remaining 73% simply leave their companies.

Once workers move to other firms or retire, it is likely that the skills which those workers acquired over many years suddenly become useless. Of course, people who do not want to work should not be forced to do so, but there are quite a few older people who want to make use of their skills as regular workers at the firms they have worked for. If one takes the broader perspective of social welfare into account, then the situation outlined above is inefficient, since human resources are not being effectively allocated in terms of quantity and quality.

In this article, we examine the survival rate for employees after the age of 50 by using the hazard model, and investigate what kind of personnel management strategy would be effective in making use of older workers' skills, and in promoting their employment. The article is organized as follows: In Section 2 we describe the framework of analysis and explain the estimation model and data. In Section 3 we then show the estimation results for the hazard rate function. Finally, in Section 4 we summarize our analysis and sketch out the policy implications.

## Framework of analysis: The Lazear model and the employment of older workers

Why is it that firms do not aggressively work on utilizing older people? In economics, one of the standard answers to this question is derived through comparison of a worker's wage and his labour productivity. In other words, the fact that the wages of older workers are high compared with their labour productivity inhibits firms from employing older workers.

E. P. Lazear (1979) indicated that a 'cheating hypothesis' supports the above. In response to the question, 'Why do firms try to set a mandatory retirement system?', Lazear explained that if firms can immediately calculate the labour productivity of each worker, then they can pay wages according to that labour productivity, as in a commission system. As a result, there will be no gap between wages and labour productivity, and a firm will neither profit nor lose by employing workers. However, when work becomes sophisticated and complex, it is not possible to immediately calculate the productivity of individual workers. Furthermore, monitoring individual productivity is extremely costly.

We are therefore left with the question of how firms can avoid underproductive workers and large monitoring costs. If a fixed amount of wages is paid regardless of a worker's tenure and workers are not monitored on how much work they do, they may neglect their responsibilities. One way to avoid this is to introduce a system of deferred payment. By warning workers that they will not be paid the deferred part of their payment if they are found to have neglected their work, workers will exercise self-control and work hard even without close monitoring. By introducing a deferred payment system, as shown on Figure 6.1, young workers are paid wages below the labour productivity (Period A in Figure 6.1), and workers with a long tenure are paid wages higher than the labour productivity (Period B in Figure 6.1). This enhances the workers' incentives to be productive.

On the other hand, if workers continue to work indefinitely, firms have to continue to pay wages that are above the labour productivity. In such cases, firms have to incur a loss for a long period of time. Therefore, firms need to set in advance a certain age at which workers are asked to resign. This is the mandatory retirement system, which effectively means the end of the period of deferred payment. In Figure 6.1, mandatory retirement is introduced at point C where the discounted present value of total wages paid and the total receipt of productivity are equivalent.

Thus, Lazear's hypothesis seems to be consistent with the stylized facts observed in the Japanese labour market: about 90% of Japanese firms

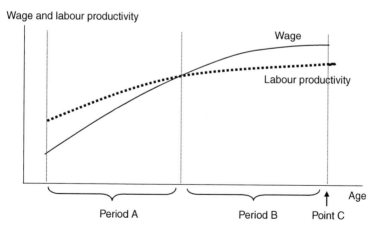

*Figure 6.1*  The relationship between wage and labour productivity
*Source*: The authors.

employ the mandatory retirement system, the wage profile is based on seniority, and firms pay extra retirement allowances when they terminate the employment contract through the early retirement incentive system before a worker reaches the mandatory retirement age. In fact, previous research has demonstrated that Lazear's hypothesis holds in the internal labour market in Japan, particularly with regard to the period of middle and old age.[1] For example, Okazaki (1993) verified that Lazear's hypothesis applied to workers of 45 and over, by estimating their wage and productivity profiles. Seike (1993) estimated the profile of the net retirement allowance gains that a worker can receive and then indicated the tendency of firms to induce workers of 40 and over to retire. Focusing on the relationship between the wage curve and the mandatory retirement age, Ohashi (1990), Higuchi (1992), Clark and Ogawa (1992), and others confirmed that the mandatory retirement age tends to be lower in firms and industries with a steeper wage curve. According to this hypothesis, the reason firms avoid employing older workers is that they have to pay wages that are above the labour productivity. The question is therefore how can we induce firms to employ older workers?

There is no other way than to reduce the gap between older workers' wages and labour productivity. One needs to either revise the system of deferred payment so that the seniority wage curve is less steep, or implement measures for raising older workers' labour productivity. For improvement in older workers' labour productivity, various ideas need to be devised in terms of personnel management. For example, more flexibility in the working system should be introduced and working methods should be improved, because workers are more susceptible to fatigue as they get older.

In the analysis that follows, we investigate whether adopting various measures to reduce the gap between older workers' wages and labour productivity promotes the employment of older people.

First, as an index for the utilization of older workers in a firm, we use the percentage of workers who continue to be employed by the same firm for one year in each age group. If the percentage is high, the firm has utilized older workers. We translate this percentage into the hazard rate (quit rate), which indicates the percentage of workers who have retired from the firm at each age. If the hazard rate is high, it means that a firm has not utilized older workers. Specifically, we define the hazard rate as 'the number of retirees (through quitting and dismissal) in the past 12 months divided by the number of employees in 12 months before the time of survey'.[2]

Next, we estimate a reduced form hazard rate function for each age group, in which the older workers' hazard rate is explained by firm characteristics such as the following: the slope of the wage curve, the rate of sales change, whether a firm has a mandatory retirement system, the mandatory retirement age (if any), whether a firm has an employment extension system and/or a re-hiring system, whether a firm has a system for providing better retirement allowance for early retirees, the ratio of short-time workers, firm size, survey year, region, personnel management measures for older workers (e.g. 'reform of wage and retirement allowance rules', 'education and job training', 'adjustment of workload', and 'introduction of flexible working hours or day'). The estimated hazard rate function is used to identify the types of firms whose hazard rates are either low or high. For example, it is shown that firms with a less steep wage curve and those adopting personnel management measures to raise older workers' productivity tend to promote older workers.

We used firm level micro data from the 'Survey on Employment Conditions of Older Persons: Firms' Survey' (the Ministry of Health, Labour and Welfare) taken in 1992 and 1996. From this survey, we obtained detailed information about the changes in the number of employees in each age group (50–54, 55–59, 60–64, 65–69) in the past year for each firm. We also used the information about employment systems such as the mandatory retirement system, employment extension and re-hiring system, and early retirement incentive system, as well as information about personnel management measures that a firm adopts for the employment of older workers. Since the survey does not include any information about wages or the financial conditions of individual firms, we used industry level data in order to make variables, such as the wage curve and the sales change. More specifically, we used data from the Ministry of Health, Labour and Welfare's 'Basic Statistical Survey on Wage Structure' for the wage curve, and the Ministry of Finance's 'Financial Statements Statistics of Corporations by Industry' for the sales change. The variables used in the analysis and their descriptive statistics are shown in Table 6.1.

In estimating the hazard rate function, we employed a maximum likelihood estimation using a logit model (see the appendix for a detailed explanation).

We should note that since we used a reduced form hazard rate function we can never ascertain the causality between the hazard rate and the explanatory variables. Neither can we identify the labour-demand and labour-supply factors. For example, in considering the wage curve, assuming other conditions are constant, the steeper the wage curve, the earlier a worker will reach Point C in Figure 6.1. Therefore, from the demand side of labour, there is an incentive for firms to induce older

*Table 6.1* Descriptive statistics

| | 1992 | | 1996 | |
|---|---|---|---|---|
| | Average | Standard error | Average | Standard error |
| Hazard rate (%) | | | | |
| 50–54 | 2.66 | 6.03 | 3.76 | 7.76 |
| 55–59 | 7.08 | 10.55 | 8.07 | 13.19 |
| 60–64 | 36.69 | 32.12 | 39.72 | 33.70 |
| 65–69 | 14.38 | 22.04 | 19.95 | 24.85 |
| Wage curve | | | | |
| 50–54 | 1.62 | 0.27 | 1.70 | 0.25 |
| 55–59 | 1.46 | 0.22 | 1.60 | 0.25 |
| 60–64 | 1.07 | 0.16 | 1.19 | 0.21 |
| 65–69 | 0.90 | 0.16 | 1.02 | 0.33 |
| Ratio of short-time workers (%) | | | | |
| 50–54 | 1.96 | 11.95 | 2.03 | 11.76 |
| 55–59 | 1.84 | 11.59 | 2.04 | 12.02 |
| 60–64 | 3.77 | 16.78 | 4.40 | 18.03 |
| 65–69 | 3.21 | 16.62 | 3.97 | 18.15 |
| Rate of sales change (%) | 3.20 | 5.73 | 2.14 | 2.87 |
| Mandatory retirement dummy (age 60, %) | 68.43 | 46.48 | 76.19 | 42.59 |
| Mandatory retirement dummy (age 61+, %) | 3.93 | 19.43 | 4.69 | 21.14 |
| Mandatory retirement dummy (by occupation, %) | 7.43 | 26.22 | 7.86 | 26.91 |
| Employment extension system (%) | 29.69 | 45.69 | 29.34 | 45.53 |
| Having used the system | 16.41 | 37.04 | 18.35 | 38.71 |
| Re-hiring system (%) | 41.86 | 49.34 | 43.60 | 49.59 |
| Having used the system | 21.48 | 41.07 | 22.73 | 41.91 |
| Having used early retirement system (%) | 6.94 | 25.41 | 6.45 | 24.56 |
| Large firm (1000+, %) | 36.08 | 48.02 | 32.55 | 46.86 |
| Medium firm (100–999, %) | 30.86 | 46.19 | 38.14 | 48.57 |
| Personnel management dummy (%) | | | | |
| Reform of wage and retirement allowance | 14.63 | 35.34 | 9.12 | 28.79 |

Continued

*Table 6.1*    Continued

| | 1992 | | 1996 | |
|---|---|---|---|---|
| | Average | Standard error | Average | Standard error |
| Introduction of job qualification and profession systems | 9.29 | 29.02 | 4.74 | 21.25 |
| Evaluating older workers' productivity | 5.56 | 22.91 | 4.37 | 20.43 |
| Redesign or development of duties | 7.34 | 26.08 | 3.84 | 19.23 |
| Education and job training | 8.12 | 27.31 | 5.19 | 22.17 |
| Devising various ideas in working system | 29.45 | 45.58 | 23.51 | 42.41 |
| Adjusting workload | 15.49 | 36.18 | 8.53 | 27.94 |
| Reallocation of workers and jobs | 28.91 | 45.34 | 16.70 | 37.30 |
| Introduction of flexible working hours or days | 13.51 | 34.19 | 7.49 | 26.32 |
| Improvement in operating procedure | 11.82 | 32.29 | 5.60 | 22.98 |
| Concerns for safety, sanitation, and health management | 23.19 | 42.21 | 12.37 | 32.92 |
| Number of observations | 7.964 | | 9.025 | |

*Sources*: Ministry of Health, Labour and Welfare, Survey on Employment Conditions of Older Persons, 1992 and 1996; Ministry of Health, Labour and Welfare, Basic Statistical Survey on Wage Structure, 1992 and 1996; Ministry of Finance, Financial Statements Statistics of Corporations by Industry, 1992 and 1996.

workers to retire earlier.[3] On the other hand, from the supply side, workers will want to stay longer because a steep wage curve means a greater rent (the gap between wages and productivity). Thus, the wage curve has both positive effects (demand factor) and negative effects (supply factor) on the hazard rate of older workers. The reduced form hazard rate function, however, can only estimate the net effects.

Similarly, regarding the personnel management of older workers, we consider variables such as 'revision of rules on wages and retirement allowance', 'education and job training', 'adjustment of workload', and 'more flexibility in work'. These variables also have an effect on the labour demand side, accompanied by the narrowing of the gap between wages and productivity, and effects on the labour supply side, resulting from changes in the marginal disutility of labour. In our estimate, we verify their net effects.

## Estimation results of the hazard rate function

The estimation results of the hazard rate function for each age group are summarized in Tables 6.2 and 6.3.

Table 6.2 indicates the estimation results of the baseline model comprised of explanatory variables such as the wage curve, the rate of sales change, the mandatory retirement system, the employment extension and re-hiring system, and the early retirement incentive system.

*Table 6.2*  Estimation results for the hazard rate function: baseline model

|  | Age 50–54 | | | Age 55–59 | | |
|---|---|---|---|---|---|---|
|  | Coefficient | Marginal effect | t-value | Coefficient | Marginal effect | t-value |
| Mandatory retirement dummy (age 60) | −0.54 | −0.13 | −13.35 | −0.80 | −0.18 | −27.35 |
| Mandatory retirement dummy (age 61+) | −0.60 | −0.15 | −8.11 | −1.34 | −0.34 | −21.51 |
| Mandatory retirement dummy (by occupation) | −0.54 | −0.14 | −10.03 | −0.90 | −0.22 | −21.57 |
| Employment extension system | −0.06 | −0.01 | −2.34 | −0.32 | −0.08 | −16.13 |
| Re-hiring system | −0.26 | −0.06 | −14.59 | −0.53 | −0.13 | −39.91 |
| Having used early retirement system | 0.39 | 0.10 | 21.28 | 0.62 | 0.15 | 45.06 |
| Wage curve | 0.39 | 0.09 | 9.80 | 0.32 | 0.07 | 10.34 |
| Ratio of short-time workers | −0.03 | −0.01 | −0.25 | −0.32 | −0.08 | −2.97 |
| Rate of sales change | −0.02 | −0.01 | −8.65 | −0.02 | −0.01 | −11.55 |

Continued

*Table 6.2* Continued

| | Age 50–54 | | | Age 55–59 | | |
|---|---|---|---|---|---|---|
| | Coefficient | Marginal effect | t-value | Coefficient | Marginal effect | t-value |
| Large firm dummy (1,000+) | −0.24 | −0.06 | −4.94 | 0.50 | 0.12 | 12.30 |
| Medium firm dummy (100–999) | −0.22 | −0.05 | −4.49 | 0.27 | 0.07 | 6.47 |
| Survey year dummy (Year 1992) | −0.40 | −0.10 | −22.14 | −0.12 | −0.03 | −8.88 |
| Constant term | −2.97 | −0.14 | −31.72 | −2.39 | −0.18 | −33.17 |
| Log likelihood | −67038.1 | | | −94529.2 | | |
| Number of observations | 16.989 | | | 16.989 | | |

| | Age 60–64 | | | Age 65–69 | | |
|---|---|---|---|---|---|---|
| | Coefficient | Marginal effect | t-value | Coefficient | Marginal effect | t-value |
| Mandatory retirement dummy (age 60) | 1.14 | 0.24 | 28.45 | 0.12 | 0.03 | 1.64 |
| Mandatory retirement dummy (age 61+) | −0.46 | −0.11 | −8.74 | 0.31 | 0.08 | 3.65 |
| Mandatory retirement dummy (by occupation) | −0.09 | −0.02 | −2.00 | 0.02 | 0.00 | 0.18 |
| Employment extension system | −0.53 | −0.13 | −34.29 | −0.22 | −0.05 | −6.06 |
| Re-hiring system | −0.49 | −0.12 | −36.36 | −0.02 | −0.00 | −0.48 |
| Having used early retirement system | 0.74 | 0.18 | 45.53 | 0.43 | 0.11 | 8.11 |
| Wage curve | 0.19 | 0.05 | 5.35 | −0.22 | −0.05 | −4.13 |

Continued

*Table 6.2*   Continued

| | Age 60–64 | | | Age 65–69 | | |
|---|---|---|---|---|---|---|
| | Coefficient | Marginal effect | t-value | Coefficient | Marginal effect | t-value |
| Ratio of short-time workers | −0.29 | −0.07 | −8.81 | −0.44 | −0.11 | −5.59 |
| Rate of sales change | −0.02 | −0.01 | −12.91 | −0.03 | −0.01 | −6.91 |
| Large firm dummy (1,000+) | 1.29 | 0.31 | 43.07 | 0.37 | 0.09 | 6.69 |
| Medium firm dummy (100–999) | 0.48 | 0.12 | 15.96 | 0.05 | 0.01 | 0.90 |
| Survey year dummy (Year 1992) | −0.26 | −0.06 | −18.28 | −0.48 | −0.12 | −13.11 |
| Constant term | −2.65 | −0.16 | −36.91 | −1.80 | −0.22 | −14.24 |
| Log likelihood | −70987.6 | | | −12462.8 | | |
| Number of observations | 16.989 | | | 16.989 | | |

*Notes*:
1. Estimated by logit model with pooled data (years 1992 and 1996). Area dummies are not listed.
2. Marginal effects are evaluated around the sample mean.
3. Standard errors are White heteroskedascity consistent estimators.

*Source*: Own calculations based on data from sources given below Table 6.1.

Table 6.3 shows the estimation results when a variety of personnel management variables are added to the baseline model.[4]

In Tables 6.2 and 6.3, if the estimated coefficient is positive, the larger the corresponding variable and so the more the employment of older workers is prohibited (because of a larger hazard rate). On the other hand, if the estimated coefficient is negative, a larger corresponding variable indicates that more older workers are promoted. As described below, for most estimation results we obtained the expected sign and statistical significance.

### Relationship with the employment system

The estimation results for the relationship between the hazard rate of older workers and employment systems (mandatory retirement, employment extension, re-hiring, early retirement incentive system) are as follows.

*Table 6.3*   Estimation results for the hazard rate function: personnel management measures

| | Age 50–54 | | | Age 55–59 | | |
|---|---|---|---|---|---|---|
| | Coefficient | Marginal effect | t-value | Coefficient | Marginal effect | t-value |
| Regarding wage | | | | | | |
| Reform of wage and retirement allowance | −0.37 | −0.09 | −14.73 | −0.10 | −0.03 | −5.98 |
| Introduction of job qualification and profession systems | −0.27 | −0.07 | −7.96 | 0.12 | 0.03 | 5.32 |
| Regarding labour productivity | | | | | | |
| Evaluating older workers' productivity | −0.02 | −0.01 | −0.41 | −0.25 | −0.06 | −5.31 |
| Redesign or development of duties | −0.01 | −0.00 | −0.52 | 0.03 | 0.01 | 1.47 |
| Education and job training | −0.40 | −0.10 | −12.61 | 0.07 | 0.02 | 3.57 |
| Devising various ideas in working system | −0.07 | −0.02 | −3.49 | −0.29 | −0.07 | −18.66 |
| Adjusting workload | 0.20 | 0.05 | 7.61 | −0.11 | −0.03 | −4.84 |
| Reallocation of workers and jobs | 0.05 | 0.01 | 2.87 | −0.09 | −0.02 | −6.06 |
| Introduction of flexible working hours or days | −0.05 | −0.01 | −1.46 | −0.24 | −0.06 | −10.07 |
| Improvement in operating procedure | −0.13 | −0.03 | −4.59 | −0.26 | −0.07 | −12.83 |

Continued

*Table 6.3*   Continued

| | Age 50–54 | | | Age 55–59 | | |
|---|---|---|---|---|---|---|
| | Coefficient | Marginal effect | t-value | Coefficient | Marginal effect | t-value |
| Concerns for safety, sanitation, and health management | −0.09 | −0.02 | −4.15 | −0.19 | −0.05 | −11.52 |

| | Age 60–64 | | | Age 65–69 | | |
|---|---|---|---|---|---|---|
| | Coefficient | Marginal effect | t-value | Coefficient | Marginal effect | t-value |
| Regarding wage | | | | | | |
| Reform of wage and retirement allowance | 0.04 | 0.01 | 2.30 | 0.21 | 0.05 | 4.41 |
| Introduction of job qualification and profession systems | −0.03 | −0.01 | −1.43 | −0.03 | −0.01 | −0.40 |
| Regarding labour productivity | | | | | | |
| Evaluating older workers' productivity | −1.08 | −0.27 | −31.34 | −0.61 | −0.15 | −9.78 |
| Redesign or development of duties | 0.22 | 0.06 | 9.97 | −0.41 | −0.10 | −5.10 |
| Education and job training | −0.19 | −0.05 | −9.35 | −0.36 | −0.09 | −6.32 |
| Devising various ideas in working system | −0.35 | −0.09 | −24.78 | −0.08 | −0.02 | −2.27 |
| Adjusting workload | −0.19 | −0.05 | −9.33 | −0.31 | −0.08 | −5.79 |
| Reallocation of workers and jobs | −0.10 | −0.02 | −6.88 | −0.07 | −0.02 | −1.72 |

Continued

*Table 6.3*   Continued

| | Age 60–64 | | | Age 65–69 | | |
|---|---|---|---|---|---|---|
| | Coefficient | Marginal effect | t-value | Coefficient | Marginal effect | t-value |
| Introduction of flexible working hours or days | −0.36 | −0.09 | −17.45 | −0.24 | −0.06 | −4.68 |
| Improvement in operating procedure | 0.18 | 0.05 | 9.34 | −0.29 | −0.07 | −4.82 |
| Concerns for safety, sanitation, and health management | −0.07 | −0.02 | −4.66 | −0.02 | −0.01 | −0.50 |

*Notes:*
1. Estimated by adding each variable to the baseline model in Table 6.2.
2. Estimated by logit model with pooled data (year 1992 and 1996). Area dummies are not listed.
3. Marginal effects are evaluated around the sample mean.
4. Standard errors are White heteroskedascity consistent estimators.

*Source:* Own calculations based on data from sources given below Table 6.1.

First, the coefficients of dummy variables on the mandatory retirement age are significantly negative until the mandatory retirement age is reached. This indicates that the hazard rate is lower before the mandatory retirement age in firms with a mandatory retirement system, compared to firms without a mandatory retirement system (base for dummy variable). Thus, we interpret that the mandatory retirement system has a job security effect until mandatory retirement.[5] Conversely, the coefficients after the mandatory retirement age are significantly positive. This implies that the mandatory retirement system has a job terminate effect at the mandatory retirement age.

More specifically, the coefficients of the mandatory retirement age of 60 are significantly negative only in the 50–54 and 55–59 age groups. However, they become significantly positive in age groups above the mandatory retirement age, namely 60–64 and 65–69. Similarly, regarding the mandatory retirement age dummy of 61 and over, we see a job security effect up to the 60–64 age group. However, we have significantly positive coefficients in the 65–69 age group, which is above the mandatory retirement age of most firms.

*Table 6.4*　The effect of the employment system on the hazard rate

| | Age 55–59 | | Age 60–64 | |
| --- | --- | --- | --- | --- |
| | Difference | STD | Difference | STD |
| Mandatory retirement dummy (age 60, %) | −5.42 | 2.43 | 18.60 | 6.32 |
| Mandatory retirement dummy (age 61+, %) | −7.46 | 3.47 | −4.95 | 2.69 |
| Employment extension and re-hiring system (%) | −3.99 | 1.69 | −17.27 | 6.67 |
| Early retirement system (%) | 4.04 | 1.86 | 14.05 | 4.18 |

*Note*: The difference between the estimated hazard rates when each dummy variable is one or zero.

*Source*: Own calculations based on data from sources given below Table 6.1.

With regard to the dummy variable for mandatory retirement by occupation, all coefficients are negative in each age group up to 60–64, which shows that firms with mandatory retirement by occupation provide more job security than firms with no mandatory retirement system.

For reference, we simulate how much the hazard rate varies depending on the difference in the mandatory retirement system in Table 6.4. The difference in the hazard rate between firms with a mandatory retirement age of 60 and those with no mandatory retirement system is about minus 5% in the 55–59 age group, and about plus 19% in the 60–64 age group. At firms with a mandatory retirement age of 61 and over, the hazard rate is about 7% lower in the 55–59 age group, and about 5% lower in the 60–64 age group.

From the estimated coefficients of the employment extension and re-hiring systems, we find that they are significantly negative not just for workers in their 60s but for all age groups. At firms that have introduced such systems, many older workers are retained not only after the mandatory retirement age but also before the mandatory retirement age. The impact on the hazard rate, which is shown in Table 6.4, is about minus 4% for the 55–59 age group and about minus 17% for the 60–64 age group.

Lastly, as regards the early retirement incentive system, the coefficients are positive not only for workers in their 50s but for all age groups. At firms that employ the system, older workers are more likely to be taken out of their firms regardless of the mandatory retirement age. The effect on the hazard rate is about plus 4% for the 55–59 age group, and about plus 14% for the 60–64 age group (Table 6.4).

## Discussion about the mandatory retirement system

As for the effect of mandatory retirement on the hazard rate, it is important to note that the effects of other employment systems (the early retirement incentive, employment extension, and re-hiring systems) are all controlled in the estimation listed in Table 6.2. Therefore, the estimated coefficients indicate the net effect of the mandatory retirement system on the employment of older workers when other employment systems remain unchanged. However, it is also possible for firms to use the early retirement incentive system or the employment extension and re-hiring system as tools for adjusting the number of older workers. For example, if many workers retire before the mandatory retirement age through the early retirement system, the job security effect of the mandatory retirement system diminishes. On the other hand, if firms maintain a lot of older workers through the employment extension and re-hiring systems, the job termination effect also lessens.

To examine this, we verified whether the mandatory retirement system actually had both effects even when the effects of the above systems were included, by estimating a model that excluded the dummy variables for those systems from the baseline model. The estimation was conducted for the 55–59, 60–64 and 65–69 age groups. For the 60–64 age group, we used dummy variables for the mandatory retirement age for each age to reveal the detailed effects of the mandatory retirement system.[6]

The marginal effect of dummy variables for each mandatory retirement age is shown in Figure 6.2.

The figure shows that the marginal effects are negative before and positive after the mandatory retirement age. For example, at firms where the mandatory retirement age is 61, the coefficients of the dummy variables for the mandatory retirement age are significantly negative for the 55–59 and 60 age groups. That is, even considering the adjustment made by the early retirement, employment extension, and re-hiring systems before and after the mandatory retirement age, the mandatory retirement system does in fact affect job security and job termination levels before and after the mandatory retirement age.

These results seem to provide important evidence on which to base a discussion of the nature of the mandatory retirement system in Japan. For example, when thinking about the proposal to legally abolish the mandatory retirement system, our results suggest that abolition might reduce the employment of older workers in their 50s who have benefited

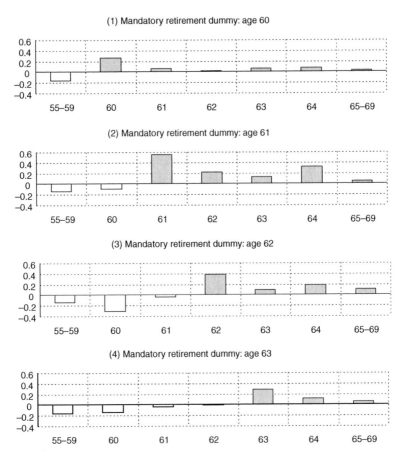

*Figure 6.2*   Job security and job termination effects of the mandatory retirement system

*Note*: Each bar indicates the marginal effects of the mandatory retirement dummy variable, calculated by estimating the model without employment extension, re-hiring, or early employment dummy variables.

*Source*: Own calculations based on data from sources given below Table 6.1.

from the job security effect of the mandatory retirement system. In an ageing society with a declining birth rate, the aim should be to bring about a situation where everybody can work regardless of age and each person can make full use of their abilities and willingness to work. In Japan, however, the time is still unripe at this stage to abolish the mandatory retirement system, because Japan does not have strict rules for dismissals or objective standards for evaluating workers' productivity. If the mandatory retirement system is abolished under such circumstances, older workers might be arbitrarily dismissed by employers, which will merely instil job insecurity.

Another example is the relationship between mandatory retirement and public pension reform. The age when one can receive public pensions is gradually being raised from 60 to 65. Based on our estimation results, this seems effective in promoting older workers aged between 60 and 64, because job security effects spread to workers over 60. However, we should be careful in making this interpretation. As explained earlier, according to Lazear's hypothesis in Figure 6.1, the mandatory retirement age is determined endogenously where the discounted present value of total wages paid and the total receipt of productivity are equivalent. Therefore, even if the mandatory retirement age is raised, if older workers' wages before the retirement age remain high, the job security effect will most likely diminish. Unless we reform the seniority wage system or prepare a system where wages can be set in accordance with each worker's productivity for an extended period, firms will try to use the early retirement incentive system or other means to lay off older workers. If firms are unable to take such measures, it will in turn have a serious impact on profits.

Taking the above arguments into consideration, it is desirable for the time being to maintain the current mandatory retirement age of 60 and promote the employment of workers who are 60 and over through the employment extension and re-hiring system. If this course of action is pursued, we expect the job security effect for workers in their 50s to stay the same because the mandatory retirement system remains unchanged. Moreover, firms will be able to set the wages of workers who are 60 and over in accordance with their productivity, because different wage and personnel systems will be applied to the re-employed and extended workers.[7] This scheme has the advantage of reducing the job termination effect of the mandatory retirement system while maintaining the job security effects.

In the long run, however, we should establish an environment in which older workers are continuously employed within firms by reforming the wage system before the mandatory retirement age, by considering the utilization of the skills accumulated before the mandatory retirement age, as well as taking into account a possible labour shortage due to the fact that Japan has an ageing society with a low birth rate.

## The gap between wages and productivity

According to Lazear's hypothesis, an obstacle to the employment of older workers is the gap between wages and productivity that arises during Period B in Figure 6.1. One way to reduce this gap is to flatten the wage curve by revising the wage system.

In fact, looking at Table 6.2, we can see that the wage curve has a significantly positive coefficient, indicating firms with a steep wage curve have workers retiring early.[8] Therefore, it can be said that flattening the wage curve to reduce the gap between the wages and labour productivity of older workers is associated with the utilization of older workers.

We also see similar findings in Table 6.3. As for the 'reform of wage and retirement allowance', the coefficients are negative for workers in their 50s. This result may imply that older workers are promoted in firms that reform the wage system so as to prevent older workers' wages from moving above productivity. In other words, we may say that reform of the wage system is necessary for the promotion of older workers. With regard to the 'introduction of job qualification and profession systems', its effect on the hazard rate is positive in the 55–59 age group, but negative for those in their 60s. This may be because firms with this program tend to select workers earlier and retain the workers who survived the screening on into their 60s. Hence, if we interpret the 'reform of wage and retirement allowance' and the 'introduction of job qualification and profession systems' as measures to reduce the gap between wages and productivity for older workers, these kinds of personnel management strategies are effective in promoting older workers.

The other way to reduce the wage-productivity gap is to increase the productivity of older workers. One possible way would be to shorten their working hours. Compared with young workers, older workers tend to become fatigued and cannot endure long working hours. Thus, introducing shorter working hours may raise the hourly productivity of older workers. In fact, we can confirm this effect in Table 6.2 if we regard the ratio of short-time workers as a proxy. The coefficients of the ratio of short-time workers are negative in each age group, which indicates that the firms with many short-time workers tend to promote many older workers as a result of improved productivity per hour due to short-time working.

Furthermore, looking at personnel management with respect to productivity in Table 6.3, the employment of older workers is maintained in each age group at firms that 'evaluate older workers' productivity'. This result also suggests that firms are more likely to employ older workers when the gap between wages and productivity is small. Likewise, the coefficients of 'education and job training' are significantly negative in each age group except the 55–59 age group, showing that retraining older workers has an effect.

Lastly, we can see that at firms which engage in providing better working systems for older workers through the 'devising of various ideas in the working system', 'adjustment of workload', the 'reallocation of workers and jobs', the 'introduction of flexible working hours or day', the 'improvement in the operation procedure', and 'concern for safety, sanitation and health management', the hazard rate is generally low in the 55–59 age groups and above. It is understood that by preparing flexible working systems, older workers' productivity is raised and the number of older workers retiring due to the reduction of marginal disutility.

## Discussion about the labour productivity of older workers

As we saw, the hazard rate was low at firms which evaluated the productivity of older workers, therefore productivity is an important element in the consideration of the employment of older workers.

Thus, what kinds of abilities do firms value in their older workers? An investigation based on occupation type, using the 'Survey on Employment Conditions of Older Persons: Firms' Survey' from the 2000 survey, provides a sense of direction.

Table 6.5 compares firms' plans for increasing the number of workers in their early 60s.

We see that whereas 11% of firms had plans to increase the number of professional and technical employees, only about 5% were thinking about increasing the number of managers or clerical workers. These figures indicate that even among older workers there is a larger demand for professional and technical workers. Similarly, comparing the firms that set different mandatory retirement ages according to occupation, the ratio of firms whose retirement age was 61 or over was more than 60% professional and technical occupations. It was about 40% for managers, and about 15% for clerical occupations. These figures imply that firms want to employ professional and technical workers longer than managers or clerical workers.

Since professional and technical workers' wages are generally higher than those of management and clerical workers, firms might view professional and technical workers as 'more expensive'.[9] However, when asked about problems related to the employment of workers in their

*Table 6.5*  Employment planning by type of occupation

| | Professional and technical | Managers and officials | Clerical and related |
|---|---|---|---|
| Ratio of firms planning the increase in older workers (age 60–64) | 11.1 | 4.9 | 4.9 |
| Ratio of firms whose retirement age is more than 61 to the number of firms that have mandatory retirement by occupation | 60.6 | 42.6 | 15.6 |
| Ratio to the number of persons who used early retirement scheme | 26.8 | 43.8 | 29.5 |
| Ratio to the number of workers being employed by employment extension or re-hiring system | 20.6 | 15.0 | 11.5 |
| Ratio of firms thinking old workers employment is a problem in that | | | |
| Their employment crowds out younger workers | 6.6 | 5.8 | 8.5 |
| Their labour cost is high | 10.6 | 15.6 | 11.5 |
| Their skills are depreciating | 8.4 | 4.0 | 6.0 |

*Source*: Ministry of Health, Labour and Welfare, Survey on Employment Conditions of Older Persons, 2000.

early 60s, relatively few firms had a problem with higher wages when employing professional and technical workers. This result tells us that the productivity of professional and technical workers matches their wages. Moreover, if we look at the actual flow of older workers by occupation, we find that not many professional and technical employees retired under the early retirement system in the past year. In addition, many of these employees were among the older workers who stayed on under the employment extension and re-hiring systems.

We should note, however, that the productivity of older workers who have been involved in professional and technical jobs is not unconditionally high. It may be high if the professional skills acquired at a younger age do not depreciate with time, that is, if those ski[l] useful in later years. However, where technological progress that the professional skills required of workers change dra..... many older workers may not be able to keep up with the technological change. As a result, their productivity may decline, so that they find it difficult to maintain employment at their firm. In particular, since professional and technical skills are more susceptible to the effect of technological progress than more generalized skills, they can sometimes be a double-edged sword. In fact, several studies that use US data have demonstrated this phenomenon. For example, Yamamoto (2003) calculated a dynamic labour supply model for older men using US panel data. The results showed that there tended to be a greater probability that older men who had been employed in industries which demonstrate rapid technological progress, or those who had been professional and technical workers, would retire earlier. In other words, older workers whose skills are more likely to become obsolete due to technological progress were more likely to withdraw from the labour market on account of their decreased productivity.[10]

Since professional and technical workers in Japan are in high demand as we have seen above, we suggest that the effect of technological progress is not evident in the Japanese labour market. It is interesting to note, however, that the ratio of firms that highlighted 'skills are depreciating' as a problem with employing older professional and technical workers was higher than for other types of worker (Table 6.5). Although acquiring professional and technical skills will raise one's employability in older age, it is particularly important to learn skills that do not depreciate with age or technological change. Consequently, it is essential for workers to make a continuous effort to develop skills so that they can adapt to future change. It is also important for firms to diversify employment practices that allow workers to build careers as professional or technical workers.

In Japan, professional and technical occupations have not necessarily accounted for a large percentage of employees. In addition, it is not easy for older workers who have worked in other occupations or as generalists to quickly acquire professional and technical skills. Considering this point, it is also important that we encourage firms to implement personnel management measures that raise the general productivity of older workers. As we saw in the previous section, preparing an environment in which older workers can make full use of their abilities, or providing education and job training for them, was effective in curbing retirement. We strongly encourage firms to conduct such measures in order to maintain and enhance the employment of older workers.

## Concluding remarks

In this article, we investigated what kinds of firms promote older workers, using micro data from the 'Survey on Employment Conditions of Older Persons: Firms' Survey'. The results obtained here are summarized below:

1. At firms that have a mandatory retirement age of 60, few workers leave between the age of 50 and 59, but many workers leave when they are 60 and over. This indicates that the mandatory retirement system guarantees employment until the mandatory retirement age, but also terminates employment at the mandatory retirement age.
2. At firms that have introduced the employment extension system and/or the re-employment system, the rate of workers who leave is low not only among workers of 60 and over, but also among workers under 60. At firms that have introduced a system for providing better retirement allowance to early retirees, the rate of workers who leave is high, not only among workers of 60 and over, but also among workers under 60.
3. The steeper a firm's seniority wage curve, the younger the workers are when they leave.
4. At firms that revised the wage system and the retirement allowance system, there were fewer workers who left at an early age. In addition, fewer workers leave between 50 and 54 at firms that have introduced a job qualification and profession system.
5. At firms where the ratio of short-time employees is high, there are fewer workers who leave at 55 and over.
6. At firms that try to properly evaluate the productivity of older workers, there are fewer workers who leave at an early age. Moreover, fewer workers leave when firms devise various ideas to improve the working system. The effectiveness of such ideas is particularly large in comparison with other measures.
7. At firms that carry out workload adjustment or the reallocation of workers and jobs, there are more workers who leave between 50 and 54, but significantly fewer workers who leave at 55 and over.
8. At firms that are concerned with improving working methods, safety, sanitation, and the health management of employees, there are fewer workers who leave in all age groups.

From these results, several policy implications for promoting the employment of older people can be derived. One of them concerns the amended April 2006 'Law Concerning Stabilization of Employment of Older Persons' to promote the stability of employment for older people. According to this amended law, firms have to secure stable employment for older people until the age of 64 by implementing either of the following measures: (a) raising the mandatory retirement age, (b) introducing the continuous employment system, and (c) abolishing the mandatory retirement system.

In the discussion over amending the law, there was a proposal that all firms should be forced to abolish mandatory retirement because it is a form of age discrimination. However, our analysis shows that the mandatory retirement system guarantees the employment of older workers until they reach the mandatory retirement age, although it also reduces the employment of workers who have reached retirement age regardless of their skills and willingness to work (see finding (1) above). It should be noted that the abolition of the mandatory retirement system poses a risk that older workers whose skills are not highly valued by firms will lose their jobs before the mandatory retirement age.

Since a system of properly evaluating workers' skills has not been established in Japan, it is likely that older workers would be subject to employment adjustment since their wages generally exceed labour productivity. If we prevent this by reinforcing regulations for dismissals, it would erode the profits and international competitiveness of firms, which may result in an overall decrease in employment. Considering these aspects, allowing firms to choose one option out of the three mentioned above seems to be the most desirable, taking into account internal issues as shown in the amended law.

Our results also have several implications as to what kind of specific measures firms should adopt in order to promote the employment of older workers. For instance, our results imply that firms should target not only older workers but also younger workers. One of the factors that prevent firms from promoting the employment of older workers is the seniority wage system (see finding (3) above). If this wage system was reformed into the performance-based pay system, where wages are evaluated in accordance with individual productivity, firms would not regard older workers as costly (see finding (6) above). In addition, if firms cared about the improvement of working methods, safety, sanitation, and the health management of employees, the job turnover rate would be lowered for all age groups, which would make it possible for firms to promote the employment of older workers (see finding (8) above).

Lastly, as future research, it is important to investigate what effects these measures would have on company performance and international competitiveness, as well as on the employment of younger workers and women, whose jobs might be crowed out due to stronger job security of older workers.

## Appendix: Estimation of the hazard rate function

In the estimation of the hazard rate function, we assume that the number of conditional retirees $s_i(a)|N_i(a)$ $(N_i(a)$ is the number of employees at age $a$ in firm $i$ $(i = 1,2,...,n))$ and follows the independent binomial distribution. Then, we employ an estimation method using a logit model indicated by Prentice and Kalbfleish (1980) and Efron (1988).[11] Based on the binomial distribution assumption, the number of retirees at age $a$ will have the following probability density function:

$$f\big(s_i(a)|N_i(a)\big) = \frac{N_i(a)!}{s_i(a)!\,(N_i(a) - s_i(a))!}\, H_i(a)^{s_i(a)}\big(1 - H_i(a)\big)^{N_i(a) - s_i(a)}$$

where the logit parameter $\lambda(a)$ is defined as follows:

$$\lambda_i(a) = \log \frac{H_i(a)}{1 - H_i(a)} \left(\text{or } H_i(a) = \frac{1}{1 - \exp(\lambda_i(a))}\right)$$

By regressing $\lambda(a)$ on firm characteristics $X_i(a)$, we can express the hazard rate function with a parameter vector $\theta(a)$ :

$$\hat{H}_i(a) = \frac{1}{1 - \exp(X_i(a)\,\hat{\theta}(a))}$$

Hence, by formulating the following likelihood function for each age group, the parameter can be estimated through the maximum likelihood method:

$$L(\theta(a)) = \Pi_i \left(\frac{1}{1 + \exp(X_i(a)\,\theta(a))}\right)^{s_i(a)} \left(\frac{-\exp(X_i(a)\,\theta(a))}{1 + \exp(X_i(a)\,\theta(a))}\right)^{N_i(a) - s_i(a)}, \quad i = 1,2,...,n$$

Note that when determining the number of older workers they employ, it is thought that firms think simultaneously about the outflow (retirement) and the inflow (employment). Therefore, we use the net number of retirees for $s_i(a)$, which is obtained by deducting the number of newly employed people from the number of people who are retiring, in order to estimate the net-based hazard rate.

## Notes

This article is based on our paper in Japanese 'Kigyō ni okeru kōreisha no katsuyō: teinensei to jinji kanri no arikata', in Noriyuki Takayama and Osamu Saitō (eds), *Shoshika no keizai bunseki* (*Economic Analysis of the Society with a Declining Birth Rate*), Tōyōkeizai Shinpōsha, 2006.

1. From the standpoint of the human investment theory of Becker (1964), Mincer (1962), Hashimoto (1981), and others, the productivity profile is, contrary to Lazear's hypothesis, steeper than the wage profile.
2. The number of employees a year before the survey was obtained by adding the net number of retirees in the past year (number of retirees – number of newly employed) to the number of employees at the time of the survey.
3. Even when the wage curve is steeper, if the intercept of the wage profile is sufficiently low, the period in which a worker will reach Point C is not necessarily shortened. However, the variation in the wages of young workers is considerably smaller than that of middle-aged and older workers (e.g. the variance coefficient of young workers' wages is less than half that of workers in their 50s and 60s).
4. Because there is no significant difference in the estimation results related to variables that are included in the base model in either case, only the coefficients related to the employment management policies are shown on Table 6.3.
5. Firms that have no mandatory retirement system are used as a base for each dummy variable on mandatory retirement age.
6. However, the data on newly hired workers are not available for each age. Thus, only the retirees were made subject to this analysis unlike in the analysis of the previous section. In other words, the hazard rate is based on gross numbers here. As before, firms that have not introduced the mandatory retirement system are used as a base for the dummy variables for each mandatory retirement age.
7. According to the Ministry of Labour's Employment Management Survey conducted in 2000, about 50% of firms replied that they lowered the wages of older workers after firms extended employment through an employment extension system. About 70% of firms replied that they decreased the wages of employees after they re-employed a worker through a re-hiring scheme. Around 30% also answered that they changed workers' positions or job qualifications after employment extension, and more than 50% did so after re-hiring.
8. It can be surmised that the effect of the labour demand side (the large gap between wages and productivity which induces firms to reduce older workers) was strong enough to raise the hazard rate for workers.
9. If we estimate the wage function of older workers using data on individual workers from the 'Survey on Employment Conditions of Older Persons', we

find that the wages of professional and technical employees are higher than those of production workers by about 30% for full-time employees, and about 40% for part-time employees.
10. In another study, Ahituv and Zeira (2000) estimated the structural VAR model using macro data and verified the negative effect of rapid technological progress on the labour supply of older workers.
11. Estimation of the hazard rate function using a logit model has also been used by Ashenfelter and Card (2001), for example.

## References

Ashenfelter, O. and D. Card (2001) 'Did the Elimination of Mandatory Retirement Affect Faculty Retirement Flows?', *NBER Working Paper Series*, 8378.

Ahituv, A. and J. Zeira (2000) 'Technical Progress and Early Retirement', *C.E.P.R.Discussion Paper*, 2614.

Becker, G. (1964) *Human Capital: A theoretical and Empirical Analysis with Special Reference to Education*, New York: Columbia University Press.

Clark, R. and N. Ogawa (1992) 'The Effect of Mandatory Retirement on Earnings Profiles in Japan', *Industrial and Labor Relations Review*, 4 (2), pp. 258–266.

Efron, B. (1988) 'Logistic Regression, Survival Analysis, and the Kaplan-Meier Curve', *Journal of the American Statistical Association*, 83 (402), pp. 414–425.

Hashimoto, M. (1981) 'Firm-Specific Human Capital as Shared Investment', *American Economic Review*, 71 (3), pp. 475–482.

Higuchi, Y. (1992) *Nihon keizai to shugyō kōdō (Japanese Economy and Labour Participation Behaviour)*, Tokyo: Tōyōkeizai Shinpōsha.

Lazear, E. (1979) 'Why is There Mandatory Retirement?', *Journal of Political Economy*, 87 (6), pp. 1261–1284.

Mincer, J. (1962) 'On the Job Training: Costs, Returns and Some Implications', *Journal of Political Economy*, 70 (5), pp. 50–79.

Ohashi, I. (1990) *Rōdō shijo no riron (A Theory of the Labour Market)*, Tokyo: Tōyōkeizai Shinpōsha.

Okazaki, K. (1993) 'Why is Earnings Profile Upward-Sloping?', *Journal of the Japanese and International Economies*, 7 (3), pp. 297–314.

Prentice, R. and J. Kalbfleish (1980) *The Statistical Analysis of Failure Time Data*, New York: John Wiley.

Seike, A. (1993) *Kōreika shakai no rōdō shijo (The Labor Market in Aging Societies)*, Tokyo: Tōyōkeizai Shinpōsha.

Yamamoto, I. (2003) *Essay on the Retirement of Older Men in the U.S. and Japan*, Ph.D.

# 7
# Effects of Support Measures on Employment of Elderly People in Japan

*Jiro Nakamura*

It is widely known that the Japanese labour participation rate of the elderly is the highest among the developed countries in the world. Table 7.1 shows the percentages of people in different age groups of 55 and above in the workforce.

One of the reasons for the high percentage of elderly people in the workforce, despite relatively high unemployment rates for middle-aged and older people, is the existence of employment support systems for the elderly. As the population has been ageing, various measures have been taken to keep elderly people in the workforce (see, e.g. Mitani 2001). Much analysis has already been conducted as to the overall effects of such measures on enhancing the opportunity to work for elderly people.

What seems to be lacking, however, is a detailed analysis of which measures are effective for which types of firm and workplace. For example, Table 7.1 reveals a significant difference between males and females of advanced age. The ratio for males in their early 60s (ages 60 to 64) is still over 70% of that for males in their late 50s (ages 55 to 59), whereas the ratio is below 70% for females. Also, the ratio for females in their early 60s has remained almost constant or shown only a slight increase at most, while that for females in their late 50s has registered a more steady growth. It is one of the objectives of this paper to analyze such gender-based differences.

In this paper, we analyze the effects of support measures on employment of elderly people in Japan by using two sets of data: the annual *Survey of Employment Conditions of Older Persons* (SECOP) (*Kōnenreisha shūgyō jittai chōsa*) published by the Ministry of Health,

*Table 7.1*    Percentage of people in workforce by age groups

|         | 1992 | 1996 | 2000 | 2004 |
|---------|------|------|------|------|
| Male    | 76.6 | 73.8 | 70.9 | 71.5 |
| 55–59   | 92.9 | 93.0 | 89.9 | 90.1 |
| 60–64   | 71.6 | 70.0 | 66.5 | 68.8 |
| 65–69   | 58.6 | 53.4 | 51.6 | 49.5 |
| Female  | 43.7 | 43.5 | 44.2 | 45.6 |
| 55–59   | 56.1 | 58.8 | 59.7 | 62.2 |
| 60–64   | 39.8 | 41.1 | 41.5 | 42.3 |
| 65–69   | 32.1 | 28.1 | 28.7 | 28.5 |

*Source*: Ministry of Health, Labour and Welfare, 'Survey of Employment Conditions of Older Persons.'

Labour and Welfare, and data on individual firms taken from *JTUC Reports on Working Conditions* (published by the Japan Trade Union Confederation: JTUC).[1]

## Facts about employment of elderly people

While the mandatory retirement system doubtlessly serves as the backbone framework for securing employment opportunities for elderly people in Japan, the labour force participation ratio drops sharply around the retirement age as shown in Table 7.1, indicating a lack of secure employment opportunities after retirement age.

Table 7.2 presents the ratios of employees in the age groups 60–64 and 65–69 to the total number of employees in the firms which set the retirement age at 60, taken from SECOP. It shows significant percentages of people employed after the retirement age. It also indicates that the number of firms employing people beyond the retirement age is growing. It is noteworthy that from 1992 to 1996, the percentage of male employees aged 60–69 rose from 6.78% to 13.2%, and that of female employees aged 60–69 rose from 3.73% to 6.63%, both significant increases. This trend continued throughout the period 1996 to 2000, with males increasing 6.78 percentage points and females increasing 7.25 percentage points.[2]

In what status at work are employees beyond the retirement age engaged then? The *Survey* (*SECOP*) in the year 2000 included a survey of status at work ((i) regular staff, (ii) non-regular staff of part-time/temporary

*Table 7.2* Percentage of elderly employees (unit: %)

|  | 1988 | 1992 | 1996 | 2000 |
|---|---|---|---|---|
| Male |  |  |  |  |
| 60–64 | 3.57 | 4.70 | 6.96 | 12.33 |
| 65–69 | 1.19 | 2.08 | 6.24 | 7.65 |
| 60–69 | 4.76 | 6.78 | 13.2 | 19.98 |
| Female |  |  |  |  |
| 60–64 | 2.26 | 2.53 | 3.33 | 9.49 |
| 65–69 | 0.82 | 1.20 | 3.30 | 4.39 |
| 60–69 | 3.08 | 3.73 | 6.63 | 13.88 |

*Note:* Figures: Restored values, Coverage: Firms with retirement age of 60.

*Source:* Ministry of Health, Labour and Welfare, 'Survey of Employment Conditions of Older Persons', various years.

workers, (iii) stay-at-home workers) for employees aged 60 and above. Among firms with a retirement age of 60, the ratios of different status at work were as follows: (i) 80.56%, (ii) 19.31%, and (iii) 0.11% for the 60–64 age group; (i) 66.29%, (ii) 33.51%, and (i) 0.19% for the 65–69. There was no data as to gender differences, nor was there any data for the period before 2000, which makes it impossible to see trends, if any. Nonetheless, this gives us an overall picture of the current situation.

For the 60–64 age group, the ratio of regular staff was high, which means that most people in this age group work under almost the same conditions as they did before retirement, whereas the ratio of non-regular workers was as low as less than 20%. For the 65–69, the ratio of regular staff dropped significantly, while the ratio of non-regular workers increased. The regular/non-regular ratio was four to one in the 60–64, whereas it was two to one in the 65–69. This indicates that more people were working as non-regular staff or on a part-time/temporary job at older ages. This means that the recent spread of part-time/temporary jobs has contributed significantly to increases in the employment of elderly people aged 65 and above.

Let us now examine the breakdown of employed elderly people by how they were employed, that is, extension of employment, re-employment, mid-career employment at the age 60 or above, external assignment, or other. This analysis covers firms which set the retirement age at 60.[3] The breakdown is as follows: 36% apply extension of employment, 32% re-employment, 27% mid-career employment, 0.3% external assignment, and 5% other measures. Extension of employment and re-employment accounted for about one third each. This means that close to 70% of employees aged 60 and above used to work for the same firm, in other words, many of the employed elderly people were actually working for their former employers after retirement.

## Effects of measures on promoting employment of elderly people

While a number of studies have reported the work style of elderly people, most have tended to analyze the behaviour of the supply side.[4] Other studies, though small in number, have focused on working patterns at the firm or establishment level (e.g. Mitani (2001), Higuchi and Yamamoto (2002) or on the wages of elderly employees, e.g. Ohashi (2000)).

This paper sheds light on how effective measures to promote employment of elderly people have been, by closely analyzing detailed company data. SECOP for 2000 reports that as many as 52% of all firms do not employ people aged 60 or above. This trend is conspicuous in large-scale firms, 65% of those with 5,000 or more employees, 64% of those with 1,000 to 4,999 employees, and 63% of those with 300 to 999 employees. A closer look at the breakdown by industry reveals that the percentage of firms not employing elderly people aged 60 or above was high (67%) in the wholesale/retail and restaurant industry; the percentage rose as high as 73% for companies with 5,000 or more employees in this industry.

### Effects of public support measures

Table 7.3 presents the percentage of firms that knew and adopted public support measures as reported in *SECOP* for certain years. The ratio of the number of firms that actually adopted public support measures to the number of those which knew them was extremely low, except for certain grants-in-aid. In fact, the public support measures that were widely adopted were limited in number: for example, incentives for introducing continued employment, incentives for employing many elderly people, and grants-in-aid for developing employment of specific job-applicants.

This section discusses how public support measures affect the percentage of employees aged 60 or above, by conducting a statistical estimation, using as the dependent variable the percentage of employees in the 60–69 age bracket among all employees in the firm. The independent variables are the firm attributes (dummies for industry, dummies for employment scale, dummies for type-of-office/factory,

*Table 7.3* Utilization of public support measures (percentage of companies)

| System | | 1992 | 1996 | 2000 |
|---|---|---|---|---|
| (S1) incentives for introducing | (a) | 49.9 | 63.2 | 63.8 |
| continued employment system | (b) | 4.7 | 8.2 | 14.6 |
| (S2) incentives for employing many | (a) | 57.3 | 63.7 | |
| elderly people | (b) | 10.6 | 16.0 | |
| (S3) grants-in-aid for developing | (a) | 56.2 | 65.3 | 61.9 |
| employment of specific | (b) | 33.5 | 29.5 | 26.9 |
| job-applicants | | | | |
| (S4) incentives for preparation for | (a) | 34.9 | | |
| transition to continued employment | (b) | 1.2 | | |
| system | | | | |
| (S5) loan of funds for improving | (a) | 39.0 | 51.3 | |
| workplace for elderly people | (b) | 1.1 | 2.1 | |
| (S6) incentives for preparation for | (a) | | 51.1 | |
| employment at high ages | (b) | | 2.8 | |
| (S7) incentives for general | (a) | | 51.9 | 53.8 |
| improvement of employment of | (b) | | 2.1 | 3.5 |
| elderly people | | | | |
| (S8) grants-in-aid for continued | (a) | | | 53.9 |
| employment of many people | (b) | | | 4.6 |
| (S9) grants-in-aid for vocational | (a) | | | 51.7 |
| adaptation to extension of | (b) | | | 2.4 |
| retirement | | | | |
| (S10) others | (a) | 32.3 | | |
| | (b) | 4.5 | | |

*Note:* (a) denotes 'know' and (b) denotes 'adopt'.

*Source:* Ministry of Health, Labour and Welfare 'Survey of Employment Conditions of Older Persons', various years.

female–male ratio, a dummy for the existence of a labour union, and dummies for area), a dummy for the existence of an early retirement system, and dummies for measures to support the employment of elderly people (a dummy for the existence of special measures concerning the employment of elderly people, and a dummy for public support measures regarding the employment of elderly people). In the estimation, two dummy variables, 'know' and 'adopt', are employed as the variables for public support measures.[5]

Table 7.4 summarizes the results of the estimation on the effectiveness of public support measures.[6] In the table, we show the values of

Table 7.4 Results of estimation by year

| | Elderly male ratio (a) | | Elderly male ratio (b) | | Elderly female ratio (a) | | Elderly female ratio (b) | |
|---|---|---|---|---|---|---|---|---|
| | Coefficient | p-value | Coefficient | p-value | Coefficient | p-value | Coefficient | p-value |
| 1992 | | | | | | | | |
| S1 | -0.03787 | 0.000 | 0.06157 | 0.000 | -0.04375 | 0.002 | 0.01434 | 0.620 |
| S2 | 0.02579 | 0.001 | 0.15453 | 0.000 | 0.09933 | 0.000 | 0.19720 | 0.000 |
| S3 | 0.02972 | 0.000 | 0.02189 | 0.005 | -0.01912 | 0.112 | 0.03095 | 0.017 |
| S4 | 0.04824 | 0.000 | 0.05794 | 0.266 | -0.02484 | 0.212 | 0.05756 | 0.459 |
| S5 | 0.01096 | 0.324 | -0.21881 | 0.000 | 0.04612 | 0.015 | -0.10087 | 0.158 |
| S10 | -0.06660 | 0.000 | -0.03619 | 0.237 | -0.08365 | 0.000 | -0.09396 | 0.181 |
| N | 5432 | | 5432 | | 5311 | | 5311 | |
| LR chi2(35) | 1225.38 | | 1389.75 | | 1169.95 | | 1232.72 | |
| Pseudo R2 | 0.1626 | | 0.1845 | | 0.1576 | | 0.1661 | |
| Log likelihood | -3154.5812 | | -3072.39680 | | -3126.83 | | -3095.4422 | |
| 1996 | | | | | | | | |
| S1 | -0.04817 | 0.000 | 0.03130 | 0.012 | -0.04420 | 0.002 | 0.00549 | 0.758 |
| S2 | 0.04499 | 0.000 | 0.06685 | 0.000 | 0.04059 | 0.004 | 0.07563 | 0.000 |
| S3 | 0.00013 | 0.987 | 0.04143 | 0.000 | -0.03544 | 0.004 | 0.00454 | 0.655 |

| | Coef. | p | Coef. | p | Coef. | p | Coef. | p |
|---|---|---|---|---|---|---|---|---|
| S5 | 0.02758 | 0.048 | -0.03852 | 0.326 | 0.01416 | 0.482 | -0.03755 | 0.568 |
| S6 | 0.01397 | 0.535 | -0.05411 | 0.449 | -0.00462 | 0.886 | -0.07405 | 0.730 |
| S7 | -0.02497 | 0.246 | -0.04626 | 0.507 | 0.01157 | 0.708 | -0.08717 | 0.686 |
| N | 2435 | | 2435 | | 2416 | | 2416 | |
| LR chi2(35) | 827.25 | | 941.04 | | 592.10 | | 624.40 | |
| Pseudo R2 | 0.4689 | | 0.5334 | | 0.2154 | | 0.2271 | |
| Log likelihood | -468.418 | | -411.52353 | | -1078.4 | | -1062.2478 | |
| 2000 | | | | | | | | |
| S1 | 0.05261 | 0.000 | 0.06793 | 0.000 | -0.00374 | 0.811 | 0.06666 | 0.000 |
| S3 | 0.03570 | 0.046 | 0.00086 | 0.971 | -0.00936 | 0.638 | 0.08997 | 0.000 |
| S7 | -0.04225 | 0.014 | 0.15056 | 0.000 | -0.04877 | 0.010 | -0.12258 | 0.024 |
| S8 | 0.00970 | 0.585 | -0.03563 | 0.342 | 0.06170 | 0.001 | -0.07067 | 0.137 |
| S9 | -0.00464 | 0.705 | 0.06335 | 0.000 | 0.06611 | 0.000 | 0.01868 | 0.085 |
| N | 1816 | | 1816 | | 1805 | | 1805 | |
| LR chi2(35) | 399.27 | | 503.96 | | 616.20 | | 641.97 | |
| Pseudo R2 | 0.2049 | | 0.2587 | | 0.2723 | | 0.2837 | |
| Log likelihood | -774.44791 | | -722.10500 | | -823.384 | | -810.49732 | |

*Note*: For the meaning of S1–S10, see Table 7.3.

*Source*: Own calculations based on data from Ministry of Health, Labour and Welfare, 'Survey of Employment Conditions of Older Persons', various years.

coefficients of the dummy variables for public measures. As shown in Table 7.3, the percentage of firms actually adopting public support measures among those which responded with 'know' was extremely low, except for a few grant-in-aid measures. Therefore, special care should be taken in interpreting the estimation result for 'adopt'. Considering the fact that a large percentage of firms did not employ elderly people at all, we estimated by using the Tobit model with the restitution factor as the weight. The table presents the results of the estimation with 'know' dummy in the columns (a), and with 'adopt' dummy in the columns (b).

Let us first take a look at the estimation results in the (a) columns. With regard to the effect on the employment of elderly males, the values of coefficients were in many cases significantly positive. However, the values of coefficients of dummy variable for measures which had a high percentage of 'know' but a low percentage of 'adopt', tended to be significantly negative. This indicates that, in the case of measures which many were aware of but found 'not easy to adopt', this awareness had little impact on the expansion of employment of elderly people.

On the other hand, only a few coefficients in the (b) columns revealed a negative sign with statistical significance, which means that the percentage of elderly people employed was high among firms that responded with 'adopt'.

A comparison of the male and female estimations reveals an intriguing fact. Whereas a relatively large number of estimation results proved positive with statistical significance for elderly males, a relatively large number of estimation results proved negative with statistical significance for elderly females. This seems to suggest a possible trend towards employing elderly males at the expense of elderly females, although it cannot be definitively concluded because of the low percentage of offices/factories responding with 'adopt'.

### Effects of private measures on expanding employment of elderly people

This section discusses the effectiveness of measures taken within firms for utilizing elderly people. Since 1992, SECOP has included the following question regarding private measures for maintaining or expanding the employment of elderly people: 'Are you currently taking any special measures to employ elderly people (aged 60 or above)?'.

Table 7.5 presents the 'special measures' accompanying the question (together with the years in which they appear). In the following, we

*Table 7.5*   Special measures taken to employ elderly people

| | Year of survey | | |
|---|---|---|---|
| Adjustment of workload | 1992 | 1996 | 2000 |
| Redesign/redevelopment of work | 1992 | 1996 | 2000 |
| Assignment to suitable job; adjustment of work assignment | 1992 | 1996 | 2000 |
| Shortening/flexibility of working hours | 1992 | 1996 | 2000 |
| Improvement in working methods/ equipment/facilities | 1992 | 1996 | 2000 |
| Revision of rules on wages or retirement bonus | 1992 | 1996 | |
| Introduction of certification or specialist position | 1992 | 1996 | |
| Consideration of labour safety and health care/ management | 1992 | 1996 | 2000 |
| Training and education | 1992 | 1996 | 2000 |
| Introduction of stay-at-home work or satellite office | | | 2000 |
| Enhancement of welfare provisions such as housing and holiday accommodation | 1992 | | |
| In-sourcing of outsourced work | 1992 | | |
| Raising retirement age; re-employment; extension of employment | 1992 | 1996 | |
| Other | | 1996 | 2000 |

*Source*: Ministry of Health, Labour and Welfare, 'Survey of Employment Conditions of Older Persons', various years.

estimate the effect of private measures on employment of the elderly by introducing a dummy variable for each of these items in the question (the value is 1 if adopting this measure, otherwise the value is 0 and by using the same explaining variables as in the previous section. A positive value of coefficient for the effectiveness of each dummy variable indicates that the corresponding measure contributed somewhat to the employment of elderly people. Otherwise, it indicates that the corresponding measure was not effective enough to meet the intended objective, suggesting the need to reassess the support for employment of elderly people.

Table 7.6 summarizes the results of the estimation on the effectiveness of private support measures. The figures in the table denote the values of coefficients of dummy variables for measures, with statistical significance. First let us examine the effects of individual measures. 'Adjustment of workload' was not significant in any year, for either males or females.

*Table 7.6*   Effects of private measures on utilizing elderly people within businesses

| | Gender | 1992 | 1996 | 2000 |
|---|---|---|---|---|
| Adjustment of workload (92, 96, 00) | M | | | |
| | F | | | |
| Redesign/redevelopment of work (92, 96, 00) | M | | | |
| | F | | −0.0841 | |
| Assignment to suitable job; adjustment of work assignment (92, 96, 00) | M | 0.0183 | 0.0179 | |
| | F | | −0.0414 | 0.0677 |
| Shortening/flexibility of working hours (92, 96, 00) | M | | 0.0255 | 0.0304 |
| | F | 0.0529 | | 0.0588 |
| Improvement in working methods/ equipment/ facilities (92, 96, 00) | M | | | 0.0892 |
| | F | 0.0429 | | |
| Revision of rules on wages or retirement bonus (92, 96) | M | | | |
| | F | 0.0362 | −0.0583 | |
| Introduction of certification or specialist position (92, 96) | M | | −0.0492 | |
| | F | | −0.0627 | |
| Consideration of labour safety and health care/management (92, 96, 00) | M | 0.0538 | 0.0470 | |
| | F | | 0.1060 | |
| Training and education (92, 96, 00) | M | | | 0.0501 |
| | F | | 0.0651 | |
| Introduction of stay-at-home work or satellite office (00) | M | | | |
| | F | | | −0.2357 |
| Enhancement of welfare provisions such as housing and holiday accommodation (92) | M | 0.0291 | | |
| | F | | | |
| In-sourcing of outsourced work (92) | M | −0.0392 | | |
| | F | | | |
| Raising retirement age; re-employment; extension of employment (92, 96) | M | 0.0166 | 0.0482 | |
| | F | | | |
| Taking no special measures (92, 96, 00) | M | −0.0113 | −0.0291 | 0.0086 |
| | F | −0.0137 | −0.0559 | −0.0663 |

*Note*: Only the results with a significance level of 5% or more are shown here. Numbers in () denote years of survey.

*Source*: Own calculations based on data from Ministry of Health, Labour and Welfare, 'Survey of Employment Conditions of Older Persons', various years.

Unlike other measures, this measure does not require any particular cost and should be regarded simply as special consideration given in everyday workload assignments. Thus, taking this measure does not in itself mean that special consideration is given to the utilization of elderly people. On the other hand, 'introduction of certification or specialist position' (1996) had a negative impact on both males and females. This suggests that, while it may have some positive impact on certain types of job, it effectively closes the door against elderly people in general.

'Shortening/flexibility of working hours' showed a positive impact on both males and females in many of the sampled years, suggesting that this measure is consistently effective in securing employment for elderly people. Also, 'consideration of labour safety and health care/management' has an overall positive impact. 'Raising retirement age, re-employment, and extension of employment' has a positive impact on elderly males, whereas it does not have a statistically significant impact on elderly females.

Next let us now examine gender differences. The first thing to be noted is that many of the results turned out to be significantly negative, although these dummy variables pertained to special measures for employment of elderly people. Of these, except for a few measures ('introduction of certification or specialist position' and 'in-sourcing of outsourced work'), many turned out to show two kinds of pattern, positive for males but negative for females and not significant for males but negative for females. The former pattern applies to 'assignment to suitable job; adjustment of work assignment'. If this implies that suitable jobs are given to elderly men at the expense of women (including, of course, elderly women), then it certainly has a positive impact on elderly males but a negative impact on elderly females.[7]

The latter applies to 'redesign/development of work' (1996), 'revision of rules on wage or retirement bonus' (1996), and 'introduction of stay-at-home work or satellite office' (2000). These all involve the revision of an existing framework or the introduction of a new system and mainly target elderly males. It implies that elderly females are disadvantaged.

As has been observed, while most of the measures taken within firms for supporting employment of elderly people have a positive impact on elderly people overall, some seem to have a negative impact on the employment of elderly female workers.[8]

## Reasons for introducing measures for supporting the employment of elderly people

Table 7.6 suggests that measures taken within firms for supporting the employment of elderly people are generally very effective. The next question is which measures are widely adopted by what kinds of firm. While it is difficult to obtain statistical data that would allow us to accurately assess such effects, federations of labour unions such as the Japanese Trade Union Confederation (JTUC) conduct a survey every year on the existence of such special measures.[9] This section analyzes in as much detail as possible what kinds of businesses instituted 're-employment or extension of retirement age' that proved to have a clear impact as shown in Table 7.6.[10]

The JTUC surveys reveal that the percentage of businesses having 're-employment or extension of retirement age' in place has been increasing at a fast pace, from 45% in 1993 to 78% in 2002. Let us examine what factors contributed to the introduction of this system. The author has endorsed JTUC's data by matching it against the financial statements of the respective firms. This employer-employee matched panel data is mainly made by Akahane and Nakamura (2008). The details are explained in their Appendix.

By matching the two sets of data, we can now employ the following as independent variables for the period from 1993 to 2002:

- A: each firm's average employee age[11] (average age of employees from the financial data),
- m1q16: the average age of male labour union members from the JTUC data,
- CR_W_L1: the rate of average wage increase for the preceding year (from the JTUC data),
- WP20_h_40: the seniority contribution to the wage (ratio of high-school graduates' wages at 40 years of age to that at 20 years of age from the JTUC Data),
- N_Profit: the ordinary profit per capita in the preceding year (from the financial data),
- F_by_M: the female-to-male employment ratio (ratio of female labour union members to male labour union members from the JTUC data),
- CR_L_S3: the rate of change in number of employees during the preceding three-year period (from the financial data), and
- firm employment scale dummies (scale-dummy1: 1,000 to 4,999, scale-dummy2: 5,000 to 9,999, scale-dummy3: 10,000 or more).[12]

The variable A was introduced as an indicator of the ageing of the company; CR_W_L1, N_Profit, CR_L_S3 and were introduced as indicators of the growth potential of the firm.

We conducted an analysis to find answers to the following three questions:

a. Are firms with an increasing population of ageing employees all the more actively taking appropriate measures?
b. Does the seniority effect on wages have any influence on the introduction of the measures?
c. Does the female-to-male ratio have any influence on the introduction of the measures?

If we assume that the greater the percentage of older employees, the greater the number of employees close to the retirement age and hence the greater the need for taking measures for expanding employment opportunities after retirement, the sign of the variables of age are positive. However, if we assume that the greater the number of such employees, the greater the cost of utilizing elderly people, the signs of variables of age are negative because firms facing greater cost of utilizing elderly people would want to avoid it by not taking measures to employ them. If we are to assume that the seniority contribution is proportional to the amount of skills investment in workers, a high seniority contribution means that the firm has a relatively large number of elderly employees with higher productivity and hence is more likely to utilize such people beyond the retirement age. We examine the effect of the female-to-male ratio to check whether the trend of favouring elderly males in expanding employment as we have suggested in the preceding sections also exists with the introduction of the 're-employment and/or extension of employment' system.

Table 7.7 is a summary of the results of the estimation based on the logit model using pooled data, with '1' assigned to 'already introduced the system' and '0' to 'have not introduced the system yet'.[13] The coefficients for N_Profit and CR_W_L1 turned out to be negative, indicating that in general, lower-growth firms were more likely to introduce such a system. This is probably because they preferred to utilize elderly people at lower wages. However, the value of coefficient for CR_L_S3 was significantly positive, indicating that companies which were reducing their employees were less likely to introduce a 're-employment and/or extension of employment' system.

Table 7.7  Results of estimation

| | (1) | (2) | (3) | (4) | (5) | (6) |
|---|---|---|---|---|---|---|
| N_Profit | -0.0258 | -0.0190 | -0.0179 | -0.0260 | -0.0310 | -0.0206 |
| | [3.96]*** | [3.40]*** | [3.26]*** | [3.73]*** | [3.62]*** | [2.84]*** |
| CR_W_L1 | -0.1262 | -0.1133 | -0.0869 | 0.0076 | -0.0350 | -0.0499 |
| | [3.52]*** | [3.38]*** | [2.66]*** | [0.15] | [0.60] | [0.95] |
| CR_L_S3 | 0.4794 | 0.4637 | 0.5954 | 0.8831 | 0.7502 | 0.6955 |
| | [2.91]*** | [3.03]*** | [3.89]*** | [4.00]*** | [3.06]*** | [3.05]*** |
| m1q16 | -0.0148 | | | | -0.0355 | |
| | [2.73]*** | | | | [4.25]*** | |
| A | | -0.0309 | | | | -0.0498 |
| | | [5.05]*** | | | | [5.64]*** |
| F_by_M | | | -0.1410 | | -0.8365 | -0.8956 |
| | | | [2.42]** | | [4.49]*** | [4.98]*** |
| WP20_h_40 | | | | 0.0485 | 0.1251 | 0.1956 |
| | | | | [0.48] | [1.09] | [1.79]* |
| Scale dummy1 | 0.2009 | 0.1733 | 0.1728 | 0.1211 | 0.1381 | 0.1382 |
| | [3.94]*** | [3.47]*** | [3.50]*** | [2.05]** | [2.24]** | [2.28]** |

| | | | | | | |
|---|---|---|---|---|---|---|
| Scale dummy2 | 0.3113 | 0.2812 | 0.2887 | 0.2799 | 0.3266 | 0.3124 |
| | [6.10]*** | [5.48]*** | [5.67]*** | [4.97]*** | [5.96]*** | [5.57]*** |
| Scale dummy3 | 0.3232 | 0.2801 | 0.2575 | 0.2918 | 0.2970 | 0.2468 |
| | [6.50]*** | [5.53]*** | [4.95]*** | [5.38]*** | [5.22]*** | [4.04]*** |
| Industry dummy | yes | yes | yes | yes | yes | yes |
| Year dummy | yes | yes | yes | yes | yes | yes |
| Observations | 1260 | 1405 | 1374 | 891 | 802 | 879 |
| Log likelihood | −785.63 | −875.226 | −864.04 | −529.098 | −448.313 | −498.419 |

Absolute value of z statistics in brackets

* significant at 10%; ** significant at 5%; *** significant at 1%

*Source:* Own calculations based on data from Japan Trade Union Confederation, 'JTUC Reports on Working Conditions', matched with financial statements of the respective firms, various years.

As for 'Question a' above, the value of the coefficient for the average age of employees was significantly negative, meaning that the higher the average age, the more reluctant the firms were to introduce the system. As for 'Question b', the value of the coefficient for WP20_h_40 was positive, although with low statistical significance, indicating that firms with a seniority-based wage system were more willing, by introducing the system, to utilize elderly people equipped with useful skills. As for 'Question c', the value of coefficient for F_by_M was significantly negative, endorsing the argument in the previous sections that the higher the percentage of female employees, the less willing the firms were to introduce a 're-employment and/or extension of employment' system.

## Conclusion

This paper has discussed the efficacy of measures for supporting the employment of elderly people after the retirement age, using detailed data on individual firms. While a number of public support measures were available, they were not widely known. Even the awareness of those public measures which were relatively well utilized was as low as about 60%. Furthermore, the utilization rates were generally not very high. According to the 2004 *Survey of Employment Conditions of Older Persons*, the biggest reason why firms did not utilize public support measures was 'do not qualify', while as many as about 30% quoted 'other reasons'. These facts point to the need for increasing the awareness and improving the procedures for utilizing such measures.

As for the private measures taken within firms, their efficacy tended to favour males. It is also suggested that firms with higher populations of older employees tended to be less willing to introduce measures for utilizing elderly people. Considering the fact that most elderly people in the work force were in fact employed by the firms they had worked for until retirement, it will become increasingly necessary not only to promote the utilization of elderly people in many firms, but also to promote a more positive stance towards the utilization of elderly people among those with an already high proportion of elderly employees.

## Appendix (supplementary note)

We would like to briefly summarize the results of the estimation using SECOP not covered in the main text of this paper. First let us take a look at the results of the estimation of dummy variables for employment scale, which are attributes of the firms. As for employment scale, we introduced two variables, for scale of firm and scale of establishment, considering the fact that re-employment and extension of employment are matters for individual establishments. We look at the situation of elderly males first. The values of coefficients for employment scale of establishment turned out to be always negative, although without statistical significance (except for 2000), meaning that the greater the establishment size, the lower the percentage of elderly people (males) employed. As for the values of coefficients for firm employment scale dummies (for each year, the reference is based on an employee headcount of 100 to 999) in 1992, the greater the firm size, the greater the (negative) coefficient in absolute value.

This means that, again, the greater the firm size, the lower the percentage of elderly people employed. It should be noted, however, that since 1996, the value of coefficient for large firms has become smaller in terms of absolute value and that in 2000, none of the coefficients corresponding to firm employment scales of 1,000 or above were statistically significant. This indicates that although at the establishment level, the greater the size, the lower the percentage of elderly people employed, this correlation tended to become weaker at the firm level. This trend can be interpreted as a sign that large firms have been stepping up their efforts to secure employment for elderly people.

A look at the results for elderly females reveals that, unlike the results for elderly males, the value of coefficient for establishment employment scale turned out to be significantly negative for all the years of the survey, indicating that the percentage of elderly females employed still varied considerably according to the scale of the establishment. The value of coefficient for firm employment scale showed trends similar to those for elderly males.

Next, we examine how the female-to-male ratio among employees before the retirement age affects the percentage of elderly people employed. The coefficient for elderly males was either not significant or positive with statistical significance in 1996, whereas that for elderly females it was significantly positive in all the years. This finding is very intriguing. In establishments where the percentage of female employees was high before retirement, it remained high after retirement (ages 60 and above). This is consistent with the observation that in the establishments suitable for females the percentage of elderly female employees is relatively high. The result, however, suggests that the percentage of elderly male employees also tended to be high in the establishments suitable for females. This can be explained without loss of consistency if we are to assume one or both of the following:

1. There are some substitute relations between elderly males and pre-retirement female employees, that is, most of the jobs that are done by pre-retirement female employees can be done by elderly males, and as a result, pre-retirement female employees may be replaced by elderly males.
2. The establishments with high percentages of female employees tend to have relatively low productivity. As a result, they find it difficult to get new recruits and make up for this by employing elderly people, in which case not only elderly males but also elderly females constitute a high percentage of headcount.

We cannot determine from the present analysis which of the above assumptions is more realistic. In studying the issue of securing employment for elderly people, however, it is important to shed light on what causes gender differences in their employment.

## Notes

This study was conducted in conjunction with the Infrastructure Study (B) 'Efficient Distribution of Labour and Human Resource Development', which is part of the Grant-in-Aid for Scientific Research of the Ministry of Education, Culture, Sports, Science and Technology.

1. Because of space constraints, this paper attempts primarily to put the facts into perspective. The present study limits its scope to businesses which apply a mandatory retirement system. The figures in the tables in this paper are taken, with some modifications where applicable and appropriate, from those presented by Nakamura (2004) based on the detailed data published in SECOP.
2. The number of businesses setting the retirement age at 60 has been increasing year by year. This fact also contributes to the increases in the percentage of employees aged 60–64.
3. Surveys for other years cover only extension of employment and re-employment. In addition, it is impossible to make an accurate judgement because, in some businesses, the total number of employees aged 60 and above minus the number of employees in the same age bracket employed through extension of employment and re-employment becomes negative.
4. For example, Ohga and Nakamura (2001) analyze the effect of public employment promotion measures on the supply of labour using detailed data on individuals.
5. Note that employing 'adopt' as a dummy variable might cause a simultaneous bias.

6. Because of space limitation, the results of the total estimation are omitted from this report. For details, refer to Nakamura (2004). For a summary discussion, see Appendix.
7. See Appendix.
8. Note that since these observations vary from year to year, the conclusions, if any, should be considered tentative.
9. This data is based on the results of JTUC's annual survey of its member unions on 'labour union member attributes, pay raises, wages by age, retirement bonuses, measures for supporting employment of elderly people, etc.'.
10. As mentioned in Section 2, nearly 70% of elderly people employed after retirement age were people who had been re-employed or whose employment terms had been extended.
11. Here, two variables are employed as data for average age, in consideration of a possible interdependency (correlation) between the average age of all employees and the female–male ratio of employees.
12. In the actual estimation, an industry dummy (category of industry) and a year dummy were added.
13. The numbers in the table are the values at which the marginal effects.

## References

Akahane, R. and J. Nakamura (2008) 'Kigyō betsu paneru dêta ni yoru chingin–kinzoku profîru no jisshō bunseki' (An Empirical Analysis of the Wage–Tenure Profile Using Firm-Level Panel Data in Japan), forthcoming in *Nihon rodō kenkyū zasshi (The Japanese Journal of Labour Studies)*, November, 2008.
Higuchi, Y. and I. Yamamoto (2002) 'Waga kuni no kōreisha koyō no genjō to tenbō' (Current Situation and Outlook of Employment of Elderly Persons in Japan), *Kinyū Kenkyū (Financial Studies)*, 21 (addition No. 2), Institute for Monetary and Economic Studies, Bank of Japan, pp. 1–30.
Mitani, N. (2001) 'Kōreisha koyō seisaku to rōdō juyō' (Policy on the employment of older workers and labor demand), in T. Inoki and F. Ohtake (eds), *Koyō seisaku no keizai bunseki (An Economic Analysis of Employment Policies in Japan)*, Tokyo: University of Tokyo Press, pp. 339–388.
Nakamura, J. (2004) 'Kōreisha koyō no genjō' (Current Situation of Employment of Elderly Persons), *Keizai kōzō no henka to rōdō shijō ni kan suru chōsa kenkyū hōkokusho (Research Report on Economic Structural Changes and Labour Markets)*, *Koyō Nōryoku Kaihatsu Kikō – Tōkei Kenkyūkai* (The Institute of Statistical Research, Employment and Human Resources Development Organization of Japan).
Ohashi, I. (2000) 'Teinengo no chingin to koyō' (Wages and Employment after Mandatory Retirement), *Keizai kenkyū (The Economic Review)*, 51 (1), pp. 1–14.
Ohga, T. and J. Nakamura (2001) 'Kōteki n nenkin kaisei oyobi koyō sokushin-saku ga kōreisha no shugyō kōdō ni ataeru eikyō' (Effects of the Public Pension Measures revision and the Public Measures for Promoting Employment on the Employment Behaviour of Elderly Persons), *Keizai to keizaigaku (Journal of the Faculty of Economics, Tokyo Metropolitan University)*, (94), pp. 27–38.

# 8
# Ergonomic Design and Intervention Strategies in Health Promotion for Ageing Workforces

*Holger Luczak and Marie-Christine Stemann*

Over the next few years, both the labour market and workplaces will change quite significantly as the average age of the workforce continues to rise. Workers over 45 will play a larger role in the workplace; and current personnel policies, centred on the employment of younger workers and the early retirement of older workers, are likely to lead to massive human resource management problems. In the future, labour force participation and employment opportunities for older workers need to gain in importance if companies are to prevent labour shortages.

At present, output, activity, and youthfulness determine the image of an employee. It is often assumed that older workers are less effective mentally and physically, and that they show lower labour productivity. For this reason, many companies have internal age limits. However, scientific research supports the claim that an increase in age does not necessarily mean a decrease in potential (see e.g. Bellmann, Kistler and Wahse 2003). Abilities change in various ways throughout one's life, and a natural loss of some abilities with an increase in age runs parallel with the acquisition of other abilities. Activities that are more suited to older people are less physically and psychologically demanding, yet promote age-distinct abilities such as experience, mentoring, communication and conflict resolution competences. Research shows that older people are often capable of fulfilling their previous job requirements to a high degree if adaptations are made to meet their needs.

In particular, ergonomics has great potential when it comes to making adaptations to job requirements according to the individual needs of older workers. Ergonomic strategies can compensate for a decrease in abilities, promote the competences of older workers, and help to establish health-promoting and salutogenic measures. This article gives an overview of various ergonomic strategies and discusses some of their implications.

## Micro-ergonomic strategies

### Compensation strategy

Compensation is a mechanism that can help to bypass changes resulting from age. The technical, organizational and personal deficits of workers are compensated for by adaptations in the workplace. Table 8.1 shows some examples of how workplaces can be adapted according to age-related physiological and psychological changes. Such adaptations should have priority over transfers to other workplaces which have easier work requirements.

*Table 8.1* Adaptations of workplace and work environment according to age-related physiological and psychological changes

| Age-related physiological and psychological changes | Adaptation of workplace and work environment |
|---|---|
| Restricted movement of joints, decreased elasticity of tendons and ligaments | Positioning of objects, control units, screens to minimize extended bending, leaning forward and stooping |
| Reduction in strength | Concrete briefing of employees on 'Lifting and Carrying' |
| Decreased physical functional capacity | Activities requiring increased energy input should not exceed 0.7 (men) or 0.5 (women) l/min oxygen consumption |
| Decreased perception; attention deficit | Longer training phases, increase of signal-noise relation at workplace |
| Weak sight, visual acuity | 50% more illumination for employees between 40 and 55 years of age 100% more illumination for employees over 55 years of age Contrast increase in display units and measuring instruments |

*Source*: Luczak 1998.

## Selection strategy

The selection strategy encompasses a useful pre-selection of load types/levels/durations depending on age. Excessive load levels requiring the maximum consumption of psychological and physical resources should be avoided. Part of this strategy is specialization as part of a value chain depending on tolerable load types. Flexible work time arrangements as well as sufficient job changes are important factors in this strategy.

## Adaptation strategy

Companies must make an extra effort so that age barriers are minimized or even completely eliminated. They must offer suitable measures for further education (e.g. in the domain of information and communication technology) and develop concepts for the promotion and activation of occupational competences for the duration of an employee's working life. In order to achieve this, companies should compile operational qualification plans for their employees. In these plans, special significance is placed on the use of know-how and social competencies, such as management ability and conflict resolution competence. Consequently, the design of work tasks for older people takes on a special role. Older workers can master some tasks better than others, so special attention should be paid to making task requirements correspond to age and ability. It is important to avoid unfamiliar, highly demanding tasks that require high motor and coordination skills, and work which makes extreme demands on vision, as well as insufficient lighting in general. Fields of activity which have an autonomous completion of tasks are preferable, as is the arrangement of work rhythms and work flows that can be set by the individual concerned, as well as complex work flows in which experience plays an important role.

## Prevention strategy

The prevention strategy entails the creation of complex safety and health concepts which are enforced through design. Primary measures, including the creation of a safe working environment, secondary measures, aiming at behavioural changes, and organizational measures are thus indispensable in reducing the dangers facing older workers. All actors such as employers, employees, work committees, work doctors, and specialists must be incorporated in such processes from an early stage. Best practices should be developed that not only comprise the consideration of prevention, but also of health promotion.

### Salutogenesis strategy

The ergonomic catalogue of goals must be centred on health and ethical responsibility. Consequences for occupational health and safety (OHS)/health promotion management should be described in detail and in accordance with morphological foundations of design. The actors in OHS must actively bring their concerns into the operational reconfiguration so that OHS becomes an integral component of operational business processes. In addition, different integration paths are possible in operational sequences. On the one hand, OHS can be anchored as a special business function. On the other hand, it is possible to solve OHS problems through special programmes and projects. The TQM philosophy that arose in the 1990s offers another possibility for holistically and continuously integrating OHS into a business.

## Macro-ergonomic strategies

### Sensitization

An important initial step in order to be able to develop goal-oriented action strategies early on is in the sensitization of companies to expected demographic changes. A short-term measure is an age structure analysis that contributes to the early recognition of problems relating to the age structure of a company. However, it is not sufficient to just calculate the proportion of the individual age groups and then carry them into the future. Instead, there is a need for future projections based on age structure analyses which relate age distribution to individual function groups, departments, and qualification levels. GfAH (Association for Occupational Safety and Humanisation Research Ltd.) has developed a means of achieving this approach so that companies can time travel in order to determine with which staff size, personnel structure, and personnel problems it will be faced within 10 years, assuming the current strategies remain unchanged. An age-structure analysis thus delivers reference points for personal reflection about future personnel, particularly at-risk employee groups.

The so-called Quick-Check represents another short-term measure, as shown by the questionnaire in Table 8.2.

If the answers of individual companies are primarily in the 'Not applicable' column, then it is highly questionable whether their current

*Table 8.2*   Quick-check for companies

| Question | Applicable | Not applicable |
| --- | --- | --- |
| The age structure is equally comprised of young, medium and older employees | | |
| Work tasks are designed so that employees up to the age of 65 can execute them | | |
| Employees are actively involved in the design of their job requirements | | |
| The business succeeds in meeting the demands for the training and recruiting of young skilled labourers without any problems | | |
| All employees – including older ones – receive the chance to qualify themselves and to expand their competences | | |
| Knowledge exchange between older, more experienced employees and newer workers is strategically promoted | | |
| All employees in the business are offered a professional development perspective | | |

*Source:* BAUA 2004: 27.

personnel policies are future-oriented, suggesting that they will have to focus more on the topic of demographic change (BAUA 2004: 26).

A typical mid-term measure is the 'age awareness workshop'. The goal of such workshops is not only to inform operational actors – depending on company size, either all employees in a small company, or selected employees and departments in a medium-size to large company – about demographic change, but also to give them the opportunity to exchange their ideas, opinions and compare interests. In doing so, they can initiate common reflection on the future business situation. The effects of demographic change on the working world should be pointed out in these workshops, and the individual operational age structure should be more closely examined. This usually delivers important insights for the creation of various future scenarios (Richenhagen 2004: 65). Furthermore, imparting worthwhile knowledge about the learning and achievement potential of older workers is beneficial, as is joint reflection on the process of 'ageing'. In particular, the awareness of managerial personnel regarding the actual potential of their older employees can thereby be increased.

Re-orientation presents itself as a choice for action in the sense of a conclusive total long-term strategy. For many companies this could mean turning away from a youth-centred culture, as they become aware that they must deal with a large number of increasingly older employees in the future. In concrete terms, such a strategy requires the following (BS/BDA 2003: 130):

- Reduction of obstacles in the way of employing older workers.
- Reconsideration of the previous qualification policies (securing the innovative abilities of older employees as well).
- Termination of both human capital wasting and indifference towards the job prospects of older workers.

### Know-how transfer

Companies have valuable, specific knowledge in the form of information about customers, processes, strategies, successes and problems. A substantial part of this knowledge is created within the companies themselves. The carriers of such knowledge are mostly individual employees (BS/BDA 2003: 106). While younger workers bring new knowledge into the business, older workers possess many years of acquired know-how. Currently, only a small number of businesses retain, adapt and secure this knowledge systematically. The systematic structuring of an organized, generation-specific knowledge transfer is, however, an important part of demography-sensitive personnel policies. To achieve this, cooperation between younger and older employees needs to be consciously promoted. In this context, some of the following strategies have proven to be effective:

'Tandems' present a particularly intense form of collegial teamwork. For example, they can be formed between experienced workers and entrants to initiate a continuous exchange of practical knowledge and know-how. Moreover, tandems are suited to the allocation of tasks among workers according to their individual strengths. Tandem creation is especially useful when older workers leave companies through partial retirement schemes, thereby enabling them to transfer knowledge to their successors. In addition to a careful selection of older workers for tandems, workers need to be carefully instructed (BS/BDA 2003: 113, 118). Employees already in retirement can still use their expertise to train workers for specific tasks. Additionally, a project-based collaboration is possible during retirement, that is, companies can reach out to former employees when customers demand extensive or specific know-how (BS/BDA 2003: 166). Older workers can also take on special roles as mentors, supervisors and coaches (BS/BDA 2003: 118). By providing support for a trainee programme or an orientation programme for career entrants, they can pass their experience on to their successors.

During the configuration of teams, or the execution of teamwork, special care should be taken to ensure that both younger and older workers are included. Older workers are able to introduce vital ideas and correctively intervene when mistakes occur, while younger workers bring with them specific skills, normally leading to cooperative teamwork in mixed-age groups (BS/BDA 2003: 112).

In order to facilitate know-how transfer, short and direct information paths and flat hierarchies are important preconditions (Pfohl 1997: 20). It should be emphasized that not every older worker is suitable for knowledge transfer to younger colleagues. Companies should thus identify suitable older workers early in order to avoid problems later. Older employees should see themselves not only as having the role of a teacher, but also the role of a student. The same is true for younger employees (Köchling 2002: 140), who should also view themselves as teachers. Only in this way will a mutual exchange be possible. Furthermore, selected workers need to demonstrate communication abilities and a willingness to participate in know-how transfer. In this context, incentives for the promotion of intrinsic and extrinsic motivation are important so that issues of prestige and threats to personal positions in the company are sufficiently addressed.

## Career development

Companies must clearly identify the need for qualifications and make professional development issues part of employee discussions when engaging in development planning. A short-term measure is a qualification needs analysis, that is, the qualification level of the employee is determined and then compared to expected job requirements (BS/BDA 2003: 160). The demand can quickly be determined through a simple questioning of employees. Self-evaluation is a further short-term measure that can be used. During a workshop, employees can estimate and weigh their own competences and how they would like to develop these in their future careers. This is supported by an intensive reflection process and an exchange of experiences with colleagues during the workshop (BS/BDA 2003: 79).

The so-called Compass Concept represents a popular model for self-evaluation. It was developed by Heusgen, the business-consultancy, and is now used in several companies, for example, Siemens, as an in-house development module application. As a result, employees learn to differentiate between self and public perception and to identify personal strengths and career values, as well as reach agreements with managerial staff and personnel management on concrete steps for career development (BS/BDA 2003: 81).

From a mid-term perspective, following the identification of qualification needs and the personal location decision of the employee, a personal development plan can be constructed. This plan should contain concrete individual development steps agreed on by the employees involved. Such a plan can contain diverse advanced training measures, but can also involve the assignment of new tasks (BS/BDA 2003: 163).

From a long-term perspective, companies should aim for life-phase oriented career planning. Companies should point out personal development and advancement opportunities within the company to their employees. This promotes employees' long-term commitment to the company, while allowing them to develop a long-term career perspective. Operational structure changes and perspectives should be analyzed in terms of scenario workshops in order to derive steps for the implementation of the personnel development approach. Researchers and scientists can provide important clues for future requirements, such as the identification of needs for future qualifications that are linked to the long-term career planning of workers (Heyer and Henkel 1995: 120).

## Professional development and life-long learning

A short-term procedure recommendation is based on taking the abilities of older workers into consideration during the assignment of tasks. Older workers tend to complete familiar, practised, and independent tasks better than younger workers. Workload, work rhythm and workflow should to a certain extent be self-determined (Pack et al. 2000: 16).

The introduction of teamwork and job rotation promotes versatility and limits one-sided work loads, which is especially beneficial to older workers; it also facilitates permanent professional and social qualifications and has positive motivational effects. Because of such effects, companies should consider more carefully which branches/ departments are suitable for job rotation and teamwork. Just as companies must choose the employees involved and the workplaces, they must also decide on the time period for job rotations. Moreover, discussions with employees should sensitize them to the targeted measures, since the success of implementation depends on the willingness, participation and support of the workers themselves (Heyer and Henkel 1995: 71).

In the long-term, companies need to ensure that the qualifications of their younger and older employees complement each other. The unique characteristics and abilities of each group should be incorporated into the solving of problems or into tasks. A bias and stereotype-free attitude towards the qualifications of different employee groups facilitates such collaboration: *Older employees + younger employees = Team = Success for business* (BS/BDA 2003: 25).

## Occupational health promotion

Companies in the production sector in particular must focus on health-promotion and age-based personnel employment in order to foster the abilities of ageing workers. Systematic occupational health promotion can – this is especially economically relevant for small to medium-sized businesses – be carried out in cooperation with institutions external to the core business (Heyer and Henkel 1995: 86). The first step entails a comprehensive stock check involving the workplace as well as the character of the employee in question. A short-term procedure recommendation consequently comprises identifying age-based workplaces 'that are particularly characterized by heavy physical demands, high environmental exposure, shift work and/or night shifts, or special psycho-mental or psycho-social requirements' (BS/BDA 2003: 95). It is imperative that companies systematically discover, evaluate and document stresses in the workplace. Companies can, for example in the context of a business inspection, have workplaces and tasks checked against the criteria mentioned, and discuss whether employees can complete their tasks successfully and without adverse health effects until the end of their employment. Such insights should be incorporated into the employee's career plan. In addition, companies should consider the extent to which employees should be offered less demanding workplaces or adequate niche workplaces (Köchling 2002: 178). Based on notices of illness and/or employee surveys, businesses can systematically gather, demonstrate, and document in a health report their employees' health problems as well as possible health risks (BS/BDA 2003: 164). A health report generates a good foundation for initiating individual health promotion.

The Work-Ability-Index (WAI) can be implemented in this context as well. Work ability can be measured as a function of age and job demands with the help of a standardized questionnaire. The questionnaire supports the compilation of current employee potential that can be collected not only through a general as-is analysis or operational diagnosis, but also through individual consultation. This procedure 'basically holds true for small and medium-sized businesses; although the latter is limited through some very restricted operating times of the work doctors and safety experts' (Ilmarinen and Tempel 2002: 94). In addition, businesses can offer their employees, after a certain age, special health-checks and then accommodate their results in cooperation with various health insurance agencies or doctors (BS/BDA 2003: 164).

This stock check, which becomes possible through short-term procedure recommendations, supports the planning and execution of comprehensive health-promotion. Work (place) design enables companies to counteract health impairments and the resulting decreases in work and efficiency. Therefore, special attention must be paid to an ergonomic workplace design. The workplaces of ageing workers should be equipped with increased lighting in order to counterbalance the limitations of their vision. The use of specialized lifting and holding aids, for example, a conveyor, helps in fighting the inevitable reduction of strength and stamina in the handling of heavy loads. Additional ergonomic possibilities exist in an age-related design of tools, work equipment, objects and operating devices, such as telephones with larger keys, computer settings for increasing display size, monofocal monitor glasses, etc. The principles of 'job enlargement', 'job enrichment', and 'job rotation' should be considered in order to avoid specialization traps and to increase room for manoeuvre. Moreover, the quantitative performance target can be reduced for employees that are already health-impaired (BS/BDA 2003: 163; Köchling 2002: 165; Luczak and Stemann 2002: 68). Night shifts and shift work in particular increase the risks of health impairment. Disturbed circadian rhythms and interferences in the temporal social structure can cause disruptions in wake and sleep rhythms as well as increased susceptibility to stress; in some cases, even long-term metabolic illnesses (Ilmarinen and Tempel 2002: 258, 265). Companies that use night shifts and shift work should offer their older employees the chance to change to regular shifts. Furthermore, shift rhythms and shift sequences should be regulated in a health-preserving manner, that is, companies should keep the number of planned sequential early, late, and night shifts to a minimum or else make short rotating shifts possible, as well as ensuring sufficient breaks. Companies should also examine whether specific work tasks can be transferred from the night shift to the day shift (BS/BDA 2003: 104; Ilmarinen and Tempel 2002: 270).

The arrangement of in-house operational health circles as a further mid-term procedure recommendation makes the increase of health consciousness among employees possible. The employees are directly involved and work precisely according to the design of the operational measures for health promotion. Aside from employees, the works committee, the manager and those responsible for occupational health and safety should take part in the circle meetings. Health issues in the company can be analyzed and evaluated in these circles. In addition, they offer a suitable framework in which the employees can develop solutions and recommendations for improvement, as well as discuss occupational strains, illnesses and disabilities. The moderation of the health circle can be taken over by an employee of the company that possesses moderation skills; often, however, external moderators, for example, employees from health insurance agencies, carry out the circle discussion. The results of the circle should be evaluated and presented (Heyer and Henkel 1995: 95).

In the long-term, companies should strive to create a company-specific programme for the systematic preservation and promotion of health (the 'healthy business' vision). Besides the maintenance of physical and mental abilities, the companies' employee illness levels can also be lowered, and responsibility for dealing with one's own health can be promoted. A 'health promotion' steering committee can be formed for the realization of the vision of a 'healthy business' (Heyer and Henkel 1995: 91).

A typical programme could contain the following options (BS/BDA 2003: 163; Heyer and Henkel 1995: 97): Back and posture/seating training; stress management seminars; the establishment of rest areas for temporary relaxation; health and nutrition counselling; gymnastics during breaks; information sessions about healthy nutrition; nutrition based on age (minimal solutions are possible even in small and medium-sized businesses, for example, in cooperation with external service offers depending on the size of the business).

## Summary

Despite a multitude of research in various academic disciplines, there is still no 'standard recipe' for implementing age-based and ageing-based working practices. It is clear, however, that companies can no longer get away with ignoring the potential of older workers. Instead, companies need to analyze their age structures with regards to demographic developments and then produce long-term personnel and business strategies to address the ageing challenge. During this process, micro- and macro-ergonomic strategies, as discussed in this paper, can be applied to overcome some of the challenges which companies now face.

## References

BAUA (2004) *Mit Erfahrung die Zukunft meistern. Altern und Ältere in der Arbeitswelt*, Dortmund: Scholz-Druck.

Bellmann, L., E. Kistler and J. Wahse (2003) 'Betriebliche Sicht- und Verhaltensweisen gegenüber älteren Arbeitnehmern', *Das Parlament*, 20 (12 May), pp. 25–34.

BS/BDA (eds) (2003) *Erfolgreich mit älteren Arbeitnehmern*, Strategien und Beispiele für die betriebliche Praxis, Gütersloh: Verlag Bertelsmannstiftung.

Heyer, K. and H. Henkel (1995) *Älter werden im Betrieb – Risiko und Chance*, Eschborn: EKW.

Köchling, A. (2002) *Leitfaden zur Selbstanalyse alterstrukturelle Probleme in Unternehmen*, Dortmund: GfAH Selbstverlag.

Ilmarinen, J. and J. Tempel (2002) *Arbeitsfähigkeit 2010. Was können wir tun, damit Sie gesund bleiben?*, Hamburg: VSA-Verlag.

Luczak, H. (1998) *Lehrbuch Arbeitswissenschaft*, Berlin: Springer Verlag.

Luczak, H. and M. Stemann (2002) 'Ab heute leben wir länger – Arbeitswissenschaftliche Strategien zum gesünderen Altern', in H. Kowalski (ed.), *Symposium bis zur Rente. Betriebliche Gesundheitsförderung für ältere Beschäftigte*, Essen: Verlag CW Haarfeld, pp. 55–75.

Pack, J., H. Buck, E. Kistler, H. Mendius, M. Morschhäuser and H. Wolff (2000) *Zukunftsreport demographischer Wandel. Innovationsfähigkeit in einer alternden Gesellschaft*, Bonn: BMAS.

Pfohl, H. (ed.) (1997) *Betriebswirtschaftslehre der Mittel- und Kleinbetriebe, Größenspezifische Probleme und Möglichkeiten zur ihrer Lösung,* Berlin: Erich Schmidt.

Richenhagen, G. (2004) 'Demographischer Wandel: Gesünder arbeiten bis ins Alter', *Personalführung,* 2, pp. 60–69.

# 9
# The Performance-based Salary System and Personnel Management Reforms in Japan

*Keisuke Nakamura*

The term 'performance-based salary system' is at the centre of a hot dispute. Some people are quick to argue that companies should construct a mechanism able to cope with the challenges posed by an ageing workforce while at the same time enabling the organization to agilely adapt to ever-fluctuating market conditions. These proponents further maintain that the performance-based salary as opposed to the traditional seniority-based system indeed serves as one such mechanism, without which it would be very difficult to survive as a business in the face of ever-intensifying global competition. Other people counter that companies should not change the current salary system, which enables long-range planning in human resource development and at the same time fosters fierce competition among employees over skills development. The vague and aggressive overtones of the very term 'performance-based salary system' fuel emotion in an already heated debate.[1]

What strikes me as odd is the apparent lack, or inadequacy, of the calm stance necessary to carefully examine how the performance-based salary system is going to change personnel management as well as human relationships inside the company.[2] The performance-based salary system may be just a temporary fad, not causing a substantial change in the personnel management systems of Japanese companies. Alternatively, it may be that we are currently at a major crossroad in history. Whatever the case may be, shouldn't we look at the signs of change that exist today with untainted eyes and observe and record what these signs mean and where they are leading? Isn't now the time for candid and serious discussion on how to interpret the observed signs, instead of a heated clash between proponents and opponents of the system?

In this paper, I would like to briefly discuss the signs I have identified thus far, and their meanings and directions, based on the insights gained through the research I have conducted, both with a colleague and by myself (Nakamura and Ishida (2005) and Nakamura (2006)). Our studies covered one electrical machinery manufacturer, two department stores, one information and telecommunications (ICT) company, and one automotive manufacturer, all considered leading Japanese enterprises. Section two will characterize three types of performance-based salary systems; Section three will shed light on their influence on the salary system; Section four will analyze their impact on overall personnel management; and Section five will discuss the challenges they pose for labour unions.

## Three types of performance-based salary systems

There are at least three types of performance-based salary systems: the simple performance-based salary system, the process-oriented performance-based salary system, and the split performance-based salary system.

### The simple performance-based salary system

The simple performance-based salary system refers to a system that links remuneration directly to quantitative results expressed in numbers such as sales, profit or cost. A very simplistic example would be a scheme which pays you ¥100,000 if you sell one car. This can be thought of as a modern version of the traditional payment by result system. Most criticism of the performance-based salary system appears to be levelled at this type of system. Since there are a number of easily identifiable problems with the simple performance-based salary system, it is readily open to criticism, and this criticism tends to be all the more vociferous.

None of the enterprises covered by the present study were using a performance-based salary system of this type. In my view, simple performance-based salary systems are adopted by very few companies and even if actually used, will disappear in due course, because – I believe – they are incapable of providing the fundamental functions of personnel management such as building loyalty among employees, raising their level of motivation, and fostering teamwork. Such systems are in a way not worth serious consideration.

### The process-oriented performance-based salary system

The process-oriented performance-based salary system refers to a system that evaluates not only the degree of success in achieving quantitative goals such as sales, profit and cost, but also the process of achieving the goals. Of the companies covered by the present study, one department store and one electrical machinery manufacturer are using this system. Let us take a look at the case of the department store.

This department store defines the performance-based salary system as follows: (1) It is not a true performance-based salary system that evaluates only end results such as sales and profit; (2) The true performance-based salary system evaluates both the end results and the actions taken to achieve them; (3) In evaluating the actions taken to achieve the end results, it is necessary to consider what approach the employees took, what ideas they came up with, and what actions they took in order to achieve those results.

This department store introduced its performance-based salary system by way of ongoing discussion between labour and management. The labour union's memo 'Agenda for Extraordinary Branch Assembly (March 18, 2002)' explains the performance-based salary system in simple terms for union members. The following is an excerpt:

> The performance-based salary system is a system which evaluates individuals' abilities based on the viewpoint of 'from action to results'. It is therefore different from the results-based salary system which focuses on 'whether you have achieved the goal' or 'whether you have completed such and such a project'. While the results-based salary system basically does not consider the process and evaluates only the final results, the true performance-based salary system takes a broader view, considering both the final results and the steps taken to achieve them. In evaluating the results, for example, the two systems take vastly differing stances as to the consideration of whether the employees achieved the results while raising customer satisfaction or ignoring benefits for the customers. In particular, the 'performance-oriented action-based evaluation' which is being proposed here is designed to evaluate individuals' reproducible actions that are expected to produce another round of results through their ideas and actions, focusing on 'what scenarios they came up with to meet their sales targets, how they consulted with their superiors, whether they managed to implement these scenarios as designed, and finally whether they met the sales target' or 'what actions or improvements they contrived to bring the project to a satisfactory completion'.

Let us now take a closer look at 'performance-oriented action-based evaluation' by taking as an example the married ladies' clothes department at this department store, which targets women in the 30 to 44 age bracket, and whose staff agreed to be interviewed.

> The married ladies' clothes department should target women between 30 and 44. Thus, actions aimed at this clientele are evaluated highly. If it is women in their 60s and 70s that are buying, it means that the action doesn't match the target. In other words, if they (the married ladies' clothes department) offer a selection of clothes targeted at those in their 60s and 70s, we don't consider it a (good) performance-oriented action. The point is whether we are appropriately addressing our customers' needs, whether we are communicating to our customers, and whether we are raising the level of customer satisfaction. The management gives guidelines. The question is whether the employees take appropriate action. (Note: The words and phrases in brackets are the author's additions.)

Missing the target means, conversely, that they are taking customers away from other ladies' clothes departments, which is no good for the total sales of the department store. Not offering a selection of clothes that meet married ladies' tastes is in itself considered a negative performance-oriented action. In addition, the selection of items is not to be determined department by department. There is an overall policy throughout the department store, and individual departments must follow it in offering their selections (e.g. items for married ladies). If they manage to increase their sales as a result of this, they are then considered to have carried out a good performance-oriented action.

Needless to say, it is not merely performance-oriented actions that are evaluated. Quantitative measures such as sales and operational profit are also evaluated. Quantitative targets are spelled out in semi-annual sales plans.

The sales target for each department is given by the department store headquarters at the beginning of each fiscal term. For departments facing a downward trend, the target is rather conservative, whereas for those facing an upward trend it is somewhat higher than for the same period in the previous year. Thus, the target is determined by taking changes in the external environment into consideration. Sales trends come from outside and are thus beyond individual employees' control. They fall therefore under the responsibility of the headquarters (the company). After taking sales trends into consideration, the headquarters prescribe a target for each department that they want it to achieve, and evaluate the degree of success in meeting the target. We were unable, to our regret, to ascertain the relative weighting scheme they apply to the evaluation of performance-oriented actions and the degree of success in achieving the target.

## The split performance-based salary system – deliberately split type

By 'split type', we mean that the degree of success in achieving a given target is not to be evaluated; in other words, the end result is not subject to evaluation. Here, performance and results are separated from evaluation. Of the companies surveyed, one automotive manufacturer (Toyota) is using a performance-based salary system of this type. Some might even question whether it is appropriate to call it a performance-based salary system. It is worth pointing out, however, that during the personnel reform for managers implemented in 1996, one of the future directions indicated was ' "the implementation of a comprehensive performance-based salary system" with diminishing weight given to seniority'. Toyota's main aim in this reform was indeed 'the thorough implementation of a comprehensive performance-based salary system'.

According to Toyota's personnel department, 'the system evaluates employees' performance (1) during the preceding year, (2) with respect to their assigned role, and (3) as output', which seems tantamount to evaluating performance. What makes it different is that 'in evaluating performance, one should not disregard the viewpoints of "conducting work from a long-term perspective" and of "exhibiting performance through cooperation and teamwork" '. Thus, 'we evaluate performance converted to its underlying abilities; in other words, we evaluate performance and work processes simultaneously'. In more concrete terms, 'we first identify as evaluation factors the abilities necessary for generating good performance, then confirm, for each evaluation factor, to what extent its underlying abilities have been demonstrated, and finally evaluate performance from those perspectives'.

In summary, they aim to implement a comprehensive performance-based salary system. In the actual evaluation of performance, however, they do not look at performance per se; instead, they first identify as evaluation factors the abilities necessary for generating good performance, confirm, for each evaluation factor, whether or not employees exercise their underlying abilities, and then use this to evaluate performance. This is a deliberate separation of evaluation from performance.

To quote one Toyota personnel officer:

> When we asked ourselves what constitutes our core competence, we thought that while we recognise the importance of performance in itself, what matters most is how we approach the target of our work

and what process we follow. Having said that, though, we cannot ignore the results of work either, and so we sort of integrated all these things in the Toyota way, so to speak. So, we ended up creating a new concept of 'abilities to exploit' and focusing our personnel evaluation on how well an employee puts his/her potential abilities to use.

The abilities identified as evaluation factors include creating challenges (i.e. items of work or assignments), meeting these challenges, managing the organization, utilizing human resources, and gaining the trust of others. These factors are further broken down into a total of ten sub-factors. For example, the ability to create challenges consists of two sub-factors, one of which is 'out-of-the-box thinking, not being limited by past practices'. This sub-factor questions whether 'the employee draws his/her own original and innovative conclusion, without referring to previous cases' and whether 'the employee makes correct judgements on matters he/she has no experience in'. Another factor, the ability to meet challenges, consists of three sub-factors, one of which is 'appropriate judgement on situations'. This sub-factor questions whether 'the employee accurately grasps and analyzes given situations by collecting appropriate information' and whether 'the employee makes valid judgements even in situations where only limited information is available'.

Another type of split performance-based salary system is one in which evaluation happens to be separated from performance without deliberate intention, as implemented by the ICT company in our study. The system itself was designed with a great deal of attention to detail. If implemented as designed, it would be a process-oriented performance-based salary system; however, in the actual workplace, it does not function as intended by the personnel department. In this regard, this should better be called a split performance-based salary system, in which evaluation ends up being separated from performance.

## Impact on the salary system

The aim of the performance-based salary system is, above all else, to reform the salary system. Therefore, the main point of discussion ought to be the changes, if any, which are occurring to the salary system. In reality, however, most discussions of the performance-based salary system centre on the basic question of 'to adopt or not to adopt', thus falling short of addressing this critical issue.

As I see it, while the performance-based salary system is significantly affecting the salaries of managers, it is having a somewhat limited impact on the wages of rank-and-file employees; its impact for them is generally limited to bonuses, and it does not affect monthly salaries to any appreciable degree. Taking the example of one department store, let us examine its impact on monthly salaries and bonuses.

## Monthly salaries

For monthly salaries, the performance-based salary system applies only to the rank of upper management (department managers and above). For section managers, supervisors, and rank-and-file employees, a skills-based wage system is used, which is part of a skills-based grade system. In the skills-based grade system, employees are classified into various grade categories, evaluated in terms of their ability to carry out their jobs using a prescribed personnel evaluation format, and are given a pay rise every year based on the evaluation results.

With the skills-based salary system, it is theoretically possible to get a decrease in wages, but in reality this seldom happens. The higher the grade category, however, the more difficult it is to get a pay rise. Also, the longer one stays within the same grade category, the more difficult it becomes to get a pay rise. In any case, it is impossible to get a pay rise unless one gets the best personnel evaluation. From this perspective, the company gives employees a strong incentive to improve their ability to carry out their jobs, which, however, is not the same as a performance-based salary system.

It is generally assumed that the performance-based salary system applies to all employees, but this is not the case, as observed with Toyota and the electrical machinery manufacturer covered in this study. The fact that it applies to employees in upper management may be easily understood if one considers the following two factors:

First, responsibility and authority should go hand in hand. The choice of brands and suppliers, the selection of merchandise items, and the methods of promotion and sales all affect performance. Only those who are authorized to make decisions on these things can take responsibility for the results. It is part of a manager's responsibility to make strategic decisions. It is unreasonable to have to take responsibility if you are not given relevant authority. Having to work under a terrible superior is unbearable enough; if on top of this, his/her responsibility is passed down to you, it would be a disaster.

Second, being young and inexperienced means being in the learning stage, as young employees must learn the ropes. They must acquire the knowledge and expertise required for their jobs, and it is through trial and error that they learn. If you kept pushing young and inexperienced employees to achieve results without giving them a chance to learn, they would feel oppressed and be afraid of making mistakes, and then their abilities would not grow as much as expected. This would have a negative impact on both the employees and the company.

Although the exact length of this learning stage depends on the company, it may be reasonable over time to expand the scope of performance-based salary systems. The department store in this study is attempting to expand the scope of its system to section managers. However, it may also be a good idea to preserve a system which encourages employees to enhance their ability to carry out their jobs until they have reached a certain level in the organization.

Let us take a closer look at the salary system for the rank of upper management (department managers and above). In a nutshell, their salaries vary from year to year depending on their performance and performance-oriented actions. First of all, they are ranked into six classes, from I to VI, according to their expected roles. Class I indicates the role with the highest value, or in simpler terms, the highest rank.

Each role or class is assigned a monthly salary range. Not all employees in each class get a flat, fixed monthly salary (e.g. ¥1 million for those in Class I, and ¥700,000 for those in Class II) since this is a performance-based salary system. Managers within each class get different salaries, depending on the evaluation based on their end results and performance-oriented actions. Figure 9.1 illustrates the salary scheme for managers.

The scheme shown in Figure 9.1 is not very complex. The columns I through VI are roles or classes, while the rankings S through D indicate the results of evaluation. The vertical axis represents the amount of the monthly salary. On one hand, the higher the class of manager, the higher the salary; on the other hand, within each class, the higher the evaluation results, the higher the salary, too. For example, within Class I, A gets ¥1 million, whereas D gets ¥700,000.

It is noteworthy that managers' salaries fluctuate year by year, depending on the results of their annual job performance. Suppose you are a sales department manager in Class III. You may have got ¥650,000 for an evaluation of Grade A last year, but your salary will go down to ¥500,000 if you get Grade C this year. Conversely, your salary will increase if you get a better grade.

Put differently, there is no regular pay rise for managers, unlike with the skills-based wage system, in which salaries increase every year, however small the rise may be. Managers' salaries may increase, decrease, or remain unchanged, depending on their end results and performance-oriented actions. It is indeed a performance-based system.

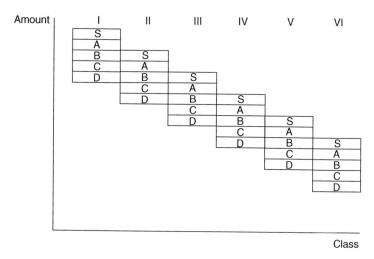

*Figure 9.1*  Managers' monthly salaries by class
*Source*: The author.

## Bonuses

The performance-based salary system affects bonuses somewhat differently. While it is process-oriented, the relative weight assigned to end results – that is, the degree of success in achieving quantitative targets – is higher, and the scope of application is wider.

Bonuses for upper management (department managers and above) consist of two parts: one based on the manager's salary multiplied by the month-linked coefficient (in number of months) and the other based on evaluation. The month-linked coefficient is determined in relation to the outcome of the labour negotiation.

Some explanation is due regarding the evaluation part. Apart from the six-class ranking scheme based on the roles mentioned above, each manager is given a skills grade, either Grade 6 or Grade 7. For each grade, the end results of all the managers are evaluated into five levels, to which the evaluation part pertains. What is evaluated here is only the end result, such as sales or operating profit; performance-oriented actions and processes are not considered. Overall, however, performance-oriented actions and processes are given some consideration, since the other part of the bonus is the manager's salary, multiplied by the month-linked coefficient. The result is a process-oriented performance-based salary system with a greater weight placed on end results.

The situation is more complicated for employees below the rank of upper management, that is, section managers and below. For young employees who are expected to gain more experience in the future, end results are not considered. For experienced employees just below the managerial rank, supervisors and section managers, end results are considered in the following manner.

The bonus for section managers and supervisors consists of two parts: one based on the skills-based salary multiplied by the month-linked coefficient (as a number of months), and the other based on evaluation. End results are factored into the evaluation part. Compared with upper management, however, the extent to which end results are considered is rather limited. For the bonus, the degree of success in achieving sales or profit targets and the degree of success in exploiting one's ability to carry out one's job are equally weighted. The former is measured in terms of the degree of success in meeting the budget. Needless to say, overachievement in terms of sales and/or profit is highly appreciated, whereas underachievement is negatively evaluated. The latter reflects the day-to-day mode of work measured by several yardsticks. Both are evaluated at five levels and added together with equal weight, to produce the final evaluation results.

For experienced employees just below the managerial rank, in addition to the degree of success in achieving targets and the degree of success in exploiting one's ability to carry out one's job, an eager attitude towards work is considered. These three measures are given weight factors of 40%, 30%, and 30%, respectively. Thus, end results have a still smaller significance. An eager attitude towards work can also be interpreted as an emphasis on the process of achieving end results.

To sum up, in evaluations for bonuses, the company's business performance and individual employees' contributions are intertwined. On the one hand, the bonus reflects the company's business results. Even though the amount of bonus is determined through a series of negotiations between management and labour union, it cannot be determined without regard to the company's business results. On the other hand, from experienced employees to employees in the rank of upper and lower management, end results such as sales and profit are factored into the bonus evaluation.

## Impact on the wage system

Thus far we have studied how performance evaluation affects the salary system at a department store. Let us now summarize, by incorporating the findings from other cases in the present study, the changes brought about by the performance-based salary system.

As for the salary system for managers, three changes are noteworthy: (a) regular pay rises have been abolished; (b) the monthly salary is no longer seen as remuneration for potential job performance abilities; and (c) the company's business performance and the individual's contribution are intertwined in bonus evaluations. A more detailed analysis of the first two changes would be in order.

Managers' salaries now fluctuate in both directions every year depending on the evaluation of their performance. In the case of the electrical machinery manufacturer, whereas the managers' salaries do not fluctuate in both directions every year, they may not increase as a result of their evaluation. Moreover, there is an upper limit to the salary increase. In any case, the regular pay rise system, which formed the core of the Japanese seniority-based wage system, has been abolished. As a result, we no longer have the traditional seniority-based wage system, where virtually automatic rises were given according to age or the length of service, although the amount of the rise varied depending on the results of personnel evaluation.

For managers today, the salary is paid according to that role or post, as opposed to the potential job performance abilities that individual employees are considered to have. In this sense, the traditional merit system designed to evaluate employees' potential abilities has been abolished.

These two changes have great significance. Although limited to the rank of management, the seniority-based wage system and a certain form of merit system, which have characterized Japanese personnel management, seem to be disappearing. Interpretations of the seniority-based wage system and the merit system vary but seem to share the following facts and views. Wages increase on the whole with age and the length of service, although there are differences among individuals. There may have been the notion of a cost-of-living salary, but the basic assumption is that the ability to perform a job increases with age and the length of service, albeit to varying degrees, even if that ability is not actually put to use. The performance-based salary system is about to change these two systems or concepts dramatically.

As for the disappearance of the merit system, some caution is necessary. One possible view is that the performance-based salary system has merely eliminated the kind of merit system that evaluates potential abilities and has replaced it with another kind of merit system, which evaluates the proven abilities. The split performance-based salary system evaluates only the abilities the employees actually demonstrate. On the other hand, the process-oriented performance-based salary system evaluates not only the end results, but also the process of achieving them, which can be viewed as a manifestation of the desire to evaluate the extent to which the individual exercises his/her innate abilities during the process (even if they have not contributed directly to the end results). This reconfirms the view that the merit system continues to form the basis of personnel management in Japan.

In summary, the performance-based salary system can be considered a major change being brought about in an attempt to maintain the merit system on the one hand, shifting its focus from potential abilities to proven abilities, and to abolish the seniority-based wage system for managers on the other.

In contrast, the wage system for staff below managers (hereafter called middle-aged and younger people) is not undergoing such a major change. Department stores continue to use skills-based evaluation systems. Other enterprises such as Toyota and the electrical machinery manufacturer in this study have introduced and based their wage systems on new evaluation systems which reflect the abilities that individual employees are expected to put to use. Another company has abolished the regular pay rise system altogether, which means an individual's wage may either increase or decrease, depending on the results of his/her personnel evaluation. I, however, do not consider these changes significant in practice for the reasons given below.

It is hard to conceive of middle-aged and younger people with a significant gap between their potential job performance abilities and the abilities they actually demonstrate before reaching the rank of management. It would be more natural to think that they actually demonstrate their potential job performance abilities as they are. Also, according to personnel officers, even at companies which have abolished regular pay rises, zero or negative pay rises are extremely rare.

Therefore, for middle-aged and younger people, wage systems which strongly encourage skills development continue to be considered healthy. In this respect, no change is taking place either in the seniority-based system or in the merit system.

There is a reason for singling out middle-aged and younger people. Although not confirmed in the strict sense, there appears to be a trend for the salary curve to level off in over middle age (typically over the mid-40s). It is inconceivable that, while managers are losing the privileges of seniority-based wages and regular pay rises, employees in the over middle age brackets who are not promoted to the rank of management (even specialists and experts, let alone rank and filers) should continue to be treated with a seniority-based wage system and a merit system that evaluates potential abilities. It appears that they are moving towards a scheme, as with managers, which abolishes seniority-based wages and evaluates abilities they actually demonstrate. As a result, the salary curve becomes flatter, while the gap between them and management widens.

Imano (1993, 1998) summarizes the above changes in a neat way: A new trend is emerging whereby skills development is emphasized for employees below the rank of management and thus their wage plan is like a loan with a long-term settlement, with wages increasing with the length of service, whereas the wage plan for managers is like a loan with a short-term settlement, with their salaries tied to their jobs. The intriguing question then arises as to what wage system will be applied to employees who are not promoted to the rank of management. My prediction and answer to this question is that a salary system similar to that used for managers will be applied to them (probably resulting in a wider wage gap).

In summary, the performance-based salary system is indeed bringing about significant changes to the Japanese wage system. The seniority-based wage system for employees in over middle ages (regardless of whether they are promoted to the rank of management) is being abolished, whereas the merit system, while remaining the cornerstone, is going to shift its focus from potential to proven abilities.

## Influence on personnel management

The scope of influence of the performance-based salary system will not be limited to the wage system itself. In my view, through changes to the salary system, it will influence all aspects of personnel management. This section discusses some of the influences as I see them.

The first is the influence on the over-middle-aged. Flattening their wage curve or letting their wages fluctuate according to the results of performance evaluations will eventually lead to the active utilization of elderly people. If wages do not automatically increase with age or the length of service, employing elderly people will not necessarily mean in itself an increase in cost. Also, if one is to pay elderly people in the rank of management according to the results of performance evaluations, the system of setting an age limit for the executive rank will lose its significance.[3] These factors may eventually help the extension of the retirement age to take root.

A crucial turning point for most employees is whether they can be promoted to executive rank. While there are more and more college graduates, the number of executive posts is limited. On the other hand, it is no longer feasible to raise salaries within the framework of the skills-based evaluation system. This situation poses two challenges to personnel management as discussed below.

The second impact will be on the development of abilities of middle-aged and younger people who have not yet been promoted to executive rank. This issue will gain increasing importance. What abilities they have managed to develop by this time depends critically on what career paths they have taken and what training they have received. It will no longer be fair to put the responsibility solely on employees. It will become increasingly necessary to give careful consideration to this issue.

One's career path is determined to a great degree by which department one is assigned to by the personnel department and what kinds of jobs one is given by one's superiors (one's immediate boss and his/her boss). It might be possible under ideal situations to listen to, and then reflect, the desires of all employees in their career plans, but this is very difficult in practice. Many factors are involved such as aptitude and the company's circumstances. For example, it would be impossible to assign all employees to the management planning department. It may also become necessary to relocate employees as a result of a change in business operation.

Another factor which should not be overlooked is the possibility that managers may be unwilling to give their subordinates challenging jobs simply because of the performance-based salary system, since challenging assignments tend to lower the department's productivity, resulting in lower performance.

Despite these difficulties, personnel departments will have to assume responsibility for giving employees the equal career opportunities they want. At the same time, from the viewpoint of respecting employees' wishes as much as possible, it will become increasingly necessary to introduce the job posting system. Alternatively, it may also become necessary for companies to increase their dependency on external resources in order to protect regular, permanent employees.

Training programs offered by personnel departments ('off-the-job training' or Off-JT) will need to take the following points into consideration:

Once equal training opportunities are offered and support for self-development is in place, employees will be responsible for making their own choices. Superiors may also need to shoulder part of this responsibility by having them take training courses the former deem necessary. The question is whether they will have the time to attend them.

Also, having an employee take a training course means a temporary setback in power to the superior, which translates into a negative, albeit temporary, impact on performance. Therefore, superiors tend to be reluctant to have their subordinates take courses which the former do not consider necessary. Thus, the challenge for personnel departments will be how to break this barrier.

Third, personnel departments will need to consider retraining their over-middle-aged people. It is not fair to give chances of executive promotion only to middle-aged and younger people. Over-middle-aged people should also be given a second chance (a 'return match') since their salary curves flatten. If the purpose of the performance-based salary system is to evaluate the employee's work or demonstrated abilities, regardless of age or the length of service, it would be absurd if age or the length of service works against over-middle-aged people, who should also be given retraining opportunities. These thoughts might be hard to dismiss. From the viewpoint of maintaining morale among over-middle-aged people, it might become necessary to address such comments, and pressure will mount to review the management of promotions, even if there are not many cases of 'return matches'.

The fourth point to consider is the increasing importance of keeping up morale. There is no question that even employees who are not promoted to executive rank continue to be assets to the company. To ensure a smooth PDCA (Plan-Do-Check-Action) cycle in business management, it is very important to keep up morale among these employees. On the other hand, pay rises and promotions no longer appear to be effective incentives. What other way is there to keep up morale without resorting to force? (It is not pleasant to be criticized, let alone scolded, by somebody younger.) This seems to be where the leadership of a manager is put into question, and perhaps a new kind of management skill might be required in this area.

Finally, personnel departments will have to consider another issue of growing importance: how to create a comfortable environment for those employees who are not promoted to executive rank and yet are working just as hard. Some such employees may feel,

I am older than you and have been working longer, but I am not as capable as you and I know that. I am, however, working hard for the company in my own way, and I make my own kind of contribution. My salary is lower than yours and is not going to go up very much, but I am not unhappy about that.

How can companies keep such ordinary people working hard and maintain their dignity? There appears to be no easy solution in sight.

To sum up, it will be necessary to find a new kind of order in the workplace which is different from the traditional seniority-based system and which matches the performance-based salary system. It will further be necessary to bring about changes in the human relationships within each company by introducing a new kind of order that will probably entail changes in the organizational culture and customs as well, although again it is hard to see what kind of solutions might appear.

## Challenges for labour unions

Labour unions are now saddled with a number of tough jobs. In addition to the issues discussed above, which all involve labour unions, they are faced with three major challenges described below.

First of all, while the management-labour relationship is becoming increasingly individualized, the fundamental question is looming up as to what role the labour union should play as an organizational body. The performance-based salary system has strengthened the link between the individual's contribution and the company's performance, at least in terms of bonuses. While this connection is more significant for managers (who are not union members), it also applies to union members to a certain degree.

Labour unions in Europe and North America have made it one of their main goals to eliminate competition among union members. Personnel evaluation, by its very nature, discriminates among union members and thus has not been accepted by labour unions. In contrast, labour unions in Japan have accepted personnel evaluation even when it has affected union members' salaries. This is not to say the Japanese system is bad. As Ishida (1990) points out, Japanese union members have long considered it fair to evaluate differences resulting due to abilities.

Thus, while Japanese labour unions negotiate average pay rises and bonuses, they do not negotiate the actual amounts that individual union members are to receive, which is considered a matter to be determined solely by management. In this regard, wages are determined not through collective, but instead through individual bargaining. The performance-based salary system has promoted this phenomenon, in that the degree of each individual union member's contribution to the company's performance is now reflected in his/her bonus. In the midst of this trend towards individualization, what is at stake now is what roles the labour union should play.

Second, it is the business target that ultimately determines the labour intensity for union members. If too aggressive an application of the performance-based salary system results in increased work intensity for union members, it would become necessary for unions to address this issue. At that point, labour unions would be required to start commenting on business targets and even business plans – in other words, to play a greater role in management. That would certainly be a major challenge for labour unions.

Third, if one supposes that the wages of over-middle-aged people will not increase to an appreciable degree, then it is conceivable that union members will make stronger demands for an increase in base wages. Although the traditional Japanese 'spring labour offensive' can be considered crumbled since the middle of the 1990s (Nakamura 2005), it may become necessary to revive it.

## Notes

1. It is probably Takahashi (2004) and Joh (2004) that invigorated the debate. These two books seem to have unleashed the pent-up grudge and anxieties of a number of people critical about the performance-based salary system who had been outshone by their proponents. The books indeed triggered an onslaught of criticism. It would be worthwhile, however, to point out that Joh (2004) did not criticize the very notion of the performance-based salary system. Those whom he did criticize were personnel staff who he thought had simply imported the American performance-based salary system intact, managers who he thought had no idea of what the performance-based salary system is, and executives who he thought tended to put blame on employees without themselves taking responsibility. He has the view that 'what we need is an advanced performance-based salary system that suits Japanese culture and custom' (Joh 2004: 197). He consistently maintains this view in his second book (2005). Takahashi (2004), on the other hand, charmed many readers, particularly those who were critical of the performance-based salary system, with the appealing title and crisp rhetoric. It appears that he based his theory on the fruit of research in experimental social psychology led by Deci (1980). What he drew upon was, however, only part of the work of Deci (1980), and he neglected or ignored the remainder. For criticisms on this point, refer to Nakamura and Ishida (2005: 269–271) and Nakamura (2006: 22–25). Incidentally, Sansone and Harackiewicz (2000) present an intriguing discussion on intrinsic motivation and extrinsic motivation. Some of the papers contained in their work attempt to depart from the notion of the two types of motivation being opposed to each other.
2. This is not to say, of course, that there has been no such research. Noteworthy are Imano (1993, 1998) and Ishida (2003, 2006), with whom my arguments resonate to a large extent. The aim of this paper is, in fact, to invigorate the discussion about the performance-based salary system (not a debate on one way or the other), including the discussion on the difference between their view and mine.

3. It may also be that this simply signifies an increased possibility of utilizing elderly people and that whether or not such changes will actually take place is yet to be seen. Inagami (2003) points out (in Chapter 3) that, in large enterprises, many salaried employees (particularly managers) over 50 are transferred to one of subsidiary or related companies, either temporarily on loan or permanently, which practically means the end of the system of life-time employment by one company.

## References

Deci, E. L. (1980) *Intrinsic Motivation, Plenum Press: New York*, translated into Japanese by N. Ando and U. Ishida, and published by Seishin Shobo, Co., Ltd.

Inagami, T. (2003) *Kigyō grūpu keiei to shukkō tenseki kankō* (*Group Enterprise Management and Personnel Transfer Practices*), Tokyo: The University of Tokyo Press.

Imano, K. (1993) 'Atarashii jinji kanri no chōryū' (New Trends in Personnel Management), *Nihon Rōdō Kenkyū Zasshi*, 426, pp. 2–14.

Imano, K. (1998) *Kachinuku chingin kaikaku – Nihongata shigotokyū no susume* (*Wage Reform for Victory: Recommendation of the Japanese-style Job-based Wage System*), Tokyo: Nihon Keizai Shinbunsha.

Ishida, M. (1990) *Chingin no shakai kagaku – nihon to igirisu* (*The Social Science of the Wage Systems: A Comparison between Japan and the United Kingdom*), Tokyo: Minerva Publishing, Co., Ltd.

Ishida, M. (2003) *Shigoto no shakai kagaku-rōdō kenkyū no furontia* (*The Social Science of Work: Frontiers of Research in Labour*), Tokyo: Minerva Publishing Co., Ltd.

Ishida, M. (2006) 'Chingin seido kaikaku to rōshi kankei' (Wage System Reform and Industrial Relations), in Rengō Sōken (ed.), *Chingin seido to rōdō kumiai no torikumi ni kansuru chōsa Kenkyū hōkokusho* (*Research Report on Wage Systems and Labour Unions' Approach to Them*), Tokyo: Rengō Sōken, pp. 11–49.

Joh, T. (2004) *Uchigawa kara mita Fujitsū – seika shugi no hōkai* (*Collapse of the Performance-based Salary System at Fujitsu – an Insider's View*), Tokyo: Kōbunsha.

Joh, T. (2005) *Nihongata seikshugi no kanōsei* (*The Possibility of a Japanese-style Performance-based Salary System*), Tokyo: Tōyōkeizai Shinpōsha.

Nakamura, K. (2005) 'Suitai ka saisei ka'(Decline or Revival?), in K. Nakamura and Rengō Sōken (eds), *Suitai ka Saisei ka – Rōdō kumiai kasseika e no michi* (*Decline or Revival? – a Road to Revitalisation of Labour Unions*), Tokyo: Keisoshobō, pp. 3–26.

Nakamura, K. (2006) *Seikashugi no shinjitsu* (*The Truth about Performance-based Salary Systems*), Tokyo: Tōyōkeizai Shinpōsha.

Nakamura, K. and M. Ishida (2005) *Howaito kara no shigoto to seika – Jinji kanri no furontia* (*Jobs and Performance of White-collar Workers – Frontier of Personnel Management*), Tokyo: Tōyōkeizai Shinpōsha.

Sansone, C. and J. M. Harackiewicz (eds) (2000) *Intrinsic and Extrinsic Motivation: The Search for Optimal Motivation and Performance*, California, CA: Academic Press.

Takahas, N. (2004) *Kyomū no seikashugi – Nihongata nenkōsei fukkatsu no susume* (*The Illusion of Performance-based Salary Systems – a Recommendation for Revival of the Japanese-style Seniority-based System*), Tokyo: Nihon Keizai Shinbunsha.

# 10
## Paradigm Changes in Labour Market Policies for Older Workers in Germany – Background Factors and Recent Developments

*Gerhard Naegele*

The foreseeable demographic developments in Germany indicate a future decline in the workforce accompanied by a considerable ageing of employees. Both developments will become markedly visible after 2015. In the future, the needs of the German labour market will thus have to be met by a smaller number of essentially older workers. This paper discusses how public awareness of and policies directed at this challenge have changed in recent years. I will first provide a short overview of the most relevant demographic and economic factors. In the second section, I will analyze recent public policy developments that affect older workers. In the third section, I will assess the overall implications, and then move on to summarize my findings in the conclusion.

### Demographic and economic context

Although projections about the development of the German workforce differ according to assumptions about factors such as future life expectancy and migration, they all point to a marked decline in the population after 2015 (Schäfer and Seyda 2004). From a medium term perspective, the proportion of Germans aged between 50 and 64 will increase significantly from about 20% to nearly 24%, whereas the proportion of the population aged between 35 and 49 will decline from about 23% to 19% by 2020 (Statistisches Bundesamt 2006).

Consequently, an extension of working life, and thus a de facto increase in the activity rate of older workers, is regarded as inevitable.

However, Germany clearly lags behind other countries in terms of the employment of older workers. The 2010 target of an employment ratio of 50% of 55–64 year olds, which the EU Commission set at the Stockholm Summit in 2004, has only been reached by highly qualified employees. For foreigners and those employed in unskilled jobs within the 55–64 age bracket, the employment ratios are currently below 30% in Germany (Europäische Kommission 2003, 2004). This data is in strong contrast to the employment rates of older workers in some neighbouring countries like Denmark, Sweden and even Switzerland, which partly reaches more than 65%.

One of the most significant forces behind the sharp drop in the number of older workers in Germany is the policy of early retirement. The trend towards early retirement started in the early 1970s, but became more pronounced in the 1980s and early 1990s. This was partly a result of low employment growth in previous decades which made early retirement seemingly an appealing method of fighting high unemployment among the younger generation.

However, early retirement was to a large extent the result of a broad 'social consensus' aimed at achieving the most effective, socially well-balanced and, above all, most inexpensive way of managing human resources. In short, early retirement was seen as a way of avoiding generational conflicts within the labour market that would otherwise spark major social conflicts. Public pension and labour market policies have strongly supported German companies in this area. Furthermore, the structural changes in East Germany after unification contributed to this trend because early retirement helped adapt the East German labour market to the process of economic transformation.

Employment policies and initiatives have only recently changed direction and are now designed to end early retirement practices. These changes are taking place at a time when the unemployment level of older workers is above average. In 2003, almost 1.1 million older workers aged between 45 and 55 were unemployed. The unemployment risk that older workers face is less the risk of becoming unemployed than the risk of remaining unemployed. Long-term unemployment among older workers is especially widespread. The unfavourable labour market conditions as well as additional factors, such as age discrimination and the comparatively high wages of older workers, are primarily responsible for prolonged unemployment. Furthermore, older unemployed people often lack up-to-date skills and are more likely to suffer from health problems. These structural challenges are not likely to disappear because of a declining population in the future. In fact, the latest forecasts show that unemployment will stay high until 2020, even though the population will shrink (Bellman et al. 2003; Ebert, Fuchs and Kistler 2006; Fuchs, Schnur and Zika 2005).

## Recent public policy developments affecting older workers

### Early exit and pension reforms

In recent years, public policies have tended to counter the social consensus on early retirement. Apart from the demographic reasons mentioned above, the core argument for this 'change of paradigm' – as it is often characterized – can be seen in growing public concern over the financial sustainability of Germany's social security systems. These are primarily based on the pay-as-you-go principle, and are part of the overall Bismarckian statutory social insurance scheme. In such a scheme, early exit results in both declining contributions and longer periods of benefit payment – a situation which is further aggravated by an increasing life expectancy.

Initiatives to stop early retirement, first launched at the beginning of the 1990s and reinforced in 1992, 1996 and 1999, are primarily centred on raising the retirement age. The current statutory retirement age at which one is eligible to receive the public pension is 65. Recently, the government decided to gradually raise the retirement age to 67, a process which will start from 2012 and will last until 2029. Early retirement is still possible, but employees will have to accept an annual 3.6% reduction on their pension until they reach retirement age. In addition, a part-time retirement law was introduced in 1996 which gives older workers the opportunity to reduce their working hours without a substantial loss of income (Altersteilzeitgesetz; BMGS 2005).

However, many labour market experts argue that an increase in the number of older workers and a higher retirement age will not be achieved by simply changing the legal framework. There needs to be both a substantial improvement in working conditions, and greater investment in older workers who want to become more employable. As a consequence of ignoring working conditions and investment in human capital, it is feared that simply increasing the pension age will not raise the average retirement age, but will only lead to a growing number of unemployed older workers who are left stranded waiting for their pensions.

Furthermore, the 2005 'Fifth Federal Report on the Situation of Elderly People in Germany' underscores the fact that simultaneously raising the retirement age and introducing benefit reductions for early exit can lead to unsocial side-effects. This is because those two measures benefit workers who can continue to work but often financially disadvantage those who are unable to do so (see for examples Behrens 2003). This leads to a worsening of social injustice affecting older people. This is already the case for employees in relatively unskilled jobs, which account for a lot of foreign workers, who are on average more likely to retire before the normal pension age due to health reasons, or due to an unfavourable employment outlook. They therefore often have to put up with pension reductions. Moreover, if one bears in mind that the average life expectancy, and thus also the term of pension payments, is lower in these groups (BMFSFJ 2006), then it becomes apparent that they are already underprivileged.

## Current labour market policies for older workers

In addition to recent pension reforms which have raised the statutory retirement age, the Federal Government – in most cases in harmony with the employers associations and some trade unions – has tried to 'modernize' labour market policies for older workers. The aim is to promote the employment prospects of older workers and move away from early retirement policies. In many cases, the new focus is explicitly on preventing older workers from becoming unemployed, and on promoting the re-integration of those who are unemployed. The following initiatives, legal measures and programmes are especially noteworthy (for details see Naegele 2002, 2004; Frerichs and Taylor 2008 forthcoming):

- Research and several Federal awareness campaigns, including public campaigns for 'good practice' (e.g. Campaign '50plus – they can do it' (since 2000); Demographic Change – Public Relations and Marketing Strategy (1999–2003); Federal Enquete-Commission on Demographic Change (2002); Perspectives for Germany – a Strategy for a Sustainable Development (2004); New Quality of Work (since 2002); the Fifth Federal Commission for Reporting on the Situation of the Elderly (2003–2005).
- The benchmarking of national, European and international policy approaches favouring an ageing workforce.
- The implementation of special financial incentives for the vocational training of older workers in small and medium-sized companies (Job Aktiv Gesetz).
- The lowering of the qualifying age, from 55 to 50, for wage subsidies for older job-seekers.

- A temporary wage guarantee for older workers to stimulate take-up of lower paid-jobs ('Entgeltsicherung').
- Exemptions for employers from contributing to unemployment insurance when recruiting an older unemployed worker ('Beitragsbonus').
- The enlargement of educational and other measures for helping the older long-term unemployed (e.g. temporary work agencies, special staff training) (Job Aktiv Gesetz).

On the other hand, current policies to promote the employment of older workers are accompanied by cutbacks in employment protection and social security due to the following measures:

- The enlargement of opportunities to use the fixed-term temporary employment of older workers (Teilzeit- und Befristungsgesetz).
- The merging of unemployment assistance and social assistance and the creation of the so-called *unemployment benefit II*. From 2006 onwards, receipt of *unemployment benefit I* for older workers will be limited to 18 months (down from 32 months). The new *unemployment benefit II*, which started in 2005, is a means-tested benefit to secure the income of unemployed workers once *unemployment benefit I* is no longer paid. In comparison with previous unemployment assistance, which on average guaranteed an income level of 50% of the last net income, payment has thus been reduced to the level of social assistance.

Against the background of EU Guideline 78 prohibiting age discrimination in the labour market, the Federal government produced a draft version of a law against discrimination in autumn 2004. This law is intended to rule out unjustifiable age-limits in job-recruitment, promotion and dismissal.

### Initiatives by employers associations and trade unions

The present *official* proposals of the Federal Confederation of Employers Associations (BDA 2002) refer to prolonging working life, although many companies are still practising the opposite by prolonging early retirement schemes (Boockmann and Zwick 2004). The Federal Confederation of Employers Associations, while supporting the Federal labour market policies mentioned above, has also made its own proposals to increase labour force participation rates among older workers. These proposals primarily aim at overcoming what the Federal Confederation of Employers

Associations sees as the most significant 'disadvantages' of employing older workers, namely high (direct and indirect) labour costs, which together with seniority-based remuneration systems and age-specific employee protection (e.g. protection against dismissal), make older workers too expensive. However, recent research, undertaken on behalf of the 'Fifth Federal Commission Reporting on the Situation of the Elderly', reveals that in Germany seniority-based wages are in fact far less widespread than assumed (Bispinck 2005). Moreover, this wage system is much more common in businesses where collective agreements are lacking, and where individual contracting is the rule.

In 2002, the Federal Confederation of Employers Associations published a guideline for employers in which they developed their 'official' arguments and proposals for better integration of older workers (BDA 2002). In particular, the guidelines highlighted the need to raise awareness of some of the benefits of hiring older workers, such as experience, motivation and reliability, and included guidelines for increasing positive age awareness in human resource management. In this context, special measures such as flexible working-time arrangements, training, health promotion, team-work comprising both younger and older workers, and job-rotation were recommended. It also urged employers and companies to replace the dominant age-related attitude towards workers by a more performance-related attitude. Furthermore, the guidelines rejected both legal regulations as well as collective agreements, and stressed the responsibility of individual employees and companies.

As far as the trade unions are concerned, they did not have an overall view that embraced both policies towards older workers and early retirement until March 2001. Strong German unions like IG-Metall, which represents the steel and iron industry, and Ver.di, which represents the public sector, continued demanding the maintenance of early exit options under financially and socially acceptable conditions (Krämer and Naegele 2002). In this context, they emphasized labour market principals in accordance with the concept of 'intergenerational solidarity', and early exit as a tool for 'humanising' the world of labour for older workers.

However, in the wake of the discussion about the economic consequences of an ageing workforce, German trade unions have since become more focused on policies that keep older workers employed longer and improve their employability. This approach is partly due to deeper insight into the ambivalences and inconsistencies of early exit as revealed by practical experience and research. For example, it has been proven that early exit might negatively affect the working conditions of future workers by increasing the workload for younger workers, leading to a vicious cycle of a shrinking workforce and therefore an increasingly unattractive workload (Naegele 1992/2004).

Awareness among Germany's trade unions concerning the effects of demographic change and the persistently high unemployment of older workers has certainly grown. Official statements (e.g. DGB 2004) increasingly express a need to strengthen in-company age-integrative approaches. These new approaches have already entered employment agreements and collective bargaining. Of major importance are the adjustment of work time according to the needs of older workers (e.g. for older shift-workers); the development of further vocational training, which is explicitly aimed at so-called 'disadvantaged' groups; support for health promotion and in-company health management, fortified by statutory measures, regulations, and financial incentives; and the promotion of group work for older workers.

Recently published proposals by leading German trade unionists aim at improving working conditions during the course of working life (Adamy 2003). This can be regarded as the beginning of a promising trade-unionist conceptualisation of policies for older-workers set within an overarching 'working life' perspective.

## Assessment of the current debate and recent policy initiatives

Although the Federal Government claims to be working on different levels to fulfil the demands of the *European Employment Guidelines*, an explicit *integrated* 'older worker's policy' (Walker 2005) is still missing. A critical assessment of existing Federal initiatives reveals three main problems (Frerichs and Taylor 2008 forthcoming).

First, the initiatives of the different Federal ministries involved are not centrally coordinated and even contradict each other. A prominent example is the ongoing promotion of early exit in the current partial retirement legislation, whereas companies are simultaneously asked to recruit and retain older workers. Second, long-term concepts promoting the employability of an ageing workforce focusing on the maintenance of qualifications, health protection and motivation on a Federal level are nonexistent. Both a national preventive health policy, as well as a national education policy favouring further adult education in an institutionalized form, following a formula of 'lifelong learning', have yet to materialize. The latter is of growing importance because the human capital factor is crucial for a country short on natural resources such as

Germany. Third, there is a lack of effort among companies, as well as few incentives, to change their personnel policies in favour of older workers and overcome traditional 'youth-centeredness'. This refers to both the integration of older workers into short-term and long-term training as well as into health-protection.

At first glance, the actions of the *social partners* (employer associations and labour unions) paint a similar picture. Although it is true that there is a paradigm shift in official statements and documents, there is ample evidence that statements and actual practices differ. For example, there is a remarkable contradiction between the official statements of employers associations and the actual treatment of older workers at the vast majority of German companies. Our own research reveals that it is very hard to identify companies with good practices in terms of explicit 'age management' (Naegele and Walker 2006). Moreover, employers associations favour a 'deregulation approach' to facilitate the employment of older workers. However, empirical research does not hold this to be effective at increasing the employment of older workers (BMFSFJ 2006). OECD experiences confirm that deregulation of protection against dismissal does not automatically lead to new jobs for older workers (OECD 2005). In addition, trade-unions have not really attempted to negotiate within a framework of more 'qualitative' collective agreements involving in-company incentives to promote older workers, such as increasing training, preventive health-protection, special working time arrangements, group-work or career-planning.

Therefore, when assessing the recent *single labour market measures* mentioned earlier, three main problems stand out. First, special measures for older workers, particularly in the field of labour market policy, are hardly used (Frerichs and Taylor 2008 forthcoming). This is partly due to implementation problems, however it also reveals that there is little demand for older workers, particularly in lower-paid jobs with heavy workloads. Second, recent cutbacks in social protection for the long-term unemployed will negatively affect older workers due to the above-average risk they face of staying unemployed once losing work. Finally, despite their variety, the single labour market measures are not effective due to the fact that they lack approaches designed to meet individual needs.

## Conclusion

In Germany, there has been a strengthening of policies aimed at the re-integration of older workers and a reversal of early retirement. This is embedded in a general trend of fostering active strategies of empowerment against the background of an ageing labour force and concerns about the future funding of pension systems. It is also partly influenced by 'moral pressure' stemming from the European Union's open method of coordination.

However, it is questionable whether active employment programmes will be a suitable replacement for early retirement. In Germany, the process of rethinking the prevailing 'youth-centred' policies of the social partners and public labour market agencies only started in 2001. A reduction of early exit strategies has not led to an adequate expansion of funding for active labour market measures. On the contrary, older unemployed people are increasingly at risk of being neglected in training programmes. Moreover, targeted programmes for this group of workers and general improvements in the job-placement structure have yet to bring positive results. Critics emphasize that the true aim of the anti-early retirement policy in Germany is the lowering of pension costs and the avoidance of employment opportunity provision for older workers.

Regarding solutions, a prolongation of working life requires that older people have a real chance of working longer. There must be improvements in both incentives and provisions that encourage older people to work, as well as improvements in measures that help employers recruit and retain older workers. At the same time, however, socially acceptable paths to early exit need to be preserved for certain 'at risk' groups of older workers whose prospects of remaining in or re-entering employment are low, for example, workers with severe health problems, disabled workers and workers in high pressure workplaces.

In addition, even if the labour force participation rates of older workers increase, this will not necessarily mean that the quality of working conditions for this age-group will be as good as it is for younger workers. 'Active ageing', which is manifested as periods of precarious employment in a narrow range of jobs with low wages, or even worse, in a long period of fruitless job-searching, may be worse than early exit. Therefore, employment targets for older workers should be amended by additional targets that guarantee a productive and sustainable integration of older workers in employment, or at the very least monitor how employment conditions for older workers develop in a *qualitative* way. What is necessary in this respect is a change in paradigm from a reactive 'elderly employee policy' to a preventative policy of employment promotion and protection which is 'age-neutral' and pursued throughout an employee's working life. This, however, does not mean that we can do without age-specific solutions in the future, for example, for the older unemployed.

The appropriate instruments for active promotion are well-known and have been partially implemented, but their actualisation requires the cooperation of all groups concerned, namely the government, employers, unions, work councils and the older workers themselves. Nevertheless, in-company approaches form the core of an 'active' and future-orientated age-management policy. Whether older workers are able to stay at work longer or not is primarily determined within companies. In this context, the arrangement of adequate workplaces which meet the needs of older workers is of importance in terms of workload, working time, work environment, and job design.

The following additional conclusions might serve as points of orientation for a strategic change in policies for older workers, and for a more future-orientated age management approach within and outside companies. These conclusions are drawn from recent research projects and scientific conferences which were led and/or organized by the author (Naegele 2002; Naegele 1992/2004; 2004; 2005; Naegele and Walker 2006; Naegele et al. 2003; Frerich and Taylor 2008 forthcoming):

- The promotion, employment and employability of an ageing workforce require action throughout one's whole working life (the concept of 'age neutrality').
- Active policy approaches should be preventive. This entails combating the typical risks that older workers face in the earlier stages of their working lives. A dual approach should be adopted which maintains the employability of individuals throughout their working lives, but which also addresses the specific risks or problems that some older workers face.
- Multi-disciplinary and coordinated approaches are necessary, taking into account education, health, training, leisure and family duties, social protection and equal opportunities. This requires attention to work organization and the work environment, and to the capabilities of the ageing workforce.
- Systematic coordination and integration of measures (e.g. training and working time adjustment, preventive health protection and career planning) is required at both the company and the public policy levels. A close coordination of public and workplace policies is warranted. However, in-company approaches are the core of an 'active' and future-orientated age-management policy. Whether older workers are able to stay at work longer or not is primarily determined within companies. In this context, the arrangement of adequate workplaces which meet the needs of older workers is of

importance (e.g. in terms of workload, working time, work environment, and job design).

- Although the overall goal is to enable older workers to remain in the active workforce and to avoid involuntary early exit, socially acceptable paths to early exit must be preserved for special 'risk' groups of older workers (e.g. the long-term unemployed, workers with severe health problems, and disabled workers).

In summary, Germany still has to develop a comprehensive strategy for active ageing to ensure that people stay in work longer, particularly after the age of 60. Germany also needs to increase access to training for older workers in the context of lifelong learning. It is therefore hoped that the conclusions above might serve as points of orientation for a strategic change in policies for older workers, and for a more future-orientated age management approach within and outside companies.

## References

Adamy, W. (2003) 'Herausforderungen einer älter werdenden Erwerbsbevölkerung. Oder: Wem nutzt eine alternsgerechte Gestaltung der Arbeitswelt?', in U. Engelen-Kefer and K. Wiesenheugel (eds), *Sozialstaat – solidarisch, effizient, zukunftssicher*, Hamburg: VSA-Verlag, pp. 86–103.

BDA (Bundesvereinigung der Deutschen Arbeitgeberverbände) (2002) *Ältere Mitarbeiter im Betrieb. Ein Leitfaden für die Betriebe*, Berlin: Bundesvereinigung der Deutschen Arbeitgeberverbände.

Bellmann, L., M. Hilpert, E. Kistler and J. Wahse (2003) 'Herausforderungen des demographischen Wandels für den Arbeitsmarkt und die Betriebe', *Mitteilungen aus der Arbeitsmarkt- und Berufsforschung*, 2, pp. 133–149.

Behrens, J. (2003) 'Fehlzeit, Frühberentung: Länger erwerbstätig durch Personal- und Organisationsentwicklung', in B. Badura, H. Schnellschmidt and C. Vetter (eds), *Fehlzeitenreport 2002*, Heidelberg: Springer, pp. 115–136.

Bispinck, R. (2005) 'Altersbezogene Regelungen in Tarifverträgen – Bedingungen betrieblicher Personalpolitik', *WSI-Mitteilungen*, 10, pp. 582–588.

Boockmann, B. and T. Zwick (2004) 'Betriebliche Determinanten der Beschäftigung älterer Arbeitnehmer', *ZAF*, 1, pp. 53–63.

BMFSFJ (Bundesministerium für Familie, Senioren, Frauen und Jugend) (2006) *Fünfter Bericht zur Lage der älteren Generation in der Bundesrepublik Deutschland. Potenziale des Alters in Wirtschaft und Gesellschaft – Der Beitrag älterer Menschen zum Zusammenhalt der Generationen*. BT-Drucksache 16/2190.

BMGS (Bundesministerium für Gesundheit und Soziale Sicherung) (2005) *Übersicht über das Sozialrecht*. Berlin: BW Bildung und Wissen.

DGB (Deutscher Gewerkschaftsbund) (2004) *Demografischer Wandel – Schritte zu einer alternsgerechten Arbeitswelt. Positionspapier des DGB zum demografischen Wandel*. DGB profil`04, Berlin.

Ebert, A., T. Fuchs and E. Kistler (2006) 'Arbeiten bis 65 oder gar bis 67? – Die Voraussetzungen fehlen', *WSI Mitteilungen*, 9, pp. 492–499.

Europäische Kommission (2003) *Beschäftigungspolitiken der EU und in den Mitgliedsstaaten. Gemeinsamer Bericht 2002,* Amt für amtliche Veröffentlichungen der Europäischen Gemeinschaften, Luxemburg.

Europäische Kommission (2004) *Mehr und bessere Arbeitsplätze für alle. Die Europäische Beschäftigungsstrategie.* Luxemburg: Europäische Kommission.

Frerichs, F. and P. Taylor (2008) 'Ageing and the Labour Market – a Comparison of Policy Approaches', in G. Naegele and A. Walker (eds), *Ageing and Social Policy in Germany and the United Kingdom.* Houndmills: Palgrave. (Forthcoming).

Fuchs, T., P. Schnur and G. Zika (2005) *Arbeitsmarktbilanz bis 2020. Besserung langfristig möglich. IAB Kurzbericht,* 24. Nürnberg: Institut für Arbeitsmarkt und Berufsforschung der Bundesagentur für Arbeit.

Krämer, K. and G. Naegele (2002) 'Recent Developments in the Employment and Retirement of Older Workers in Germany', *Journal of Aging and Social Policy,* 13 (1), pp. 69–82.

Naegele, G. (1992/2004) *Zwischen Arbeit und Rente,* Augsburg: MARO-Verlag.

Naegele, G. (2002) 'Active strategies for older workers in Germany', in European Trade Union Institute (ed.), *Active Strategies for Older Workers,* Brussels: ETUI-Eigenverlag, pp. 207–245.

Naegele, G. (2004) 'Verrentungspolitik und Herausforderungen des demographischen Wandels in der Arbeitswelt. Das Beispiel Deutschland', in M. von Cranach, H. Schneider, and E. Ulich (eds), *Ältere Menschen im Unternehmen. Chancen, Risiken, Modelle,* Bern: Haupt Verlag, pp. 189–219.

Naegele, G. (2005) Nachhaltige Arbeits- und Erwerbsfähigkeit sichern – dargestellt am Beispiel älterer Arbeitnehmer, *WSI-Mitteilungen,* 4, pp. 214–220.

Naegele, G., C. Barkholdt, B. de Vroom, J. Goul Anderson and K. Krämer (2003) 'A New Organization of Time throughout Working Life. Integrated Report', European Foundation for the Improvement of Living and Working Conditions, Forschungsbericht der Forschungsgesellschaft für Gerontologie e.V. Dortmund 2003, Dublin.

Naegele, G. and A. Walker (2006) *A Guide to Good Practice in Age-Management,* Dublin: European Foundation for the Improvement of Living and Working Conditions.

OECD (Organization for Economic Cooperation and Development) (2005) *Ageing and Employment Policies Germany,* Paris: OECD Publications.

Schäfer, H., and S. Seyda (2004) 'Arbeitsmärkte', in Institut der deutschen Wirtschaft (ed.), *Perspektive 2050 – Ökonomik des demographischen Wandels,* Köln: Deutscher Institutsverlag, pp. 97–120.

Statistisches Bundesamt (2006) *Bevölkerung Deutschlands bis 2050. 11. koordinierte Bevölkerungsvorausberechnung.* Wiesbaden: Statistisches Bundesamt.

Walker, A. (2005) 'The emergence of age management in Europe', *International Journal of Organisational Behaviour,* 10 (1), pp. 685–697.

# 11

# Towards 'Ageless' Employment Policies – a Union's Experience of the Extension of the Mandatory Retirement Age

*Nobuyuki Shintani*

This paper describes how Japanese labour and management tried to cope with changes in employment conditions brought about by ageing in the workforce. The focus is on the gradual extension of the mandatory retirement age. The aim of achieving 'ageless' employment policies is a slight exaggeration. In substance, it implies employment policies that do not discriminate against workers because of their age.

The JEIU (Japanese Electrical Electronic & Information Union) was established in 1953 and is the third largest private-sector industrial federation in Japan. It is composed of unions belonging to companies in the electrical appliance, electronics and information sectors, and is a member of the International Metalworkers' Federation and the International Confederation of Trade Unions (see Figure 11.1).

The JEIU has been at the forefront of negotiating and enforcing many practices now taken for granted in Japan, such as the five-day week and childcare leave, even before there was legal recognition of these issues. The extension of the mandatory retirement age has been one of such issues, which the federation took up in the mid 1960s. The JEIU's efforts contributed to the extension of the mandatory retirement age from about 55 to over 60. This struggle required great persistence in the face of widespread opposition and eventually took about 40 years to resolve.

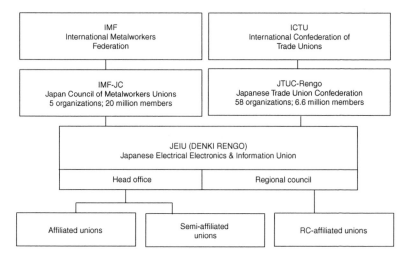

*Figure 11.1*   The affiliation of the Japanese Electrical Electronic and Information Union

*Source*: The author.

## The structure of labour relations and collective bargaining

Let us first look at the structure of labour relations in the electric industry in Japan. The trade unions in Japan, unlike those in Europe or the US, are in-company unions. In most industries, the industry-based unions that are commonly seen in Europe and the US are not present. In the electric industry, the JEIU does not have a labour pact with the employer association at present.

There are more than ten employer associations in the electric industry, such as the Japan Electrical Manufacturers Association (JEMA), and the Japan Electronics and Information Technology Industries Association (JEITA) to name but two. Although labour relations are based on company unions, the federation applies 'industry-based united bargaining' to improve labour conditions across the industry. Through industry-based united bargaining, the federation tries to coordinate for all member unions: (a) the schedule of the bargaining process, (b) the setting of the deadline for employers' replies, (c) items to be demanded, (d) minimum acceptable levels for management offers, and (e) standardized action in case a management offer is unsatisfactory. When any offers fall short of the agreed level, the member union of the respective company must go on strike. United bargaining therefore aims at generating multiplier and spin-off effects through the integration of negotiations.

Industry-based united bargaining in the electric industry is conducted every year for salaries and lump-sum payments during the so-called 'spring offensive', and every other year for collective labour agreements, such as work rules and employment rules that are about to expire and need to be renewed. To enable the integration of negotiations on such agreements, the federation requests that member unions have the agreements last for two years expiring at the end of March in even-numbered years. The extension of the mandatory retirement age was also dealt with in the framework of industry-based united bargaining for labour agreements.

The structure of industry-based united bargaining in the electric industry is shown in Figures 11.2 and 11.3. Industry-based united bargaining is implemented by the Central Bargaining Committee (Chuto, see Figure 11.3) composed of the 17 major unions and of executives from the JEIU. Chuto represents the core of the united bargaining approach. The mid-sized unions form the Expanded Central Bargaining Committee (Kakuchuto), and small and local unions form the Local Bargaining Committee (Chito).

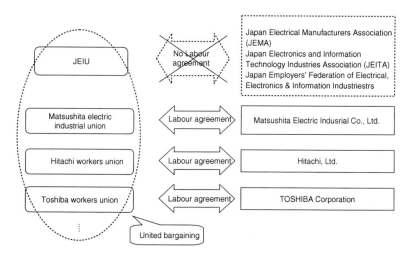

*Figure 11.2*   Industrial unions align demands to improve overall conditions
*Source*: The author.

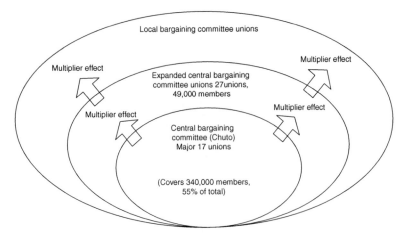

*Figure 11.3*   Denki Rengō's united bargaining
*Source*: The author.

The Central Bargaining Committee, which mainly consists of large unions, decides the first unified deadline for replies from management. The Expanded Central Bargaining Committee, in principle, applies the same deadline. The Local Bargaining Committee's unified date for the reply from management is one week after the Central Bargaining Committee's unified date. The Local Bargaining Committee refers to the conditions that major unions extracted from management, trying as much as possible to achieve equally good conditions. The negotiation results of the Central Bargaining Committee are thus fed to the Expanded Central Bargaining Committee and to the Local Bargaining Committee to ensure that the labour conditions of smaller unions can be improved all together.

Company unions engage in negotiations at each company, but because the financial performances of each company are different, unions will confront different limits during negotiations. The industry-based united bargaining was conceived to overcome this kind of limitation. All unions that are negotiating work together, to achieve maximum leverage. On the other hand, much in the same way as the JEIU unites the unions by facilitating communication, the management side also exchanges information and agrees on a common policy of negotiation before coming to the table to discuss labour conditions.

The right to strike, the source of bargaining power, is not directly held by the federation, but by each member union in accordance with the date set in the united bargaining process. The demands of member unions are composed of demands that are unique to each union as well as demands that are part of the united bargaining. The member unions of the Central Bargaining Committee transfer the right to order a strike to the Committee if any of the replies from employers that relate to the united bargaining demands do not meet the agreed minimum level, known as the 'ratchet'. When a certain company makes an offer that does not reach the level of the 'ratchet', the Central Bargaining Committee orders the union of that company to go on strike. The authorization to order a strike is confirmed through secret ballot by individual union members. In the 1960s, and up to the early 1970s, most of the federation's individual members, who numbered 300,000 to 400,000, did strike mainly trying to achieve higher salaries. However, strikes to achieve higher salaries have stopped since 1980.

## Extension of the age of mandatory retirement

In the mid 1960s, the federation started using industry-based united bargaining for collective labour agreement related issues, mainly to demand the extension of the mandatory retirement age. The process of achieving a retirement age of 65 can be subdivided into three phases.

### Phase 1: Tackling extension to the age of 60

The federation first included the extension of the mandatory retirement age, which most large companies had adopted, in its demands in 1964. However, at that time, the age for mandatory retirement was mostly 55 for regular male full-time employees. For female employees, it was 50. Contrary to Europe's movement towards earlier retirement, the JEIU wanted to match the retirement age with the age at which a person would be eligible to receive their pension. This meant raising the retirement age. At the time, the age of eligibility for employee pensions was 60, and therefore extending the mandatory retirement age to 60 was critical in facilitating life after retirement. The JEIU was aware that a later retirement age might affect the employment opportunities of younger people, but the need for older workers and their eagerness to continue working could not be ignored.

The JEIU's demand to raise the retirement age above 55 started in the united bargaining for a labour agreement in 1964, and continued in 1966 and 1968. The demand was phrased 'Mandatory retirement at 60'. There was no notable progress in 1964 or 1966, but in 1968 the JEIU included the demand in its 'unified demand standard' and backed it up with the possibility of a strike. Through negotiations, some unions of large companies achieved an extension from age 55 to 56.

The demand for 'Mandatory retirement at 60' was again put forward in 1970 as part of the 'unified demand standard'. Specifically, the demand stated that 'the extension of the mandatory retirement age should be up to the age of 60 and any resignation after the age of 55 should be treated as retirement'. While the negotiation proved to be difficult, in the end most large companies agreed to raise the mandatory retirement age to 60.

The reason behind this concession might have been the labour shortage caused by the rapid growth of the economy. In any case, this was a breakthrough in Japan, as no other industry in the country had so far achieved such an agreement. In 1970, the number of companies that adopted the mandatory retirement age of 60 was 22 out of 124. The number grew to 61 out of 125 in 1972, when the same issue was taken up again.

### Phase 2: Extension beyond the age of 60

After several major unions succeeded in raising the retirement age in 1970, the JEIU continued its efforts to increase the number of companies applying a mandatory age of 60 through the labour agreement bargaining in 1972 and 1974. The JEIU further demanded that new retirement systems do away with gender discrimination and improve the conditions of workers aged 56 or older, who typically had their salaries reduced to 80% or 90% of their previous salary levels. Gender discrimination with regard to the retirement age was mostly rectified by 1983.

From the late 1970s, the ageing of the population was starting to be recognized as a social issue and the quest for the extension of employment beyond 60 began. At the JEIU's annual convention in 1981, the 'directive on policies for upper-middle-aged workers' designated skill re-development, job re-designing and employment after 60 as priority areas. The convention decided to accept the transfer of workers to affiliates and related companies for re-employment or contractual employment in return. It also suggested a diversification of employment patterns including 'partial employment', or daily employment of only a few hours a day.

In the labour agreement negotiation of 1983, the JEIU demanded that this 'directive on policies for upper-middle-aged workers' become part of the agreement. It was the first attempt by a Japanese industrial federation to extend employment beyond the age of 60. The labour agreement negotiation after 1985 also included such demands, and by the end of 1980s, about half of the larger companies had some employment schemes for workers over 60. This did not, however, guarantee the employment of all workers over 60.

## Phase 3: The realization of employment up to the age of 65

While the very fast ageing of the population and workforce was the main factor behind an extension of employment beyond the age of 60, the revision of the Employee Pension Act that pushed back the age of eligibility for pensions had a direct and substantial impact. The effort to revise the law started in the 1980s. In 1994 it was finally decided that eligibility would be gradually raised to the age of 65 from 2001 onwards.

The labour unions' activities on government policy and regulations such as social security and labour laws are mostly handled by Rengo, the national centre of labour unions in Japan. When Rengo was founded in 1989, it represented 7.98 million employees, which corresponded to 65% of the 12.22 million organized workers belonging to both private and public sectors in Japan. The postponement of the age of eligibility for pensions implied by the reform of the Employee Pension Act took place without any change in the mandatory retirement age. It meant that workers would face five years without a job or a pension. Such a situation was not acceptable for Rengo.

In Japan, the ministry in charge of social security policies and labour laws is the Ministry of Health, Labour and Welfare. The ministry usually holds Policy Discussion Meetings to produce draft legislation. Members of the Policy Discussion Meetings are academics and representatives of management and labour.[1] Rengo used to have a seat in the Pension Discussion Meeting of the Ministry of Health, Labour and Welfare, but the reform of the law in 1994 was approved by the Meeting in spite of Rengo's opposition.

As one of the major players within Rengo, the JEIU participated in these initiatives and also provided its own opinion directly to government bodies like the Ministry of Health, Labour and Welfare, the Ministry of Public Management, Home Affairs, Post and Telecommunication, and the Ministry of Economy, Trade and Industry, as well as to political parties like the Democratic Party of Japan, the Liberal Democratic Party, and Komeito. In the policy dialogue of 2000, the JEIU submitted the statement 'Urgent Consideration of Eliminating the Age Condition in Recruiting' to ministries concerned and to political parties.

In the united bargaining for a labour agreement in 1992, that is, even before the reform of the Employee Pension Act, the JEIU demanded the establishment of 'a system to guarantee the employment beyond 60 if the worker so desires, or the formation of a labour-management consultative body to discuss the introduction of such system'. However, the management side showed little interest in the issue. While management agreed on the establishment of the consultative body, there was not much progress. This demand was repeated after the reform of the Employee Pension Act. Specifically, in the bargaining of 1994 and 1996 the JEIU demanded:

a. matching of the retirement age with the pension age;
b. prevention of the bankruptcy of pension plans;
c. fulfilling work-lives;
d. securing of an adequate workforce and the maintenance of economic vitality.

The negotiation in 1996 resulted in the establishment of a labour-management consultative body in about 50 unions, but they did not lead to the actual extension of the retirement age.

The federation's annual convention in July 1996 specified the demand for 'retirement extension for full-time workers and union members'. The convention of the following year also confirmed that the retirement age should gradually be extended to eventually match the age of eligibility for pensions so as to cope with the ageing society. It also requested that the work hours, compensation and other conditions for the extended period should be decided through consultation between labour and management at each company.

To prepare for the reform of the Employee Pension Act that would take effect in 2001, it was necessary to agree on the extension of the retirement age in the labour negotiations of 1998. In 1998, the extension of the retirement age to 65 was included in the 'unified demand standard' that was backed by the determination to strike for the first time in 18 years if the demand standard was not met. The management side, however, replied that they had doubts about extending the retirement age across the board and that a change in the retirement age was too significant to be accepted on an 'as-demanded' basis. In fact, in 1998 the performance of the electric industry was worsening. At the end of the deadlocked negotiation, a compromise was worked out that implied the commitment to continue the labour-management consultation towards the establishment of a system to extend retirement to

65 by fiscal year 2000. As a result, consultations were to continue in 75% of the unions (118 unions) that had originally submitted the demand.

However, the labour-management consultations produced no agreement. Since the federation's annual convention in July 1997, the focus had been on extending retirement to 65, the tactic was now changed to the more general demand of extending the period of employment.

The JEIU made it clear that any failure at the labour-management consultations to generate results would provoke an extremely rigid attitude in the labour negotiations in 2000. The JEIU suggested the following three principles of employment extension to its member unions:

a. The company should provide working opportunities for those willing to work;
b. Retirement should be extended at least until the age when the worker becomes eligible for a pension;
c. The status of the older worker should be stable and comparable to that of a regular employee.

The JEIU also decided to accept that, in principle, the workers eligible for extension would be those with union membership prior to retirement. If they continued work with a company other than their previous employer, they could become special union members entitled to special treatment in terms of rights and responsibilities. Labour and management reached an agreement at the end of 1999, in which a system based on the above three principles of employment extension were to be established. The three principles of employment extension were agreed upon in 49 companies. By the end of May 2000, consultations had led to an agreement in 97 companies. The activities toward the extension of the retirement age to 65, which had begun in 1983, were thus successfully completed one year before 2001, when the reform of the Employee Pension Act started to take effect.

This achievement was not only the result of persistent negotiations, but in many unions the revision of lump-sum retirement payments and company pension plans were also on the table, thereby contributing to the willingness of employers to come to an agreement. A change in accounting rules forced companies to state any outstanding obligation to provide lump-sum retirement payments in their balance sheets starting in the fiscal year 2000. Companies desperate to reduce obligations wanted unions to agree on a revision of the terms of lump-sum retirement payments and company pension systems. Management was

willing to accept the extension of the retirement age to induce unions to agree to such revisions.

In the same period, there were some individual cases outside the electric industry in which the extension of the retirement age was agreed upon, nevertheless to reach such an agreement in 50 large and small unions in the electric industry had a notable social impact.

## Details of the agreements achieved and remaining challenges

As of 1 February 2005, 20 unions belonging to the JEIU had achieved an increase in the mandatory retirement age to over 60. In all the unions that introduced this extension, the retirement age was raised to the age when the pension payment would start. However, the number of unions where the extension would be applicable to all willing workers remained at 74 (62%).

The extension of the mandatory retirement age requires that both labour and management re-design jobs and develop adequate working conditions. There should be no preconditions like 'when there are jobs that are adequate for workers eligible for extension' or 'when there are appropriate jobs'. Some companies limited the eligibility of workers to those recognized as qualified by the company. All in all, 25% of companies still had room for improvement. The systems introduced can be classified into three types (Figure 11.4).

---

**Three patterns of employment extension systems**

- **Type A: Re-employment through limited time contract**

    –After retiring at previously set age, the company would sign a yearly contract that would be repeated until specific age.

    –Matsushita Electric Industrial, Hitachi, Sharp, Matsushita Electric Works, Pioneer, etc.

- **Type B: Early change of employment status and no-limit re-employment**

    – The type of employment for those expressed willingness for extension will be changed at mid-50s (the worker would resign and be hired again under different contractterms) to be kept employed until the extended retirement age.

    –Toshiba, Mitsubishi Electric, SanyoElectric, etc.

- **Type C: Active selection of retirement extension**

    –The retirement age is extended for those willing. Fuji Electric adopted this pattern.

---

*Figure 11.4*   Three patterns of employment extension systems
*Source*: The author.

The structure of Type B is explained in Figure 11.5. The salary after the extension is either discounted from the previous salary, in which case there is a relation between the previous salary and the current one, or one that is completely reset to match current market conditions without any reference to the previous salary. In some cases, the two methods are combined.

All systems combine the government allowance or the company pension plan to maintain the actual total income of the worker while trying to reduce personnel costs.

Although the business environment is unpredictable, being able to retain skilled workers at an attractive cost while facing an expected labour shortage is an attractive option for companies. For workers, on the other hand, the income may decrease, but if public allowances and pension plans are wisely used, actual income can be kept at a relatively stable level. Their personal disposable income may even increase as their children mature and require less financial support.

The government allowance consists of the Old-Age Pension for Active Employees and the Allowance for Retention of Old-Workers. The Old-Age Pension for Active Employees is a good example of the retirement extension contributing to the funding of the pension plan, without representing a mere substitution, because the amount of the pension payout decreases as the salary level of the worker increases.

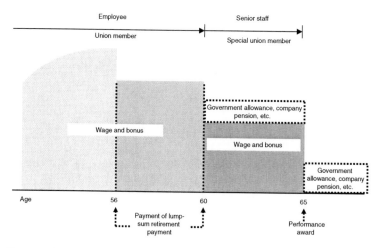

*Figure 11.5*  Early change of employment status and no-limit re-employment
*Source*: The author.

The Allowance for Retention of Old-Workers compares the salary at 60 with salary levels after 60. If the post 60 salary level is less than 75% of the salary at 60, then up to 15% of the age 60 salary level is paid out from the employment insurance scheme (it was up to 25% in 1999). The scheme is very effective in stabilizing income (see Figure 11.6).

We do not know much about how the schemes have been used after 2001 because most unions are not publicizing the operational results. One of the reasons for this hesitance is that 2002, the year following the establishment of the retirement extension scheme, was one of the worst years the electric industry has ever experienced.

The slump in the IT industry caused by the demise of the dot-com bubble in the US threw many of the Japanese electrics and electronics companies into the biggest deficits of their corporate histories. The change in accounting rules that required the listing of obligations regarding the lump-sum retirement payment further worsened the financial situations of companies. Thus, companies were hit by a two-fold shock; one affecting their profit and loss condition, and another worsening their debt position.

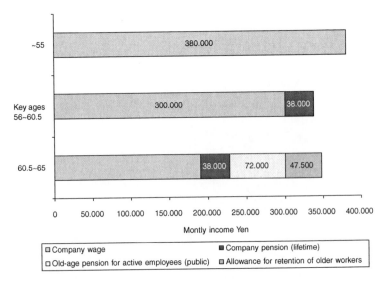

*Figure 11.6*   Example of a system that combines company pension and government allowance

*Source*: Calculations by the author based on case of company D salary table.

Even in the largest electrics companies in Japan, various changes which lowered the level of labour conditions, including pay-cuts and employment adjustments, were reluctantly introduced as a temporary measure to cope with the severe economic environment. In some cases, the introduction of early retirement schemes resulted in retirements of over 10,000 employees in a single company (see Figure 11.7). Those who applied for early retirement were mostly people in their 50s. In one large company, 70% of the workers who retired were in their 50s.

To motivate workers to accept early retirement, it was not unusual to offer inducements worth up to 40 months salary on top of the regular lump-sum retirement payment. Among the JEIU's member unions, the largest inducement payment involved 72 months salary. It can be assumed that in such an adverse business environment management was not paying a high priority to securing jobs for workers past their retirement age.

The application of the employment extension agreement over this period can be grasped by looking at the cases of 11 companies as depicted in Table 11.1.

The JEIU not only addressed the period without pension or salary income, even though that was an important issue; the main goal was the extension of the mandatory retirement age. For those capable and willing to work, securing the option to continue working is essential for a fulfilling life.

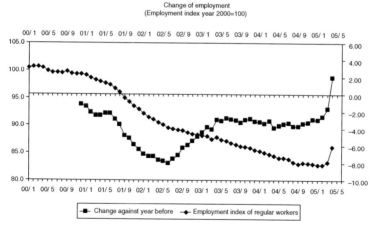

*Figure 11.7*  The employment trend in the electric industry (adjustments after 2001)

*Source*: Own calculations based on data from Statistics Bureau, Ministry of Internal Affairs and Communications.

*Table 11.1*  Actual utilization of extension system (accumulated record until 2004)

| Company | Type of extension | Eligible workers | Applicants | System utilization ratio |
|---------|-------------------|------------------|------------|--------------------------|
| Co. #1  | A |       |       | About 2 |
| Co. #2  | A | 84    | 17    | 20,2%   |
| Co. #3  | A | 93    | 37    | 39,8%   |
| Co. #4  | A | 51    | 16    | 31,4%   |
| Co. #5  | A | 827   | 13    | 1,6%    |
| Co. #6  | A | 99    | 77    | 77,8%   |
| Co. #7  | A | 26    | 9     | 34,6%   |
| Co. #8  | B | 2.067 | 490   | 23,7%   |
| Co. #9  | B | 680   | 380   | 55,9%   |
| Co. #10 | B | 79    | 30    | 38,0%   |
| Co. #11 | B | 400   | 15    | 3,8%    |
| Total   |   | 4.406 | 1.084 | 24,6%   |

*Source*: Own calculations based on company cases.

## Conclusion

To maintain the vitality of the economy and a rapidly ageing society, the government recently adopted fairly drastic policy measures to promote the hiring of older workers. On 1 April 2006, the Revised Aged Worker Employment Stabilization Act went into effect. The Act required companies to keep on hiring willing workers at least until they become eligible for government pension payments. The government also phased in various subsidy programs and advisory services to encourage the hiring of older workers.

The Revised Aged Worker Employment Stabilization Act mandated that all employers have to apply one of the following schemes:

• extend the mandatory retirement age to the age of eligibility for pensions.
• introduce an employment extension system whereby willing workers are re-hired after they reach the mandatory retirement age, where the mandatory retirement age in this case can be decided by agreement between labour and management or in the rules of employment.
• abolish mandatory retirement.

Based on the revised Act, the JEIU demanded that management agree to extend the employment of willing older workers including non-full-time workers and managers in the negotiations over labour contract related issues. Management agreed to this for 70% of the unions that made this demand.

As was pointed out at the beginning, the common lifetime employment practice in Japan implied a mandatory retirement age. The JEIU fought for the postponement of the retirement age and for the extension of the total period of employment within the framework of lifetime employment to accommodate the rapidly ageing workforce.

Promoting the postponement of the retirement age and the extension of the employment period within the existing employment system affected the supply-and-demand balance of labour markets. In the period starting in the late 1990s, when Japan's GDP recorded a minus growth rate, the labour market was characterized by a condition of oversupply. Therefore, all of the above activities were especially tough going both for labour and management.

In spite of the difficulties, the JEIU did not strike or initiate lockouts to resolve the situation. Even though it took time, it engaged in an extensive dialogue with management to produce steady results. The system of labour-management consultation that took root in most large companies in Japan may be considered a 'social infrastructure' of which the JEIU can be proud.

Japan now faces the 'Year 2007 Problem', namely the massive retirement of the Japanese Baby Boom generation that was born right after the Second World War. These workers possess an extensive amount of knowledge and skills. As the ageing of the population and decreasing number of children are bound to lead to a labour shortage in the near future, it is essential to preserve such knowledge and skills not only for the economy, but also for society. At the same time, and for the same reason, the participation of female workers needs to be improved.

In order to realize 'ageless' employment that can cope with the challenges of an ageing society, the revision of compensation systems, including those for younger workers, and personnel systems is inevitable. In larger electrics companies, the seniority element of the compensation system is being reformed. This step should be taken further to achieve a longer employment period and an extension of employment of older workers. This would imply a change in the very structure of the system. At the same time, implementation of human resource programmes to develop workers' capabilities to handle diverse tasks prior to their reaching the retirement age is important in preparing them for jobs after mandatory retirement. In that sense, there remains a lot to be done to fully adjust employment conditions and human resource practices to not only cope with, but also benefit from, an ageing work force. The JEIU will continue to support necessary adjustments in its negotiations with the aim of ensuring that older workers have a fulfilling life.

## Notes

The presentation is based on the author's professional involvement. The history is documented in Denki Rengō (1992, 2005, 1995–2006, and 1992–2007).

1. A few years ago, under the Koizumi Administration that took charge in 2001, this authority was transferred to the Council on Fiscal and Economic Policy to reduce the influence of ministries and to increase the power of the Prime Minister.

## References

Denki Rengō (1992) *Undōshi* (*History of Campaigns*), 4th Edition, Tokyo: Konpōzu Yuni.

Denki Rengō (2005) *50 nenshi* (*50 Years History*), Published on CD-Rom.

Denki Rengō (1995–2006) *Teikitaikaigiansho* (*Proposal of The Periodic Conference*), 43th–54th conference, internal source.

Denki Rengō (1992–2007) *Chūōiinkaigiansho* (*Proposal of The Central Committee*), 78th–93th meeting of the central committee, internal source.

# Index